Teaching Genius

Dorothy DeLay, 1992. Photo: Christian Steiner.

TEACHING GENIUS

Dorothy DeLay and the
Making of a Musician

by Barbara Lourie Sand

aϕ

Amadeus Press

Originally published in hardcover by Amadeus Press in 2000

Paperback edition published in 2005 by

AMADEUS PRESS, LLC
512 Newark Pompton Turnpike
Pompton Plains, New Jersey 07444, USA

For sales, please contact

NORTH AMERICA

AMADEUS PRESS, LLC
c/o Hal Leonard Corp.
7777 West Bluemound Road
Milwaukee, Wisconsin 53213, USA
Phone: 800-637-2852
Fax: 414-774-3259

UNITED KINGDOM AND EUROPE

ROUNDHOUSE PUBLISHING LTD.
Millstone, Limers Lane
Northam, North Devon EX39 2RG, UK
Phone: 01237-474474
Fax: 01237-474774
E-mail: roundhouse.group@ukgateway.net

E-mail: orders@amadeuspress.com
Website: www.amadeuspress.com

Printed in Singapore

The Library of Congress has cataloged the hardcover edition as follows:

Sand, Barbara Lourie.
    Teaching genius: Dorothy DeLay and the making of a musician / by
    Barbara Lourie Sand.
        p.   cm.
    Includes bibliographical references (p.   ) and index.
    ISBN 1-57467-052-2
    1. DeLay, Dorothy, 1917–   2. Violin teachers—United States—
    Biography. I. Title.

ML423.D35 S36   2000
787.2'092—dc21
[B]
                                                                99-056004

To the memory of my father,

Arthur Lourie

Contents

Foreword

by Zubin Mehta

I first heard of Dorothy DeLay when I was in my teens. She was a colleague of my father, so that from the start my story with her has not been about going out for coffee every day but about her tremendous gifts.

Dorothy is this fountain of plenty that never stops. She just keeps on bringing these little genii — geniuses — to me: Midori, Sarah Chang, Gil Shaham, and others. I have worked with many of her former students, including Itzhak Perlman and Shlomo Mintz.

On the American scene, she is absolutely one of the foremost violin teachers. She has the great good fortune of collecting talent from all over the world, and not just soloists. Ninety-five percent of violin talent goes into orchestras of all kinds, and these excellent products of Dorothy DeLay's studio at Juilliard go not only to the greatest orchestras but to all kinds of orchestras everywhere. So we are all very, very grateful to her.

Soloists are something else. The soloist is one you cannot stop, like a meteor. The soloist will go his or her own way, so it is especially important that Dorothy is also a mother figure to everybody. She is there every day for them and guides them through their early life. She is not just a violin teacher: she *takes care* of the younger talent. There is *no* question of exploitation. She is extremely careful — otherwise the comet burns itself out.

When she brings a child to me, she just wants me to meet him. I give some of these gifted youngsters the opportunity to play once with the orchestra, usually for children's concerts. They get a taste, and then they have to go back to school.

Dorothy is very careful that the young violinists' parents do not keep disrupting their lives. What we do is to nurture them. Dorothy is there at the rehearsals; we talk about what they need to work on; we have to accompany them in a different way. It is like having a diamond: they are dealing with the highly emotional experience of the music itself, and we are dealing with a human life.

Acknowledgments

My gratitude to Dorothy DeLay for her openhearted cooperation in letting me into her teaching life for more than ten years is expressed more fully in the opening chapter of this book. I want to extend my particular thanks to her husband, the writer Edward Newhouse, for having been ready to talk, or to listen, whenever I felt the need. Newhouse is not only blessed with total recall for names and dates, but has the storyteller's gift for making seemingly dull facts riveting. He has been of enormous assistance in the course of researching material for this book.

I wish to thank the following musicians for having given their time so generously in being interviewed: Laurie Carney, Heidi Castleman, Min Soo Chang, Sarah Chang, Catherine Cho, Rohan De Silva, Cornelius Dufallo, Kikuei Ikeda, Hyo Kang, Masao Kawasaki, David Kim, Cho-Liang Lin, Robert McDuffie, Peter Oundjian, Itzhak Perlman, Mark Peskanov, Gil Shaham, Evan Solomon, Arnold Steinhardt, and Isaac Stern.

Thanks, also, are due to managers Tom Gallant of MCM–Musicians Corporate Management, Ltd., Lee Lamont of ICM Artists, Ltd., Edna Landau of IMG Artists, Inc., Susan Wadsworth of Young Concert Artists, Inc., and Nancy Wellman of Herbert Barrett Management, Inc. Others in the music world whose help is acknowledged include Joseph Polisi, president of The Juilliard School; Stephen Clapp, dean of The Juilliard School; Andrew Thomas, director of the Pre-College Division of The Juilliard School; William Parrish, assistant director of the Pre-College Division of The Juilliard School; Robert Harth, president of The Aspen Music Festival and School; Peter Schaaf, many of whose photographs appear in this book; Johanna Keller, editor of *Chamber Music*; Toby Perlman of the Perlman Music Program, and Patty (Mrs. Boris) Schwarz.

Shirley Fleming, editor of *The American Record Guide*, unwittingly started this project in 1988 when she asked me to write an article about Dorothy DeLay for the late, much-lamented journal *Musical America*, of which Fleming was then editor.

My warm thanks to Eve Goodman, my editor at Amadeus Press, who had an immediate understanding of this book from the time we first talked about it, and gave me every encouragement. I am also grateful to Reinhard Pauly, who provided valuable suggestions for the text. Joshua Leventhal contributed to its final shape.

Invaluable help of a diverse order that each of them will understand was provided by Geary Ahern, Barbara Anderman, Sarah Bayliss, Curt Carlson, Dudley Carlson, Carla Lynton, the late Ernest Lynton, Shihoko Niikawa, Cindy Russell, Halina Sand, Louise Schiller, Margaret Spanel, and especially Janice Papolos and John Winterbottom.

My deepest gratitude goes to Gila, Jordan, and Michael Sand, writers all, for their support. Without the untiring enthusiasm and editorial intelligence of Michael Sand, this book would not have been written, and I would have missed out on a fascinating adventure.

Certain portions of this book originally appeared in different form in *The Strad*, published in England; permission to use that material is gratefully acknowledged.

My thanks also to *The American Record Guide* for permission to use material from an article about Peter Oundjian that appeared in the September/October 1997 issue, and a portion of an article written by Robert McDuffie that appeared in the July/August 1997 issue.

Acknowledgment is made to Angel Records for permission to quote some text from the video of Sarah Chang in London, produced by Ian Stoutzker.

Gratitude is also due to S. G. Phillips, Inc., for the use of excerpts from "The Awakening" by Isaac Babel, translated by Walter Morison, from *The Collected Stories by Isaac Babel*. Copyright © 1955 by S. G. Phillips, Inc. For the title to chapter 13, "Enormous Changes at the Last Minute," I thank Grace Paley.

Introducing Miss DeLay

Itzhak Perlman is wearing a wig and a long-skirted dress. He is in the middle of giving a violin lesson, and has a cellular phone in one hand and a pencil in the other. "That was simply wonderful, sweetie," he says in a little-girl voice to virtuoso performer Robert Mc-Duffie, who has just given an execrable performance of the opening of the Mendelssohn Violin Concerto. Almost without missing a beat, Perlman continues his phone call to the Shun Lee Palace, an elegant Chinese restaurant near Lincoln Center. "Please send over thirty dumplings," he whispers into the mouthpiece. "No. On second thought, make it forty—and don't forget the extra sauce." He pauses for a moment, and says, "Actually, I think you had better send fifty. OK? Thank you, sweetie." In almost no time, concert artist Nadja Salerno-Sonnenberg arrives by bicycle with the order, and the two immediately get into a heated argument over the number of dumplings and the amount of sauce provided.

The occasion is a private party for Dorothy DeLay's eightieth birthday in 1997, and just about every major violinist in New York City is present. Many, including Perlman, McDuffie, and Salerno-Sonnenberg, are former students of this world-famous teacher. Perlman's impersonation is only one of many skits that have everyone in the room, including the honoree and her husband, laughing to the point of helplessness. Dorothy DeLay's refusal to give voice to an out-and-out negative is as familiar to them as the generic name "sweetie" and her enjoyment of food. Following the opening skit, Robert McDuffie and Nadja Salerno-Sonnenberg proceed to read aloud the very worst reviews that either of them has ever received from the press. At the conclusion of each brickbat, they bow toward the guest of honor, and solemnly intone, "And, thank you, Miss DeLay."

Almost all of today's major violinists spent their musical childhoods under the watchful eye of this plump, motherly woman. Appearances are deceiving, or at the least, wholly inadequate. DeLay is hardly just a nice lady who teaches the fiddle. For more than half a century, she has been a power-behind-the-throne, unknown outside the classical music world but a legend within it. It is a world in which all the standard emotions — ambition, greed, hunger for power, desire for self-expression, approval, recognition, friendship, love, and so on — are present in greater or lesser degree as they are when it comes to striving for a major career in any field.

DeLay is besieged by parents from all over the globe begging her, often at enormous personal sacrifice, to teach their children — they see her as holding the key to professional paradise in America. Where her students are concerned, this kindly presence is capable of behaving more like a lioness, defending them from outside predators, such as overambitious parents or managers; insisting that they listen to their own musical instincts; and finally, making sure that they gain the skills and independence they will need to survive and flourish in the jungle of the professional concert world that awaits them.

DeLay's influence extends far beyond the practice room. A top New York manager has described her as one of the great power brokers whose word can make or break a career. Orchestra conductors come to her for advice about soloists. She is the first port of call for a journalist on the track of a story in the violin world, or for an advertising firm looking for a cute whiz-kid to perform in a commercial. DeLay has taught at the Juilliard School of Music in New York since 1948, and is the only native-born American and the only woman to have entered a previously all-male bastion and be ranked among the world's great violin pedagogues. Beyond the confines of the concert world, most people have never heard of her.

Around the time of her seventy-fifth birthday, I asked DeLay if she could give me a list of her students who were performing in the upcoming season. The next time we met, she rummaged around in an unbelievably overstuffed notebook that was about three inches thick, which contained her records of her students, and produced a sheet of paper on which the ink had run. A powerful and pleasant scent filled the air. "I brought you these names," she said, "but I've messed them up by spilling perfume on them, so I'd better read them to you."

Adding that the names were not in any particular order, DeLay proceeded to run through a list that included Itzhak Perlman, Nadja

Salerno-Sonnenberg, Robert McDuffie, Cho-Liang Lin, Gil Shaham, Midori, Joseph Swensen, Sarah Chang, Mark Peskanov, Nigel Kennedy, Shlomo Mintz, Peter Oundjian, Kyoko Takezawa, Christian Altenburger, Christian Badea, Anne Akiko Meyers, Chee-Yun, Robert Chen, Chantal Juillet, Jaap van Zweden, Mila Georgieva, Livia Sohn, and Kurt Nikkanen. "I'm sure I've forgotten some," she concluded with a worried frown. No wonder those pages from DeLay's notebook smelled so good.

These artists shared the common goal of wanting to play the violin as beautifully as possible, but the routes they traveled with DeLay in their pursuit were as diverse as their individual personalities. What was vital for one was of minor importance for another. Contrary to the general mythology that has sprung up around her, DeLay does not teach only the stars. All her pupils are advanced players—they have to be to get into Juilliard to begin with—but within the group there is a considerable range of ability. DeLay's unorthodox style of teaching applies to everyone who studies with her, not just the handful of virtuosos who may make it to Carnegie Hall.

When I began sitting in on DeLay's lessons in the late 1980s, I noted in my diary:

> Watched DeLay teach for the afternoon. Second time. Class of four teenagers. We talked between breaks. Still can't figure out what she does that is so extraordinary. Feel torn between taking her reputation on faith and being a thorough skeptic.
>
> She's a very accurate reader of human nature, plus a touch of a cynic. Ample. Settles into chair comfortably. Pushes lips out. Peers over glasses. Sings, whistles, beats time on table. Lower jaw thrust forward. Scarf around neck seems to be a trademark. Crutches.
>
> After class DeLay got a bit weepy talking about a tragedy in the life of one of her students. "It gets me every time." Quite natural and unremarkable at the time, but with hindsight I suppose it is unusual. She is also a shrewd, hardheaded businesswoman with no illusions about what it takes to succeed. She doesn't miss a chance to tout one of her students.
>
> Judging from today, she seems to have particularly strong sympathy for those students who are unsure of themselves or frightened—she talked about Mark Peskanov as a little boy, for example, and also Itzhak Perlman when he first came to the U.S. at the age of thirteen. Reminiscent of herself when young?

Thinking back, in the course of the afternoon she cried a few tears, laughed a lot with her students, gossiped, listened intently, talked about musical structure, suggested various bowings, fingerings, and interpretations. No startling revelations, no mysteries unveiled. What is she up to? Why does it work?

The answers to those last two questions form the basis for this book. They emerged only after I became a lesson junky and found myself heading more and more often for Room 530, DeLay's studio on the fifth floor of the Juilliard School, where, for nearly ten years, between 1988 and 1998, I enjoyed a unique window onto her relatively unknown world. During that time I was writing articles about a number of her students and ex-students for several music periodicals in the United States and in England, an activity that dovetailed neatly with my interest in DeLay herself.

All the material quoted from DeLay and her husband, Edward Newhouse, derives from notes and tape recordings of conversations either at their home in Rockland County, at the Juilliard School, or at the Aspen Music School in Colorado, where DeLay has taught during the summers since 1971. DeLay was unstintingly generous in giving her time for interviews and in letting me sit in on her lessons virtually at will. She managed to combine an astonishing degree of openness with extreme caution in talking about her students out of concern for their private and professional well-being. There was never any hint of her steering me toward or away from a particular student or situation—the individuals who appear in the following pages do so entirely by my own choice. Whom to include was a subject we simply never discussed.

The important mentors in one's life are memorable for characteristics such as their individual quirks, their personal magnetism, and their obsessive devotion to a subject, attributes that are a thousand times more compelling than any amount of learned educational method. DeLay's particular strengths lie not only in her absorption in the learning process itself, but in her intuition, her humor, and her clarity of thought, qualities that would have made her a great teacher in any field, from astrophysics to medieval literature. It happened that inclination and force of circumstances led her to choose music.

Most of our children are not prodigies, or even particularly gifted in any one field, but they all have the potential to shine as individuals in some way if given the right conditions. A striking quality of the products of DeLay's studio is the absence of uniformity in the way her students play—each speaks in his or her own voice. The skepticism with which I initially viewed DeLay's teaching has been replaced over the years with a profound respect for who she is and what she does. DeLay may teach geniuses in music, but her way of doing so is relevant to just about any kind of learning in any subject at any level and at any stage of life.

Itzhak Perlman impersonating Dorothy DeLay at her seventieth birthday party, with "student" Paul Rosenthal, director of the Sitka Summer Music Festival in Alaska. Perlman again donned wig and falsetto voice for DeLay's eightieth. Photo: Peter Schaaf.

Part One

Dorothy DeLay—

Her Life and Legacy

1 DeLay's Life: A Limitless Sense of the Possible

"She has a limitless sense of the possible," the writer Edward Newhouse has said of his wife, Dorothy DeLay, whom he married in 1941. "It is a Midwestern trait. Here is the empty prairie—let's build a city. And eventually a city gets built, along with all the various urban problems thereunto. Dottie has a way of overlooking obstacles, and sometimes, if you overlook them long enough, they tend to disappear."

DeLay was born on 31 March 1917 into a family of teachers and preachers in Medicine Lodge, Kansas, a cattle town near the Oklahoma border that had been, in DeLay's grandmother's time, an Indian stockade. Those family members who were not teachers were circuit riders, ministers who went from one town to the next on the frontier, where there were communities that had no churches.

Medicine Lodge today has a museum with a replica of that stockade, and among the items prominently on display are the enormous kettle the family used for making soap from the fat of their cattle, some clothing, and the sword that belonged to DeLay's maternal grandfather, William Osborn, at the time of the Civil War. DeLay's maternal grandmother, Jennie Stoughton Osborn, was a voluminous letter writer who learned to type when she was in her late eighties. She became a menace to the family by inundating them with correspondence—a situation that was astutely resolved by her son, who suggested that she write her memoirs. These were eventually bound and printed, and include a description of Jennie Stoughton Osborn's granddaughter, Dorothy, who was taken by her mother to see the King of Belgium as he passed through Kansas in 1919 on a whistle-stop train tour of the United States. "Dorothy was only two years old, but she wanted to see the King, too," her grandmother wrote, "and was handed up to the platform by her mother, where she put her little arms around [the King's] neck and hugged and kissed him."

DeLay's mother, Cecile Osborn DeLay, was born in 1882, and when she was about eight years old, she was one of several little girls who accompanied Carry Nation around the state on her crusade against liquor. The little girls wore angel wings on their backs as they trooped after their formidable leader—Carry Nation was a robust six footer—on her rounds of calling the drunken sinners to repent. In the heat of her missionary zeal, Carry would invade the local barrooms to urge the patrons to take the pledge, and if she was ignored, she took her ax to the barroom shelves and mirrors. Grandfather Osborn had no patience with either Carry Nation or her cause, and once he knew what was happening, saw to it that his little daughter Cecile, perhaps to her distress, was stripped of her wings.

Kansas is a part of the world to which DeLay still feels strongly linked, and she has said that if the East Coast were to break off from the United States and sink into the ocean, she would go right back to the place where she was raised. "I would get a whole bunch of little tiny violins and a whole bunch of little tiny kids together, and we would build a violin school from the bottom up," she said, already overlooking obstacles.

When she was growing up, DeLay, who was the eldest of three sisters, always swore she would never become a teacher herself. She says she slid in by the back door, having initially planned a solo career. Her father, Glenn Adney DeLay, was the local school superintendent and an amateur cellist; her mother played the piano. Both parents were devout members of the Methodist Church, which did not prevent their little four-year-old Dorothy, an individualist from early on, from being suspended from Sunday school for refusing to believe that Jonah had been swallowed by a whale—she felt that, realistically, it just didn't make sense.

"I was brought up in a very authoritarian, religious, rigid background," said DeLay when we were talking one afternoon in her studio. "There were definite things that were just right and wrong as I grew up. They were fixed in my philosophy. The first time I consciously realized that there are many different ways of judging things, it shook my faith in the universe." DeLay rocked back in her chair and laughed.

A light dawned and I thought, My goodness, if things aren't what they are, well, what is? From the time I was very small, I knew that

DeLay at the age of about two, sitting on the lap of her great uncle
Stoughton, in Medicine Lodge, Kansas. Courtesy Dorothy DeLay.

God was sitting up there in the sky with the book of my life in his lap, and every time I did something bad I got a black mark. By the time I was five I had black marks all over my poor book. It was just terrible. I sometimes think I understand people who are schizophrenic. There would be times when I would think to myself, I'm the only person living on this earth. All the other people are angels sent to watch me and report me when I make mistakes.

DeLay's childhood fantasy of God and his book may have resonated for her through the years. As a teacher, she scrupulously avoids making any lasting black marks on the music of her students.

I asked DeLay if her sisters felt the same way about God and the book.

No, I don't think so, because I was the eldest. My next sister is Nellis, and the youngest is Louise. My mother used to get terribly upset with my sister Nellis and me when we were naughty, when I was around six or seven, and she would say, "I don't know what's happening. My two good little girls are gone and there are these two horrible little girls in my house. I am going out, and when I come back"—only it never sounded like "when I come back," but "if I come back"—"I hope those horrible little girls are gone, and my good little girls are here again." And she would go sailing out to have tea with a neighbor. So I would be sitting on the floor with my feet in front of me and big tears rolling down my cheeks, and my sister Nellis, who was much smarter, being the younger, would say, "Good. I'm glad she's gone. Now I can do what I want."

DeLay said that, this story notwithstanding, she got tremendous support and encouragement from her mother. DeLay's father, by contrast to her mother, was never particularly approving of her. He appears to have been a man who was difficult to please and judgmental of many of the people around him. DeLay clearly inherited her mother's optimistic nature and adventurous spirit.

My husband laughs at me because I have always had the feeling that nothing is impossible. My mother used to tell me life is so full of opportunities—there are so many things you can do. You can do just anything you want. She was exaggerating, but I took it literally. When I first met my husband, we got to talking about how people feel about doing things, and I said, "Well, you know, given enough time, I think I could do anything that anybody has ever

DeLay and her cousin Nelson Turnbull, outside the family farmhouse in Medicine Lodge, Kansas. DeLay, Nelson, and Nelson's brother, Dick, dug a hole in the yard deep enough for them to sit in. The family's prize cow fell in and had to be shot. Courtesy Dorothy DeLay.

done." He started citing the great sculptors of the past, and I said, "Sure, I just need enough time"—a bit like the ape principle that given enough time they could type out all of Shakespeare.

At the age of three, DeLay was already reading. She started taking violin lessons when she was four and gave her first concert at a local church the following year. She said she can still remember how good it felt to have her mother be so proud of her on that occasion. When she was attending Neodesha High School, DeLay was found to have an IQ of 180 and was among a group of a hundred students nationwide selected for a survey by the Stanford-Binet research team that was gathering information to check the accuracy of IQ ratings. The study tracked those one hundred students for a period of ten to twelve years following their graduation from high school, to see how they fared compared to a control group of the same number. Neither the high-IQ children nor the parents were told who had been selected. The only person who knew the identity of the chosen students was the school principal, whose responsibility it was to complete the necessary documentation and pass it on to the local superintendent of schools—who was, in DeLay's instance, her father, so the cover of secrecy was inadvertently blown.

DeLay was the top student in all her classes, either because of or in spite of her notion that she had to be the best, or something terrible would happen: "If I came home with a score of ninety-six, the response was 'Who got a hundred?'" She was also the concertmistress of the high school orchestra. By this time, Neodesha, where the family lived, had come a long way from its dusty frontier town origins, and the orchestra included roughly a hundred of the school's four hundred students—a statistic that any school today would envy, if it is lucky enough to have an orchestra at all.

Because of the disparity in age between herself and her classmates—DeLay entered her senior year of high school at the age of fourteen—DeLay says she had difficulty making friends. The seventeen- and eighteen-year-old girls in her class were mainly interested in discussing their boyfriends, the last thing in DeLay's mind at the time, and her presence cramped their style. Being so extremely bright did not help, either. She described herself as the kind of person who knew all the answers—hardly a social asset under any circumstances. DeLay had to wait a year and a half after graduation before entering college since her parents felt that she was still too young to be away from home.

DeLay entered Oberlin College in Ohio at sixteen, and took violin lessons with Raymond Cerf, a student of Eugène Ysaÿe, but at the end of her freshman year her father decided that a conservatory education was too limiting, and DeLay transferred to Michigan State University, where the violinist Michael Press was on the faculty. Press, a product of the Moscow Conservatory, had emigrated after the Russian Revolution and in 1922 came to the United States, where he proceeded to make a considerable reputation as a violinist, conductor, and teacher. DeLay studied with him until she graduated from Michigan State at the age of twenty, and then, this time defying her parents' wishes, she headed for the Juilliard School in New York with thirty dollars in her pocket.

The most prominent teacher in the violin department at Juilliard at the time DeLay entered the school in 1937 was Louis Persinger, who had been appointed to the faculty in 1930 as successor to Leopold Auer. DeLay studied with Persinger for a short time, but her chief teachers were Hans Letz and Felix Salmond. During her years as a graduate student,

DeLay had to earn her living and was sometimes hard-pressed for time to practice. "There were times I went to class unprepared," she said. "I would be sitting in Felix Salmond's chamber music class, trying desperately to read my way through a trio, and all of a sudden these fingers would come down right in front of my nose, snapping the rhythm." DeLay stopped to demonstrate vigorously. "I couldn't see the notes on the page because this hand was going up and down and I was afraid to move. I would be still trying to play my part and from above I would hear, 'What are you composing there, girl?'" DeLay laughed. "It was just dreadful."

DeLay did four years of graduate work at Juilliard, where she earned her Artist's Diploma. She also began getting concert dates, both as a soloist and as a member of the Stuyvesant Trio, an ensemble that she and her sister Nellis, a gifted cellist, formed with pianist Helen Brainard. Nellis had come to join her sister in New York, and for a while the two shared an apartment, living basically on potatoes. Nellis went on to have a long and successful career as a cellist with the New York City Ballet Orchestra. She married the singer Clifford Harvuot, who was with the Metropolitan Opera for some forty years.

"If ever a girl worked her way through college and Juilliard graduate school, that was Dottie," said Edward Newhouse. "She baby-sat in exchange for room and board. She would be the concertmistress of a Broadway show for a year or more, while studying full time. These were Depression years—she and Nellis played for their dinner at restaurants, they played weddings, they did everything," Newhouse laughed.

> I remember Dottie seeing a notice on the bulletin board at Juilliard from some agent or manager downtown, name unknown, saying "Girl Violinist Wanted." Here was this guy right out of central casting, feet on desk, cigar in mouth, who said, "All right, well, what do you do?"
> Dottie said, "I'm answering your ad for a violinist."
> "Yes, yes, I can see the violin case, but what do you *do?* Do you do tap or what?" So she didn't open her violin case. She just said good-bye. Besides, I think tap dancing while playing the violin might be a trick beyond her.

Dorothy DeLay and Edward Newhouse met in late 1940 on a Missouri-Pacific Railway train en route to New York. She had been playing in Leopold Stokowski's All-American Youth Orchestra, which had chartered a ship and was going around to large port cities in South America.

At the end of the tour, the ship docked in Los Angeles, and the orchestra stayed on to make a couple of records. On her way back to New York, DeLay stopped in Kansas to see some of her family, and then got on the train in St. Louis. Newhouse was already on board, having come from Houston, where he had gone to visit his younger brother who had just graduated from the Colorado School of Mines. He was looking fairly disreputable, having checked his luggage, with everything but the clothes on his back, through to New York.

As Newhouse described the event, by the time DeLay got on in St. Louis, the train was practically empty, and he could not help noticing her as she sat down.

> She had a lovely head of hair—a real mane. After the train got started, I pretended to be thirsty, so I could get a better glimpse of her on my way to the water cooler. She saw me looking at her rather intensely, and carefully moved her handbag to the other side, next to the window. It took me a while, but finally I asked if I could sit with her. Dottie has always been very polite, and said, "Yes, I guess so." By then we were in Harrisburg and we chatted for the rest of the journey. She told me she was a violinist, and I told her I wrote novels and stories for *The New Yorker*. Being shy, I didn't ask her to marry me until Trenton. She didn't say yes until New York, and in the tunnel before arriving in Pennsylvania Station, we decided we would have one son and one daughter, and she gave me her phone number.
>
> I telephoned the next day, and when Dottie answered, she put her hand over the phone and called to her sister Nellis, who was in the shower, "It's that man from the train—what do I do?" Nellis said, "Hang up. Just hang up." Well, she didn't, and we got married four months later.

DeLay and Newhouse were married on 5 March 1941, and they in due course carried out their early decision about the number and gender of the children they would have. Their son, Jeffrey, is a professor of radiology at Columbia Presbyterian Hospital and lives in Bronxville with his wife and two children. Their daughter, Alison, is a children's librarian and storyteller, and her husband is a doctor at Massachusetts General Hospital; they have two children. Newhouse likes his son-in-law's style of medicine—whatever ailment you have, he says "Soak It." You have a sore elbow? Soak It. You have a brain tumor? Soak It.

At the time she and Newhouse got married, DeLay was still a student at Juilliard. She was also doing more and more concerts, and a newspaper photograph of the Stuyvesant Trio from that time shows DeLay carefully placed in such a way as to conceal the fact that she was in an "Interesting Condition."

The Stuyvesant Trio, 1941, with cellist Nellis DeLay (Dorothy DeLay's sister) and pianist Helen Brainard. The group had several successful seasons and considerable press attention. DeLay was carefully placed behind the piano in this picture to conceal her visible pregnancy. Photo: J. Abresch, New York.

"I did quite a nice season," said DeLay, "and then, because of the war, our whole life was shattered, the structure was gone." Newhouse joined the army and DeLay followed along as much as she could as her husband was transferred to various parts of the country. Newhouse ended up in Washington, D.C., at the Pentagon as aide to Air Force General Henry H. "Hap" Arnold, writing his reports and speeches, and now and again accompanying him to conferences.

Living in wartime Washington proved fascinating but difficult. "I was not really equipped to deal with it terribly well," DeLay said. "We had one baby and then when the war was over we had another, and I discovered I didn't like being a soloist. I always felt stricken after a concert because I never felt I had done particularly well. Then to be faced with people in the Green Room congratulating me, and to have to go to a party afterward!" DeLay clasped her hands in mock horror. "You know how you project your feelings onto other people? I expected the audience to be knowledgeable about music and I thought, If they are knowledgeable, how can they have liked it? I didn't understand the simple fact that they came to the concert because they loved to hear live music, and that that was the most important thing."

Increasingly, DeLay found herself looking for reasons to turn down concert engagements, or even losing letters inviting her to play. It took some time for her to realize that she was setting traps for herself, and that what she really wanted was to be out of concert performance altogether. From the time their first child was three months old, DeLay and Newhouse always had a housekeeper, which enabled DeLay to pursue her performing career, but no small additional consideration was that she was loath to be away on tour from her two young children for any length of time. At this point DeLay actually considered going to medical school, but dropped the idea after a few months when her husband confronted her one day with the question of whether she really wanted to go back to college and do four years of math and the sciences. The answer, she said, was No, although it would have been Yes to chemistry or physics.

Back in New York after the war, DeLay decided to return to serious study of the violin. "I had done my four years of graduate work, but I was not satisfied," she said. "I was very uncomfortable. I just did not like very much what I had done so far, and felt there were too many things I did not know."

DeLay described herself as having gone through a period of terrible insecurity and self-consciousness at around this point in her life, which must have a great deal to do with her ability to empathize with students who are going through similar miseries. "When you feel that way, it is awfully hard to look at someone else and think about how to help that person, because you are so desperate for help yourself," she said. "I think it is because you don't understand the real purpose of being alive. You are just worried about whatever people are going to think of you."

Early in 1946 DeLay started interviewing teachers, including the legendary Ivan Galamian, who had just been appointed to the Juilliard School. She characterized him as having been a very shy person, and said she liked him the best because he was the most direct. Starting that spring, DeLay had about six lessons with Galamian over a period of three months, in the course of which they became friends. DeLay would meet regularly with Galamian and his wife, Judith, for supper on Monday nights, and most of the talk would revolve around students and teaching methods. "He listened so carefully to what I said, and responded so thoughtfully," DeLay recalled. "I really had to think very hard about what I was saying. I admired him a great deal."

DeLay's lessons in Galamian's studio were followed by a couple of weeks at his summer place near Westport, New York, in the Adirondack Mountains, to which Galamian would invite a few of his students. Hard work was the order of the day in the Galamian household, and the fortunate few who were invited spent most of their time practicing. This was the very beginning of Meadowmount, the summer camp that Galamian and his wife established in 1944. At the time that DeLay went to stay with the Galamians, she still had no thought of becoming a teacher herself. She was wholly concentrated on her violin studies, but she was deeply impressed by the intensity of Galamian's devotion to his school. Whether she was aware of it or not, the seeds of her future career were being planted.

> I wanted to go on with my own work, and I wanted to see what he was doing. I sat in the studio in Meadowmount sometimes and watched the process, and then I thought: something very special is happening in this room. So I said to Mr. Galamian, "Why do you come up here and break your back working so hard, when you can stay in New York and work half as much and make more money?" He was just pouring all his energy into that school. He thought for a while and then he said, "Because I would be proud of it." He had never talked that way to me before, and I thought, That's wonderful, that's really wonderful!

In the fall of that same year, a friend of DeLay's invited her to teach one day a week at the Henry Street Settlement School in Manhattan, and she decided to try it just to see what it was like. Right from the beginning, DeLay, to her surprise, discovered that she loved teaching. It appealed to her sense of adventure—of watching something change before your very eyes—as well as to her fascination with how people's minds work. She took so much pleasure in the job that the two-and-a-half-hour bus journey from her home to the school bothered her not in the least.

Three or four months after DeLay started teaching at the Henry Street Settlement School, fate threw a similar opportunity in her path, this time at the Juilliard School, where she was already well known to the faculty and the administration from her graduate student days. The Preparatory Division, as the Pre-College Division was then known, was in the process of expanding its staff, and the person in charge of the program, Fred Prausnitz, called and asked DeLay if she would teach there part-time. DeLay told him she would be delighted.

At Juilliard, as at the Henry Street Settlement School, DeLay had some little kids who were not particularly gifted. From her description, they were making the kinds of sounds that keep families from starting their children on the violin. Nevertheless, "Suddenly, I realized that I was having a good time, and that they were having a good time, and that the day I did my three hours of teaching was the nicest day of the week," she said.

Within the year more work came along. The conductor Hugo Fiorato, who was a friend of DeLay's, was teaching chamber music at Sarah Lawrence College in Westchester, New York, and needed a violinist and a cellist for a couple of hours a week. He offered the job, which paid five dollars an hour, to DeLay and her sister Nellis, and the two young women accepted with enthusiasm. DeLay started out at Sarah Lawrence as a violinist, but she stayed on as a teacher and was a member of the faculty from 1948 to 1987.

In 1948 Galamian invited DeLay to join him as his assistant at Juilliard, as well as at Meadowmount. The Newhouse family, Dorothy, Edward, and their two children, would rent a house on Lake Champlain, eleven miles away, and settle in for the summer. DeLay continued to work with Galamian summer and winter for more than twenty years. The eventual rupture between the two in 1970 over teaching methods caused a permanent upheaval in the classical music world. But that is another story to emerge in the following chapter.

Studio portrait of DeLay, 1950. Courtesy Dorothy DeLay.

Although DeLay says she slid into teaching by the back door, there seems to have been some grand design in the way the door—or doors—opened. Curiosity made her push open the first door to the Henry Street Settlement House, but the others, including Sarah Lawrence, Juilliard (1947–), Meadowmount (1948–1970), Aspen (1971–), the University of Cincinnati (1974–), the Philadelphia College of the Performing Arts (1977–1983), the New England Conservatory (1978–1987), and the Royal College of Music (1987–), unlocked as though predestined.

Edward Newhouse was born in Budapest and came to the United States at the age of twelve. He became a writer and published several novels as well as a great many short stories, almost all of them in *The New Yorker*. "I just wrote a lot of fiction for them, for maybe thirty years," Newhouse says. "I would have eight to ten stories a year. I haven't published a word there or anywhere since the mid-sixties." Newhouse's circle of friends was composed of many outstanding writers of the time, not only because of his life at *The New Yorker*, but because the part of rural Rockland County where he and DeLay settled (now the bustling community of Nyack) became a center for people in the arts. Their friends and neighbors included the writers Charles MacArthur, Carson McCullers, and Countess Alexandra Tolstoy, as well as distinguished actors, artists, and composers.

A current of gentle teasing runs through much of the conversation between DeLay and Newhouse—they are obviously not in the least bored with each other after a lifetime together. They argue, they interrupt each other, they ask each other's opinion, and they defer to each other. "Well," DeLay will say about some past incident, "the first thing that happened is that she arrived here—"

"The first thing that happened, sweetie," Newhouse interrupts, "is that before she came—" "And John said—" DeLay continues imperturbably.

"No!" Newhouse insists.

"OK, well you tell it. You give the absolute and accurate truth."

"Well, there is my version, and then there is that of my associate here," says Newhouse, turning to me as DeLay rolls her eyes and says "Oh, Eddie!" in mock despair.

"Mr. Newhouse is a very sage adviser," said the virtuoso violinist Cho-Liang Lin, a former DeLay student. "He is a wonderful man—easygoing and thoughtful. There is a terrific give-and-take between them. If

I need to talk about a business question or a career move, I go to him. He has a clear view from the sidelines. There is Miss DeLay out there at the center of the world. Mr. Newhouse knows he's very important to her, but he has no interest in sharing the spotlight."

After Newhouse retired from *The New Yorker,* his book-lined study at home became a hub from which he helps DeLay's students to write grants and applications, dispenses practical advice, fields some of the innumerable phone calls, and serves as a general store of information. If one calls Juilliard for news about a DeLay student, one is frequently referred to Newhouse as a more up-to-date source. He has always had a particularly soft spot for the youngest ones and long cherished a Christmas card to DeLay from then-six-year-old Sarah Chang: "I like the Juilliard school. I like it because you teach there. Also, I like the bending [sic] machines." ("I can't tell you how much better her handwriting is than my son's," Newhouse added.) He also likes to tell of a phone call from a very self-possessed ten year old whom he had not yet met. "I have heard so many good things about you, Mr. Newhouse," the child said. "I want to write to you so I would like your address and also your zipper code." A letter he passed on to me from another child is a model of realism in the face of possible disappointment: "I think that if I can't get a puppy I'll get a kitten and if I can't get a kitten I'll get another hamster." The writer of this note, by the way, was also about ten and already a formidable soloist.

Newhouse is soft-spoken and courtly. He is also enormously erudite and a splendid raconteur with a fondness for history as well as the arts. He is unabashedly proud of DeLay and is adept at providing an interviewer with catchy quotes: "William Schuman [the composer and Juilliard's first president] called her the Dottie Appleseed of the violin world," referring to the large number of her students playing all over the globe; useful pegs for writers: "I thought you might be interested to know that no fewer than five of her students will be playing with the New York Philharmonic this season"; and jokes: "Dottie has just received the Sanford Medal from Yale University. Since she is a direct descendent of Thomas J. Hooker [Hooker (1586–1647) was a Puritan clergyman and the chief founder of Hartford, Connecticut], I am suggesting that when she accepts she should say, with downcast eye, that she imagined this was the first time such an honor had been bestowed upon a Hooker."

The gentle manner can suddenly turn sharp if Newhouse feels his wife is in any way under attack. Shortly after we first met, Newhouse and

I talked about a particular student who, like many, studied with both DeLay and one of her associates. I asked about the difference between what went on in the two lessons, and remember feeling as though I had stepped on a hornet's nest. "If you go that route you'll be walking a high wire and you'd better have a big net under you," Newhouse replied coldly. "Why?" I asked. "Some writers like to say that so-and-so specializes in technique, and so-and-so in musicality. None of the students they teach in common are confused," he added. "There is so much to be taught. They do not work at cross purposes." Since, in fact, I had heard no complaints of mixed signals between DeLay and her assistants, I could only assume that some previous experience had led Newhouse to regard the question as provocative.

At home in Nyack, the telephone starts ringing at nine o'clock in the morning and continues throughout the day and evening. The callers are current students with problems, both personal and professional, ex-students on tour who just want to check in, deans of conservatories looking for faculty, managements, conductors—an endless parade of people who are in one way or another connected to the violin world. After DeLay escapes to Juilliard, Newhouse remains captive to the telephone. "I impersonate somebody who knows something, although after all these years there has been a certain process of osmosis," he said.

> There is this mare's nest next to the phone that she calls her address book, although actually it's more like an outrage. A conductor will call and say, "My soloist came down with tendinitis, have you got somebody?" and Dottie will start phoning around. Or a string quartet may want her advice if they have to replace one of their violinists. Sometimes one of the students is desperate for a bit of hand-holding: "Miss DeLay, he asked me to marry him, should I?" or, "He *didn't*"—tears dripping down chin. "What should I do for encores?" "Should I do encores?" "Will they expect me to do encores?" Or "My arm hurts. Should I stop practicing?" Those questions, of course, I leave to Dottie.

Newhouse gives an amiable smile and says, "Part of my function is to convince all the girls in the class that they are beautiful. When the kids are having their exams, the phone sometimes goes nonstop. It is reminiscent of Secretary of State Kissinger saying 'This isn't governing—this is crisis management.'"

At the time of these particular conversations with DeLay and Newhouse, DeLay was about to be eighty-one. In addition to her Juilliard classes, a forty-five minute trip from her home, which she drove herself, she still flew regularly to the University of Cincinnati College-Conservatory of Music, where she was the Starling Visiting Professor, and spent her summers in Aspen, where she holds the Dorothy DeLay Chair. Back in New York, conductor and violinist Peter Oundjian said he saw her driving along the parkway doing seventy miles an hour. He tried to catch up with her to give her a wave, but couldn't keep up. "Absolutely characteristic," he laughed. "She was perfectly focused, knew exactly where she was going, and was doing it at speed."

While DeLay has generally kept a low public profile in the course of helping her students to get their names in lights, she is not without honor at home or abroad. She holds honorary doctorates from Oberlin College, Columbia University, Duquesne University, Michigan State University, and the University of Colorado. Yale University has bestowed on her the Sanford Medal, their highest award for "Distinguished Contributions to Music." She has received the Artist Teacher Award of the American String Teachers Association, the National Music Council's American Eagle Award, and the King Solomon Award of the America-Israel Cultural Foundation. She is a Fellow of the Royal College of Music in Great Britain.

In 1994 DeLay, along with fellow musicians Harry Belafonte and Dave Brubeck, received the National Medal of the Arts, presented by President Clinton at a White House ceremony. She was nominated for the award by the Aspen Music Festival and School, and letters of support came from her students, including Itzhak Perlman, Robert McDuffie, Gil Shaham, and others, as well as Carnegie Hall's then executive director, the late Judith Arron, and DeLay's friend and former Supreme Court Justice the late Harry Blackmun.

Newhouse likes to describe the ripple effect that DeLay's teaching has had, and even without the bias of a fond husband, the legacy is impressive. Quite apart from the star soloists, she has taught the concertmasters of orchestras all over the world, including the Berlin Philharmonic, the Philadelphia Orchestra, the Amsterdam Concertgebouw Orchestra, and the Chicago Symphony; violinists of the Juilliard, Tokyo, Cleveland, American, Takács, Mendelssohn, Blair, Muir, Fine Arts, and Vermeer String Quartets have studied with her; her former students teach, passing on her ideas as well as their own, at the major music conservatories in the United States and abroad; and four violin concer-

DeLay, seated in a wheelchair, receiving the National Medal of the Arts from President Clinton in a White House ceremony in 1994. Official White House photograph.

tos, written by major composers in her honor, have become part of the repertoire.

All in all, the little girl from Medicine Lodge, Kansas, has lived her life pretty much in keeping with Newhouse's description of the Midwestern character. Gradually, over the years, DeLay has built not just a city, but, through her students and the teachers she has trained, an entire network of cities that continues to grow.

2   Teaching Geniuses: Auer, Galamian, and DeLay

"By the way, who *is* Miss DeLay? I've never heard of her," a reporter from a British newspaper asked Edward Newhouse on the telephone, when trying to reach DeLay with a query from his editor. Newhouse's astute response was to identify his wife as the teacher of Nigel Kennedy (formerly known as "the Nige" and now simply as "Kennedy"), England's most famous violinist, whose early incarnation as a punk-rocker with orange hair, earrings, and far-out clothes, both on stage and off, had, in combination with his virtuosity, made him a household name in Britain. "Really? How fantastic! How absolutely incredible!" exclaimed the reporter, instantly bowled over with DeLay's status.

Music teachers do not make their pupils famous, but the reverse — teachers owe their reputations to their successful students, and even the greatest pedagogues are usually known only within the music world. Most people know the name of Jascha Heifetz, for example, but how many are familiar with that of his teacher, Leopold Auer, who was the most influential violin teacher in the world in the earlier part of the twentieth century? Or Ivan Galamian, who inherited Auer's mantle during his long tenure at Juilliard, which lasted from 1946 until his death in 1981? Galamian became an almost legendary figure to musicians in his time, but he, like DeLay, remained largely unknown to the general public.

Auer, Galamian, and DeLay are the most prominent names in the roster of great violin pedagogues in the twentieth century, and all three taught at the Juilliard School. Auer was there comparatively briefly, about twelve years, since nearly fifty years of his career were spent at the St. Petersburg Conservatory in Russia. Galamian also taught at his studio in Manhattan, at the Curtis Institute of Music in Philadelphia, and at

Meadowmount, the school he established in the Adirondacks. While DeLay has taught at a half-dozen major institutions, Juilliard has been her base since 1948.

The other celebrated violin teacher at Juilliard in the twentieth century was Louis Persinger; as mentioned in chapter 1, Persinger was appointed to the faculty in 1930 following Auer's death; he remained at the school for the next thirty-six years. Persinger originally became famous as the teacher of the five-year-old prodigy Yehudi Menuhin. He was also an accomplished pianist, and when Menuhin began appearing on stage, Persinger traveled with him and served as his young student's accompanist. Persinger, who also taught Ruggiero Ricci, was much respected, and while his influence at Juilliard did not match that of either his predecessor, Leopold Auer, or his successor, Ivan Galamian, he remains an important figure in that world.

There were, of course, other teachers of distinction in the United States during the middle of the twentieth century, such as Naum Blinder in California, who taught Isaac Stern from the age of ten to eighteen (Blinder was the only teacher Stern ever had), and the much beloved Josef Gingold at Indiana University, whose students included Jaime Laredo (also a Galamian pupil) and Joseph Silverstein. In spite of the number of outstanding music schools—including the New England, Peabody, Oberlin, and Cincinnati College conservatories, the Cleveland Institute of Music, the Manhattan School, Mannes College, and the Curtis Institute, the real seat of stringed instrument power when it comes to producing solo virtuosos has remained at the Juilliard School.

LEOPOLD AUER

Leopold Auer, who was born in Hungary in 1845 and died in 1930 near Dresden (but was buried in New York), spent most of his life in Russia. At the outbreak of the Russian Revolution in 1917, a vast population of Russian Jews, including many of Auer's students, fled to the United States, and Auer, who was in Norway at the time, decided to come to America rather than return to the chaos at home. At the age of seventy-two, and by then world famous, Auer settled in New York, where he was known and warmly welcomed, and started teaching and giving a few concerts, including a performance at Carnegie Hall. Students flocked to him as they had in Russia, but more for the name than the instruction, as he was no longer in full health and vigor. For the final twelve years of his life, Auer taught both privately and at the Juilliard School as well as at the Curtis Institute.

One has only to look at the names of Auer's students—not just Heifetz, but also Mischa Elman, Efrem Zimbalist, and Nathan Milstein —to realize in what a rich period he lived and what a giant he was in his field. Auer is popularly known as the founder of the classical Russian school of violin playing, but so many musicians, before, during, and after his time, were part of the process of bringing this style of playing to the world's attention—the recognized centers having hitherto been in Belgium, France, and Germany—that the title of founder is really a form of convenient shorthand. What is indisputable is Auer's stature as a teacher and artist. In 1868 Auer was appointed to the faculty of the St. Petersburg Conservatory at the recommendation of Anton Rubinstein, to replace Henri Wieniawski. Auer was then twenty-three, and he remained at the conservatory for forty-nine years in the course of which he is reputed to have taught more than five hundred students, many of whom undoubtedly made important reputations as concertmasters, chamber musicians, and orchestral players, but as usual, it was the big-name soloists who made the Auer name famous.

Auer, the son of a house painter, was a violin prodigy who spent his teen years touring in the provinces in order to support himself and his father. In his book *Violin Playing As I Teach It*, Auer describes the difficulties confronting a budding musician in mid-nineteenth-century Russia, with little or no access to the great cultural centers. "I was only a young artist then, whose musical education was as yet uncompleted, handicapped at first by my lack of a sufficiently large and varied repertory," he wrote. "Little by little, however, I built up my repertory by using every opportunity that came to me to hear genuine virtuosos play while 'on tour' and by hearing them play in Vienna during my rare visits to that city." The touring virtuosos so sought after by Auer—he mentions Henri Vieuxtemps, Ferdinand Laub, and Antonio Bazzini—rarely performed outside the big cities in any case, because of the slowness, practical difficulties, and discomforts of traveling from one town to another— significant obstacles to ponder for today's performer who grumbles about crisscrossing the country by airplane—not that that is a bowl of cherries, either.

One cannot help wondering what Auer, starved for role models, might have done with a CD player. Today, no matter where you live, you have instant access to the greatest artists and orchestras of the world without stepping outdoors. DeLay routinely advises her students to get hold of as many different recordings of a work as they can find, not in order to learn the repertoire, but to compare the various performance styles. Of the Mendelssohn Violin Concerto alone, they can listen to some *sixty* versions. In addition, most of these children have attended live concerts with their parents since they were able to sit still. One result of all this exposure is that students in the wunderkind category usually have between fifteen to twenty different concertos under their little belts by the time they are eleven or twelve.

While Auer had a distinguished career as a performer, it was as a teacher that he secured his place in history, and in this area, his reputation began to grow only at the turn of the century, when he was already in his mid-fifties. The early 1900s saw many Jewish students from the Pale—those areas where Jews were allowed to live in czarist Russia—making their way to the music conservatory at St. Petersburg. Odessa in particular was a major breeding ground, in part due to the presence of Piotr Stoliarsky, a magnetic teacher who had a particular gift for producing child prodigies—the records are sketchy, but his method appears to have relied largely on a sort of good-cop–bad-cop approach, praising them lavishly at one moment and threatening imminent extinction the next. Stoliarsky's star pupil was David Oistrakh, one of the few eminent Russian violinists who did not study with Auer. Of Auer's students, Mischa Elman was from Odessa (the family moved there when he was six, following a pogrom that all but demolished their town); Nathan Milstein was also from Odessa; Efrem Zimbalist was born in Rostov; and Jascha Heifetz came from Vilna.

The families of these and other prodigies were drawn to the St. Petersburg Conservatory, and to Auer, in the hope that through their children they might be able to struggle out of the poverty and harsh conditions of the ghetto. Once a child was admitted to the conservatory, he and the accompanying parent were eligible to obtain permits as temporary residents, somewhat akin to being granted visas for a foreign country.

Auer was a teacher who involved himself in the lives of his students outside the studio, advising them on matters such as concert attire and the social graces as well as on professional advancement—those who hoped to play on the international circuit, for example, were virtually required to learn a foreign language. The few fortunate Jewish students who were permitted to leave the Pale to study in St. Petersburg got there through the influence that Auer wielded with government officials in charge of those districts.

Boris Schwarz discussed the kind of teacher Auer was in his valuable book, *Great Masters of the Violin.*

> In technical matters, he was no teacher at all; he left the technical preparation of his students to his assistants. . . . Clearly, Auer had no "method" of general validity; his greatness lay in sizing up the potential of each student and developing his peculiar individuality. . . . Though he valued talent, he also demanded punctual attendance, intelligent work habits, and attention to detail. Auer was stern, severe, even harsh.

Apropos of this last statement, among the many anecdotes that make up the Auer legend is his purported yardstick for the amount of time a student should practice: "Three hours if they are any good, four if they are a bit stupid, and if they need more than four, they should try another profession."

IVAN GALAMIAN

Ivan Galamian, who took center stage after Auer, charmed, instructed, and intimidated two entire generations of violinists, and his influence on performance style continues undiminished. For nearly forty years, until his death in 1981, Galamian served on the faculties of both the Juilliard School and the Curtis Institute in Philadelphia, although most of his teaching took place in his West 73rd Street apartment in Manhattan. Galamian's immense prestige rested in part on the fact that no fewer than seven of his students won the Leventritt Award: Betty Jean Hagen, Sergiu Luca, David Nadien, Itzhak Perlman, Arnold Steinhardt, Kyung Wha Chung, and Pinchas Zukerman. For many years the most important violin competition in America, the Leventritt Award carried a fairly modest sum of money and, more significantly, a great deal of exposure in the form of appearances with major American orchestras. Other students were winners of the Queen Elisabeth, the Tchaikovsky, the Carl Flesch, the Wieniawski — in fact, all the international competitions of note.

Born in 1903 in Tabriz, Persia, of Armenian parents, Galamian was taken at the age of two to Russia, where the family settled in Moscow. His father was a successful businessman, and both parents encouraged Gala-

Ivan Galamian in 1977 in his Manhattan studio, where pictures of history's greatest violinists glared down upon his students. Galamian was DeLay's world-famous predecessor at the Juilliard School; she was his assistant from 1948 to 1970. Photo: Peter Schaaf.

DeLay with Yehudi Menuhin in 1975, when both were serving as jurors of the Queen Elisabeth Competition in Brussels. Courtesy Dorothy DeLay.

mian's early interest in the violin. At the age of thirteen, Galamian was admitted to the Moscow Philharmonic School as a student of Konstantin Mostras, who was himself an Auer disciple. Galamian remained with Mostras for the next six years, all through the First World War and the Russian Revolution.

Galamian was fifteen when Lenin moved the government from St. Petersburg to Moscow, with the Communist regime in full control. Families like the affluent Galamians were stripped of everything they owned, and young Galamian was thrown in jail. He was, at the time, a member of the opera orchestra of the Bolshoi Theater, and this proved to be the youth's saving. Only the arts, and music in particular, were exempt from the repression of the Bolshevik regime, and it was the opera manager's insistence that Galamian's musical participation was essential that rescued him from an open-ended prison term.

In 1922 Galamian emigrated to Paris, where he studied with Lucien Capet, professor of violin at the Paris Conservatory and a great authority on the bow, an area of expertise that later became Galamian's trademark. Capet took Galamian under his wing, introduced him to the music world in Paris, and helped him to arrange his debut recital in 1924. Galamian concertized for a while and started teaching at the Russian Conservatory in Paris, which became his focus. Galamian moved to New York in 1937 and initially did some teaching at the Henry Street Settlement House while establishing his studio.

Galamian's studio became a mecca for gifted students almost from the beginning. Word of mouth on the part of both parents and teachers produced an unending stream of young hopefuls who made the weekly pilgrimage to his teaching studio—nicknamed "the torture chamber" by his wife, Judith Galamian—in their Manhattan apartment. Galamian's teaching style is generally characterized as "old school authoritarian," and his students were meticulously prepared. Heavy emphasis was placed on technical work, and Galamian was notoriously intolerant of students who deviated in any way from the particular bowings and fingerings he advocated. Nothing was left to choice or chance. A standard joke among his students was to say, "I'm off to see the Doctor. He'll give me a prescription." Galamian had precise ideas of what he wanted, and there was no technical problem for which he did not have a solution. Similar discipline was imposed in matters of interpretation, and while some chafed under the regime, others found him inspiring and blossomed through his teaching.

"Cry Now, Play Later" was the headline of an article about Galamian in *Time* magazine in 1968. The article, which also refers to him humorously as "Ivan the Terrible," goes on to say, "His speech is soft, and the softer it gets, the more ominous it can be." It states that Galamian believes that "suffering through exercises" is liberating for students, allowing them to go on to develop their own musical personality later. At that period in his career, Galamian was seeing roughly a hundred students, including old graduates who would stop in for a check-up, anywhere from once a week to once a month. He taught seven days a week from eight o'clock in the morning until six o'clock in the evening, with an hour out for lunch. Lessons lasted precisely fifty-five minutes, no matter what the circumstances. In the last years of his life, Galamian made the concession of cutting back from a ten-hour to an eight-hour day. According to the *Time* article, he had no outside interests and never took a vacation. Judith Galamian said that she once persuaded him to go to the theater, but he was so bored—the show was *Oklahoma!*—that he wanted to leave at the intermission.

Politics is as rife within conservatory music departments as it is in the rest of academia, and the great pedagogues who come to represent a particular style of teaching—no matter what instrument is involved—accumulate their partisans and their critics. They are like the leaders, if not of a religious community, at least of a political party, and the feelings of their followers about the merits of their ideas and personalities can run high. In June 1997 I interviewed some of Galamian's colleagues and former students for an article for *The Strad* magazine, published in England, and found it to be like discussing someone who had died only a month before instead of nearly twenty years earlier. There were many vivid memories and few disinterested observers. The quoted material from these artists that follows derives from those conversations.

Arnold Steinhardt, first violinist of the Guarneri Quartet and a veteran of several summers as a teenager at the Meadowmount School of Music, recalled that at Meadowmount Galamian liked to joke, "This is a concentration camp. This is where you learn to concentrate." Steinhardt also described the place as exquisitely beautiful. "It was like being in a prison camp in a national park. It was not fun and games—you had to practice six hours a day." Steinhardt added, "Mr. Galamian was very old-fashioned about girls and boys. He would say, in his heavy Russian accent, 'Keep out of zee bushes! I don't vont to find you in zee bushes.'" Another ex-camper, Laurie Carney of the American Quartet, was at Meadowmount studying with DeLay and shared some of Steinhardt's remembered dread. She had met Judith Galamian on her first day at the school when she walked into the cafeteria. Mrs. Galamian told Carney that if she didn't put her hair back she would chop it off. Carney was ten years old at the time and found the tone of the threat entirely believable.

"He didn't speak a lot during a lesson, and he hardly ever smiled," continued Steinhardt, who studied with Galamian for several years:

He never threatened or cajoled—he had enormous presence. His basic feeling was that anybody could become a fine violinist. The stage was already set in his studio with all those photographs of Vieuxtemps and Corelli looking down at you, and your lesson would last precisely fifty-five minutes, never more, never less. To be late was unforgivable. One time he telephoned me to say, "Your lesson has been changed, you will come at seven o'clock in the morning instead of eight o'clock." I set two alarm clocks and slept through them both. I tore over but another student was already playing when I arrived. Galamian's eyes flashed sparks and he waved me out in spite of my apologies.

All Galamian's students were given two basic principles which he delivered in a heavy Russian accent: one was "More bow!" and the other was "Play so that the last person in the last row of the hall can hear you." Both excellent pieces of advice. Later, after I had "graduated," I came to know him socially and found he could be both kind and funny. Sometimes we would play chess together at Meadowmount and he would like to have a glass of vodka with the game. "One glass is good," he would say. "Two is better. Three is not enough." When I was no longer a student, he was very friendly.

David Nadien, who later became concertmaster of the New York Philharmonic and held that post for some years before devoting himself full-time to teaching and freelancing, was among a handful of students who lived with the Galamians. His recollections of Galamian are much warmer than Steinhardt's, perhaps because he came to know him on a more intimate basis from being at such close quarters. "The Galamians' apartment had great long hallways and a lot of rooms," he recalled. "Galamian had his studio in the front, and we—Helen Kwalwasser, Yura Osmolovsky, and myself—had rooms in the back where we practiced three or four hours a day. It was a very relaxed atmosphere, and all of us had fun." Nadien recalled that Galamian had two beautiful boxer dogs of whom he was enormously fond, who were a big part of the household. At one time, it seemed that somebody was stealing food from the fridge. "Galamian stayed up in the dark in the kitchen one night to catch the guilty party," Nadien said. "One of the boxers had actually figured out how to manipulate the handle and open the fridge door."

Nadien described Galamian as a good musician with excellent taste in musicality. "The students who played the best did not always do what he suggested, but if they sounded well, he was wise enough to leave them alone. He stressed warmth and good sound, and I think he unquestionably deserves a major place in the history of violin teaching."

"Not a day goes by that I don't talk about him as a teacher," said the distinguished violinist James Buswell, who teaches at the New England Conservatory of Music. "Once you have been under a master, it pervades all your work." Buswell characterized Galamian as a man with an analytical mind who held a profound philosophy of order that he tried to instill in his students. "Galamian had a revolutionary technique for the bow arm, which was based on his deep knowledge of the laws of physics and anatomy," said Buswell, adding that the ability to project the violin sound at a time when halls are getting bigger, and recordings can be adjusted to the listener's taste, has become ever more critical. "Galamian's burden was the acoustical survival of the stringed instrument as we know it," Buswell concluded.

DOROTHY DELAY

In 1948, two years after his appointment to the Juilliard faculty, Galamian and DeLay were joined in what ultimately became an impossible relationship. At that time, Galamian invited DeLay, who was already doing some teaching at Juilliard, although not yet on the faculty, to serve as his assistant—an arrangement that was to continue for the next twenty-two years.

During those years, while DeLay also established her own studio, she and Galamian gradually became something of an odd couple as their views about teaching methods diverged more and more sharply. Galamian's style was austere and disciplinarian, while DeLay's was democratic and flexible. They even looked the parts—Galamian being thin and somewhat dour, while DeLay was plump and bubbly. Eventually, fundamental differences between the two, both practical and philosophical, led DeLay to assert her independence and to emerge from behind Galamian's powerful shadow.

The breaking point arrived in the fall of 1970 when DeLay telephoned Galamian to tell him that rather than return to Meadowmount, she had decided to take up the invitation of Gordon Hardy, then the Aspen Music School's president, to teach at Aspen the following summer. Galamian is said to have listened in silence to DeLay's decision, and then hung up the telephone without a word.

The following day, he went to see Peter Mennin, Juilliard's president at the time, and demanded that DeLay be fired from the faculty, adding that he would see to it that she got no more students if Mennin did not accede. Mennin, not surprisingly, refused, and although DeLay and Galamian both continued to teach at Juilliard and even to serve on the same committees for the next ten years, Galamian never spoke to her again, pointedly looking the other way when she came into the room. The split created an uproar in the music world at the time. DeLay and Galamian had been teaching roughly thirteen or fourteen students in tandem, and Galamian called them in, one by one, and told them they had to make a choice, which many found a painful experience. Galamian apparently assumed that they would all elect to remain with him, but the overwhelming majority went with DeLay.

Gordon Hardy was in the somewhat delicate position of being both dean of students at the Juilliard School and president at Aspen. "Dorothy's coming to Aspen did indeed cause a split with Galamian. In fact, his relationship with her just stopped," said Hardy in a telephone conversation in July 1997. "At Juilliard, I had to handle both of them, which turned out not to be a problem. I made a strong point of telling faculty members that if they did not want a particular student who was also studying with Galamian to go to Aspen, then that student could not make the move." But move they did.

One student who was at Juilliard when all this upheaval was going on said that there was a lot of talk around the school that students who went with DeLay would not be treated well by Galamian on examination juries. "Cello juries were a breeze by contrast," she said, "because the department got on well with each other. But when Itzhak Perlman only got a B-plus at a violin jury, we couldn't believe it. If you studied with both and chose her, Galamian wouldn't speak to you again." Isaac Stern's much-quoted comment on the episode was that "the branch office had taken over." Galamian died in 1981, a full ten years after the break. By then, DeLay was well established in her own right.

In spite of the bitterness of the break, DeLay has always spoken of Galamian with great respect. She talked about him in some detail one afternoon in her studio:

> He came from southern Russia from an Armenian family, and in those families the father's word is law. If anyone in the family disobeys, it is a powerful insult to the father and makes him feel terribly lacking in dignity if his authority is questioned. Mr. Galamian felt that formalities must be adhered to and that in a situation with a child, he was the authority—that children were there to do as they were told. I just don't feel that way about children, but then I'm an American and I'm a woman, and I have two children of my own. Mr. Galamian had no children, unfortunately, because I think he would have been a wonderful father. So there was that cultural difference between us.
>
> I always have the feeling that if you know the style of the person you're working with, you can work inside that style. You just have to

understand the style first. I prefer to have these kids researching, thinking, seeing what the options are, and I tell them to go and find out. So we differed that way. He preferred to work in very straight-forward ways on technique, and his area of expertise was the bow, and he was excellent with it—his students had good sounds. Big healthy sounds, and they were beautifully organized.

I asked DeLay whether she consciously made a plan and set a goal at the time she separated from Galamian and found her own way of teaching, or whether it evolved on its own. At first she replied that it had evolved, but then she was silent for a bit and her tone changed:

> I guess I set a plan. I asked myself a question: What do I want my students to be able to do? And I thought, I want them to be able to work independently and know what they are doing. So I thought, Well in order to do that, what will I have to know?
>
> And so I made this imaginary circle of people in my mind listening to a performance, and those people included Toscanini, Heifetz, Casals, somebody from the Met—I forget which singer I chose—a pianist, and so on. They are all sitting there listening to this performance and now the performance is finished, and what will they say? And I thought, Well, Toscanini will say "Oh, it didn't follow the score at all. Didn't pay any attention at all to what was in the score." Or, maybe they *did* pay attention, but that would be his emphasis. And I imagined what Heifetz would say, what he would be interested in himself, and what he would comment on. And I went around the whole ring of people, imagining the reaction to this performance from each person's standpoint. So after I made a list of these possible reactions, I thought, Well, this is what my kids have to know when they play, and the practice sheets I made up are a condensation of those ideas.

DeLay's practice sheets include a schedule: the first hour is spent on basics—articulation, shifting, and vibrato exercises for the left hand, and various bow strokes for the right; the second hour is for passages from repertoire, arpeggios, and scales; the third for etudes or Paganini; the fourth on a concerto; and the fifth is for practicing Bach or the student's recital repertoire. Students are instructed to limit themselves to the first, third, and fourth hours on orchestra rehearsal days, and to rest at least ten minutes between hours.

Later in this same conversation, DeLay returned to one of her favorite subjects: how we learn.

I found myself being interested in how certain talents can be developed because I have always had the desire to believe that environment is more important than heredity. So I said to myself, If somebody doesn't play in tune, it is because he hasn't learned how. Mr. Galamian would say, "Oh, he has no ear. Don't waste your time." I would say to myself, I want to find out if I can get this person to play in tune, and I would experiment with all kinds of things, and Mr. Galamian would say, "You don't have time for that," and I would think, Yes, but I want to know, and I would go on trying.

Mr. Galamian was very much interested in editing—in the bowings and fingerings. I have been invited to do that a lot and it bores me. I can't do it. He also wrote a couple of books. I have been invited to do that, but that bores me, too. I'm just not interested.

If there was a hint of disdain in these last comments of DeLay's as well as in the nature-nurture argument between her and Galamian, I found it a breath of fresh air in view of his behavior toward her after their split. This was the closest I had ever heard DeLay come to voicing a criticism of him. How could she not have been subject to powerful feelings about Galamian's attempt to get the president of Juilliard to fire her, and his refusal to speak to her or even acknowledge her presence at department meetings for all those years? While DeLay goes out of her way to look for the best in everyone, she can be very outspoken when she thinks the occasion warrants, and keeping to herself her reactions about Galamian's treatment of her must have cost her considerable effort.

Isaac Stern, who is surely among the most gifted as well as the most influential violinists of our time, was close to both Galamian and DeLay. While not himself a teacher, Stern has played an enormous part in helping young violinists find their rightful places on the concert stages of the world. Starting in the late 1950s, as the leader of the group known affectionately within the music world as the Kosher Nostra and with the help of the America-Israel Cultural Foundation, he made it possible for many Israeli youngsters such as Itzhak Perlman and Pinchas Zukerman to come to America and study with Galamian. Shlomo Mintz was the first of the Israeli contingent to come specifically to work with DeLay, and Perlman, who worked with both teachers, later made the switch to DeLay's studio.

In a telephone interview in January 1998, I asked Stern about his role with these students, and his views about both Galamian and DeLay

Isaac Stern congratulating DeLay at her surprise seventieth birthday party. DeLay had been lured to the event by Itzhak Perlman, who asked her to set the evening aside as he was going to receive the greatest honor of his life — which was, as he later explained, to honor her. Photo: Peter Schaaf.

as teachers. He said that he was "a guide rather than a teacher" for the Israeli musicians.

> I had neither the talent nor the patience to sit down every week and continue on and on to prepare the physical part of the primary training. I brought them over to study with Ivan Galamian, who had an extraordinary teaching ability. DeLay was an assistant to him, but [the students] actually worked with him in those early years around 1958 and 1960. There was a year when we were all in Israel and I had asked Sasha and Mischa Schneider from the Budapest [Quartet] to listen to these "Young Turks," and they were all bowled over. They came over, and as others came along I sent them on the same route.
>
> Galamian was extraordinary in the way he could teach basic discipline and bring out the maximum ability of a young player. It was never his forte or basic interest to teach a very large musical style, and he and I had many discussions—we were very close friends—because he felt the first thing was to play the instrument

and to do all the technical work, and the repertoire connected to the technical work, and then you could worry about becoming a musician. I always had the point of view that you couldn't separate the two from the very beginning. That you had to know not only how, but why you play.

He came to me at one time and asked me if I would be interested in taking the best of his students and taking them through the literature musically while he took care of them technically. It was very flattering but at that time I didn't have the time to do so. I of course listened to many of the students—Jaime Laredo, Arnold Steinhardt—there were many. Perlman did not start with Dorothy, he continued with her, as I remember it. Later on, don't ask me what the circumstances were, but there became a difference of opinion between Dorothy and Galamian.

That is when she began her individual life as a teacher, with extraordinary success. Dorothy had an instinct for young people. She had all the feeling for what they could do and how to teach them, more than she had in remembering their names—buttercup and pussycat and what-not, because she had so many. I think that has changed—she has come to focus on a few. But Dorothy became an institution. As Perlman and Zukerman and a few others began to have extraordinary success, everybody wanted to study with Dorothy DeLay. She had a talent for picking out really extraordinarily gifted young players. They are now, of course, getting younger and younger and more and more Far Eastern than ever. I don't know if Dorothy has less than 150 students, but I would be surprised, between New York and Cincinnati and wherever else she teaches, and her forays into Europe, Israel, and the Far East. She has become a magnet for the gifted, and particularly for the parents of the gifted who want their kids to succeed where they could not.

She has been really remarkable in her ability to have the talents play really at their optimum and, I must say to her great credit, not all the same. They have individual characteristics. She allows them a certain amount of freedom to express themselves as long as they use the basic equipment that she feels is necessary to be free, because only from a disciplined base can you really be free—and she has done that brilliantly. She has, in the last few years, brought me every single talent that she has ever had. I can't count the number of students. Pinky and Itzhak I knew on my own. They would come and play for me from time to time and we would sit and discuss. The same thing happened with later generations—

with Sarah Chang, with Midori—I've listened to thirty or forty of them over the years. (I don't want to be specific because I'll make mistakes.)

Dorothy has worked out a very simple series of basics that she insists on, and these are basics that started with what she learned with Galamian, and continued to grow as she taught more and more, and of course, she is both observant and intelligent. She developed what could now be called her own approach toward a young talent. It was not something that happened by explosion, but more by osmosis. As her students played, I think she also learned in judging what they could do, and applied it to all the others as they came along. Of course, the apple of her eye is Itzhak, and he adores her, deservedly.

Dorothy and I have known each other for a long time. We met in the 1940s. Later on, I got to know her better—much, much later on—when she became the only game in town, to put it bluntly. We have remained very close friends. I am very fond of her and I respect her enormously, and I think she feels the same way about me.

Itzhak Perlman, who studied with both DeLay and Galamian, described Galamian's teaching method as "Scare You to Death." "You had better play it perfectly or else his eyes are going to glare down on you and make you feel like that's *it*," he said, adding that as a child he found Galamian's authoritarian style extremely frightening.

With Galamian, there was almost no room for give and take, because he had a particular system that actually he applied to everybody. Some of his greatness lies in the fact that he could teach anybody, no matter how talented or untalented they were, how to play the violin very well. Some would be more inspired, some would be better, obviously, but they would be proficient at what they do when they studied with him. But he did apply the same method with almost no variations for everybody. Miss DeLay was much more flexible, was much more into the person, and into their background, into what makes them tick. I would come and play for her, and if something was not quite right, it wasn't like she was going to kill me.

That's where we come to the differences between the two. She would ask questions about what you thought of particular phrases —where the top of the phrase was, and so on. We would have a very friendly, interesting discussion about "why do you think it should sound like this" and "what do you think of that?" I was not quite used to this way of approaching things. In a sense, because of the teachers I had had in Israel, I was almost more familiar with Galamian's teaching method. With my first teacher, who was of Russian background, I would play something and she would say, "That's wrong. You do this and you do that." It was more like you'll play and I'll give you instructions, and Galamian was in a sense the same way.

With Miss DeLay, I would go in and we would disagree about things. We could have a good discussion and we could have a good fight—forget about doing that with Galamian! For example, if there was a note out of tune, I would play for Galamian, and he would say, "What's the matter, it is out of tune!" Miss DeLay would say, "Sugarplum, what is your concept of F-sharp?" which means your F-sharp is out of tune. It is a different style of teaching that puts the student at ease.

Working with both teachers gave a fantastic variety. For example, Galamian would only teach a particular repertoire, and he wouldn't teach anything else—he wouldn't try to teach anything out of the ordinary. Whereas Miss DeLay has an adventurous attitude. I would say to her, "Listen, I would like to bring you a concerto by Castelnuovo-Tedesco," and where Galamian would say, [Perlman lowers his voice and mumbles in a heavy Russian accent] "Oh, Tedesco. Oh, well, that is nothing but [rumble, rumble, rumble]," Miss DeLay would say, "Sure, sugarplum. Let's hear it." So I had both, which was very good—the kind of freedom with the one, and the kind of rigid system with the other, and the system for me was the best possible one-two punch.

"People always said Galamian could make a violinist out of a table," said conductor-violinist Peter Oundjian, who studied with Galamian, Perlman, and DeLay. "He really had a method of position for the bow arm. He understood so well the mechanics of the violin. I still have some of his bowings, for example in the Vieuxtemps Concerto, and I see his suggestions, and I think, that's exactly right. They are always exactly right. But I never heard him teach vibrato. Miss DeLay used to give me terrific vibrato exercises—fantastic bow and vibrato exercises." Oundjian added that Galamian took him through a lot of repertoire very quickly, a routine for which he was famous—some students would be asked to learn a new concerto every few weeks. "He gave you all the fingerings and all the bowings, and you did it, and you learned. And he knew what to give you," said Oundjian. "If you had a weakness in your spiccato, he'd give you a piece with a lot of spiccato."

> I remember one particular lesson where I was having trouble with a passage in the Lalo Violin Concerto. Galamian did not say anything. I played through the whole four etudes I had been assigned, and the whole Bach and the whole Lalo, and he just went, mumble-mumble-mumble—no real words. I said, "Mr. Galamian, in this passage in the last movement of the Lalo, I am really having difficulty—can you make some suggestions how I can make it better?" Galamian's response was to say, very soberly, "When you have played it two thousand times it will be much easier."
>
> Unfortunately, it's not true. As I get older, I think it is more important to find out what you are doing wrong than to play it two thousand times and see if it gets easier. Miss DeLay, in that kind of situation, would observe that one of your fingers was lagging behind, or that you are getting your hand into the wrong position, or that you are tightening at a certain point, which is preventing your hand from being free to move.
>
> Even though Itzhak has got this outrageous talent himself, he makes you feel that your talent is extremely worthy. You feel that you are important to him. That's part of being a great teacher. When you are in the room with a student, they are the most important thing to you. I didn't feel entirely the same way with Galamian, but that may have been because of the stage in his career—he was in his seventies. But it was really not Galamian's style. It was a more imperious kind of relationship. You practiced because you were scared not to.

The different styles, both personal and pedagogical, of Leopold Auer, Ivan Galamian, and Dorothy DeLay invite comparison. Auer's lack of method—even Heifetz was at a loss to describe it—has its counterpart in DeLay. She is the first to say she has none, in terms of working with a set of rules. Galamian, on the other hand, was and is famous for his method which he codified in detail in his *Principles of Violin Playing and Teaching*, which deals with the entire range of bowing and fingering problems faced by the performer. Although all three teachers had several assistants, Galamian spent far more lesson time working directly on technique than did either Auer or DeLay, who, particularly in her later years, has relied more and more on her cadre of helpers for scale classes, ear training, and the like.

All three had the gift of "sizing up the potential of each student" and all of them "valued talent" (to borrow Boris Schwarz's assessment of Auer), but where Galamian regarded talent as inborn, DeLay sees it as a quality than can be acquired. In terms of demanding punctuality, Auer and Galamian would have been soulmates, while DeLay's schedule is notorious for being honored in the breach. As for relations on a personal level, Auer and DeLay shared an active interest in the lives of their students beyond the studio. Galamian certainly cared deeply about his students but maintained more of a barrier between himself and them on nonmusical matters. Schwarz wrote that Auer was "stern, severe, even harsh," and many of Galamian's students, including his greatest admirers, would describe Galamian the same way, but no one could connect these adjectives even remotely with DeLay, although "demanding" would certainly apply.

Whatever the specific traits possessed by these three individuals, there is no one combination that would have served to guarantee any of them a spot in pedagogical heaven. Nor is there any way to copy them and achieve the same results—their effectiveness lies in those intangible and still unclonable qualities that constitute a magnetic personality. One may try to duplicate everything one can observe about another person, but one cannot learn how to have the same intuition, or sense of humor, or presence.

DeLay has long been accorded her place in the ranks of history's great violin teachers. While there is speculation on who will eventually become her successor, no one particular name is in the ascendant. Perhaps more than one individual will emerge, or perhaps someone from outside the United States. Perhaps in the twenty-first century the center of violin study will shift away from America to some other part of the world.

Part Two

IN THE STUDIO

3 The Power of Primitive Thinking

"What *fascinates* me," said DeLay one afternoon in her studio at Juilliard when she was taking a break between students, "is watching somebody come in here and stand in front of that music stand and suddenly discover that he can do something that he didn't think he could do." She paused for a moment, looking for an example.

> I had one student who always played chamber music but who did not have particularly facile fingers—not like Perlman's or Peskanov's, or like Gil Shaham's. He came in one day and said, "Miss DeLay, I've been invited to play a virtuoso piece at a summer festival, and I don't know what to do. I've never studied it—it's the *Scherzo-tarantelle* of Wieniawski."
>
> I said, "Well I think you can play that—why don't you think you can play it?"
>
> "Well," he said, "I don't think I can play fast enough."
>
> I said, "I think you could play it fast enough for the festival. Anyway, let's find out. How fast would you like to go?"
>
> "I would like to go as fast as Itzhak Perlman, but I could never!"

DeLay smiled at the recollection of the scene and continued, "I had a record of Itzhak and we clocked it on the metronome and got the speed. We started practicing slowly because he had never seen the music before." DeLay had the student play through the opening two pages in this fashion, sometimes in different rhythms, as she gradually increased the speed of the metronome.

> Pretty soon he said, "You know, it's getting faster," and I agreed, and we went for another ten or fifteen minutes, over and over on

the first two pages. A bit later he stopped me and said, "You know, I think I could play this," and I said, "Let's keep going." We worked on the first two pages for about forty-five minutes and I had the metronome in my hand, and finally I said, "Do you want to see how fast you're going?" And I showed him, and he was right on the speed where we had clocked Itzhak.

DeLay rocked back in her chair and nodded her head slowly. "I know so surely that if he had been handling that metronome, as he approached that number he would have said to himself, I can never do this as fast as Itzhak Perlman, and he would have stopped himself. So I thought about that a lot—how we stop ourselves from doing things. In his case, I sneaked up on him. It is just fear that keeps us from being able to do these things—that's all."

Unlike most conservatory teachers, DeLay has no particular teaching method to which she adheres—she prefers to describe what she does as an approach rather than a system. She knew very well the likely outcome of that metronome experiment with that particular student, or she would not have suggested it. It worked for him, where it might have been absolutely wrong for someone else. There is no Procrustean couch on which a student is expected to lie, even if it means chopping off the head or the feet (or, God forbid, the fingers), in order to fit properly.

These budding virtuosos do indeed have to put in hours and years on building technique. All DeLay's students, big or little, have to do their scales, their arpeggios, their etudes, their Bach, their concertos, and so on; by the time they reach their teens, they are expected to be practicing a minimum of five hours a day. But where many teachers advocate the practice-makes-perfect philosophy, DeLay focuses on finding the root of a problem, be it technical or interpretive, rather than in promoting its repetition. She has an extraordinary intuition for pinpointing what a student needs, and helping him in the course of time to discover it for himself. One benefit of this strategy is that the student, not incidentally, gains conviction and an individual style in the process of learning.

Initially, DeLay also taught all the scale and ear-training classes herself, but delegated the task as she became increasingly involved with other aspects of her students' lives, helping them to get established in the profession. Among other things, this meant fostering relationships with managers, conductors, heads of conservatories, and university music departments—in fact any area where there might be a good slot for one of her "babies." DeLay is a very long-range planner, and these connections, along with her track record, are why she is so often turned to for recommendations about artists.

The merits of teaching by the carrot versus the stick continue to be debated endlessly by parents, politicians, university professors, and the like, and nowhere more fiercely than within the music world. Does a child learn better by the imposition of strict discipline or by gentle nurturing? Some of my initial mystification about what DeLay was up to, and why it worked, came from thinking that I was watching the carrot side of this old controversy—that she believed that students who were told they were wonderful and marvelous, instead of having their knuckles rapped, would just naturally play better. Since other famous teachers, including, for example, the arch knuckle-rapper Ivan Galamian, were mentors to some of today's greatest artists, this was obviously impossible, but I was so busy looking at the backdrop—at the encouragement and support that she provided—that I failed to pay proper attention to the foreground, to what she was saying and not just how she was saying it.

Trying to describe how DeLay teaches is complicated by the fact that a lot of what transpires in a lesson is invisible to the eye, although it becomes evident to the ear as her students make progress. There would be lessons in which nothing much seemed to happen. A student would play, and she would say, "That's very nice, dear. Next time, how about trying the fingerings we talked about?" Only later, when I had watched the same student in the course of many lessons, did I see that each situation had its own history. It would turn out, for example, that the subject of fingerings had come up in different ways for the past several lessons, and DeLay was biding her time until the penny dropped and the student really heard what she was saying. Or, indeed, that the student was not practicing enough, or well enough, for any of a hundred reasons—problems at home, a period of rebellion, lack of comprehension—and that DeLay wanted to approach the problem sideways rather than head-on for the moment.

The secret of DeLay's success seems obvious to me now, but it was a long time before I saw it. DeLay is basically in the business of teaching her pupils how to think, and to trust their ability to do so effectively. This is a much more difficult undertaking than telling them to copy what she does, or to repeat a passage over and over until it—at least in theory—gets better. To DeLay, learning and thinking are inextricably connected, and the core of her philosophy lies in continually challenging her students to look for their own answers. This requires tremendous imagination on the part of a teacher, because what may serve as a catalyst to understanding for one student may be a turn-off for another.

DeLay's lessons are punctuated with questions: What do you think Beethoven was trying to say in this passage? Can you see a way to make a better transition from this theme to the next? Why don't you experiment a bit with the bowings and see what you can come up with to give this section more vitality? Do you think the phrase would sound better if you take more time with the down-bow?

DeLay may stand a problem on its head, turn it inside out, break it into tiny bits, and lay out ten different possibilities, but the final choice of a solution is left to the student. "Do it my way" or "Do it this way" are simply not in DeLay's lexicon. She is a committed individualist, and rather than imposing her own ideas, she insists, gently, cheerfully, but relentlessly, on making her students think for themselves.

Sometimes when I was sitting in on DeLay's classes, she would take time between lessons just to talk. These conversations were on general topics of the moment: the development of a particular student, or somebody's research about how the mind works, or, indeed, the nature of the universe. Discussions on less lofty matters included a fair bit of backstairs chit-chat—sex and violence being every bit as much a part of the classical music world as any other. The conversations were, in fact, about anything that came to mind. I taped many of them with the open understanding between us that if DeLay said something she wanted kept confidential about one of her students, or anything else for that matter, I would turn off the tape recorder at her request and not make use of the material. The system worked out fine for both of us, and as time went by, somewhat to my amusement, DeLay would herself sometimes lean over and push the stop button without warning.

But there were other times when DeLay would be silent for quite some time before she spoke, and in the beginning I found this awkward, until I realized that she was really thinking with great care about what she wanted to say. These talks went to the heart of how DeLay's mind works and what she regards as important as a teacher. The excerpts that follow are drawn from my tapes of conversations that took place over several years, some at her home in Rockland County, some in her studio at Juilliard, and some in a variety of settings in Aspen, Colorado, where she has taught in the summers.

Kids Become What You Tell Them They Are

We had a little neighbor across the street when my kids were little whose father used to call him "bucket-head," and that's what he grew up into—a bucket-head. Every time I heard that man say that word, I just wanted to hit him. That is a terrible thing he did. If you are sitting in the studio and you want a kid to do something, and he's a very sensitive child, and rather timid, the best thing to do, I think, is to wait until what you want happens by accident. And you say, "Hey, look what you did. Isn't that wonderful! I *like* that." Then a child will repeat it and repeat it and repeat it.

Teaching by Example

I used to have teachers who tried to teach me by example, and what they would do is say, "No, no, do it like this"; and I would think, Well that is different from what I am doing, but I can think of a hundred ways it is different. I wonder which one they are talking about. I would try something and the teacher would say, "No, no, do it like *this*," so I would try it again, change it, do something else, and that wouldn't be what was wanted either, and I would go home very upset. I never could figure out which aspect of what they had done was what they meant. It was the most frustrating experience I have ever had. Also, I don't like the idea of one person's perform-ance being the supreme influence on a young person. I don't think it is healthy. I think they need a tremendous diet of listening to many, many different people so that the intake is spread out over many styles.

The Power of the Spoken Word

Communicating is a very difficult thing to do. When students start using words in a sloppy way, I try to pin them down: "What exactly do you think that means?" so they get the habit of understanding what they are doing when they speak. Words are so powerful. Musi-cians are the worst criminals in being careless about what they say. Musicians will say, "Oh, that goes so deep!" OK, "deep." Presum-ably, they mean something inward, but "deep"? Inward what? There is no information in that word. It is a sloppy word. It is like "love." We don't know what the word *love* means.

I try to tell them that you can use words to communicate, you can use words to conceal, you can use words to impress—you can use words for many different motives. When somebody speaks to you, you try to figure out which this is, and if somebody is really trying to communicate something, it is a gift—it is a great gift when somebody tries to tell you something, because a lot of the time, that is not what they are doing. They are not interested in sharing something. They are interested in trying to conceal or to impress or to do something else.

I find it difficult to teach someone who doesn't talk back. Working with one of the kids today, I was thinking that I get as much from his ideas as he gets from mine. I was trying to keep things in balance, but every so often I would slip up and say, "Oh, I don't think I would do this," and then I would think, Shouldn't have done that, DeLay, shouldn't have done that, because it doesn't open up thinking and reasoning. I love to watch the kids think. I do not find giving instructions very satisfying.

Asian students have a totally different take on the use of words than the Americans. I try to tell some of my kids, "Stop being a nice Asian girl, and start being an American woman. There are certain things you don't have to put up with, and I will teach you naughty language with which to tell people off." So I do, and they do, and they feel wonderful.

The Barrier of Fear

People can be terribly afraid that nobody is going to have any respect for them. Many people go through a period in their teens and early twenties when they find getting instructions extremely threatening because being corrected implies that you have a job and you are not capable of doing it properly. You have got to believe you can do this job properly or you will have absolutely no self-respect. There can be any number of years where they are struggling to establish their own autonomy, and trying to prove to themselves that they are capable of making decisions of their own. During that period of time, they seem to be very afraid of other people's opinions, and sometimes they throw the baby out with the bath and they refuse good advice when it's available.

I can sympathize with that. I can remember going through it. I could not hear criticisms from my teachers—they frightened me terribly. If I recognize something like that going on with a kid, I try not to make a statement. I say, "Well, what do you think about that?" Or, "That is very interesting." Or, "I like this very much."

What stops some people from making the transition to thinking independently? If you are a child who has been put down, you start to feel small. You start to feel unimportant, and as a result, you start to feel fear. It is a very frightening thing to feel that you are unimportant to everyone. You feel you may cease to exist. You have to know that you have been terribly important to one person at least—maybe more—but very important to one person who gives you tremendous support.

The Pleasure Principle

Fear can provide a spur, but the moment the source is out of the room, the spur is gone. Success stays with you. When you are successful, you remember how nice that was, and you do it again. I think people who are successful have learned to be proud of what they are doing—at least intermittently—but always with the hope of doing better.

Perseverance

Are there particular qualities one looks for in a student? If you get someone who is really staggeringly better than other people, you have the feeling that it may be easier for that person than it would be for someone who may be more borderline. I don't know what it is that makes it possible for people to go on in the face of discouragement because no matter what you do—music, politics, art—you are going to face times when you are not successful, so I suppose the ability to go on anyway is the most valuable. One of my friends who taught used to say that determination and drive were the most important. He thought the important thing was to keep going, keep going, not get too excited, just keep going—and I think he had something there.

Making Plans; The Meaning of Discipline

There has to be a transition point where we realize that our own reactions have validity. We have to realize that our own thoughts, our own ideas, our own emotions, really are all we've got. But because we are intelligent people, they are very reliable, very valuable, very interesting. I think that when we are very small we assume that there are certain things we can't do, that we have to be told every move. I have always felt that it is necessary to respect children's minds, because they are so incredibly intelligent and so knowledgeable, without realizing it. They are so imaginative—they have such wonderful ideas. When you start doing your own planning in an independent kind of way, you begin to realize that there are certain mental processes that you have to go through.

I know that this sounds strange, but I remember the point at which I became really conscious of the fact that if you're going to make a good plan, you have to set your goal first. It sounds like a primitive piece of thinking, and perhaps we do this all our lives on some subconscious level, but I remember the day on which it suddenly became conscious with me—light bulb above my head, you know?—and I thought, Wow! You set a goal and then you know what you're doing. Rather like that *New Yorker* cartoon of the young wife watching her husband filling in the stubs on his checkbook and saying, "What a good idea—that way you always know how much money you have. What a good idea!"

People are always talking about discipline—another of those obvious things—and I had this image of some horrible sort of Simon Legree person with a whip standing over me, and then I realized that discipline is very simple; after you set this gorgeous goal, you say, "OK, now this is where I want to get, and now how do I get there?" So you say, "Step one, step two, step three, here I am— I got there, that's my plan." So discipline is just the process of carrying out your plan. I don't know how to describe it except that something that ought to be obvious to us has not been obvious and then suddenly becomes obvious, so that everything comes together in your mind. But the only way that can happen is if you are feeling comfortable and not feeling some kind of demands are being made on you; if you are feeling that you can trust your mind, and that it's a good instrument, and that what you need to do is to figure out how it works.

I swear to you, it is in the concentration. If you take any task, and it looks like it's too big and it's not working, you have to break it into small steps, and take it in small steps. You just have to find those small steps, and I do find that process fascinating.

An Unimpeded Vista

Is musical sensitivity innate? I think it is too easy for a teacher to say, "Oh, this child wasn't born with it, so I won't waste my time." Too many teachers hide their own lack of ability behind that statement. I don't like that statement. It gets my back up. I don't want it to be true that a quality like that is inherited, because you can't do anything about it. I want it to be true that we can all learn anything.

At the same time that DeLay believes passionately that the best learning takes place in an atmosphere of support and encouragement (That's great, sweetie-pie! Wonderful, sugarplum!), she can be as tough as old boots in the demands she makes of her students and in refusing to settle for less than somebody's best. Being a master of psychology, she knows precisely what that "best" is and how to elicit it—in particular, when to speak and when to keep still. "Most of the time," DeLay once remarked, "I am just sitting here thinking of things to say and then stopping myself from saying them."

4   Saturday's Children: The Pre-College Kids and Their Parents

Dorothy DeLay teaches at the Juilliard School of Music six days a week, and on the seventh, meaning Sunday, a chosen few of her students travel out to her home in Rockland County. During the week, DeLay gets to Manhattan at about three o'clock in the afternoon, and parks in the garage adjacent to Alice Tully Hall, which is directly under the Juilliard School. Because of her difficulty walking—she has had to use a crutch for some years—she is usually met by a student or a piano accompanist, who helps her up to her studio by giving her an arm and taking her briefcase. When DeLay was in her seventies, she would still teach until around midnight, so it would be one or two o'clock in the morning before she got home. Now in her eighties, she has cut back, finishing between ten and eleven, and still has to drive herself back to Rockland County. Her concentration during these marathon sessions is extraordinary. The teaching seems to energize her, and the later it gets, the more animated she becomes. The students, fifty or sixty years her junior, begin to wilt long before she does.

The students in Juilliard's Pre-College Division come for their lessons on Saturdays, some from as far away as Boston, Philadelphia, or Cleveland, but most from New York. "Pre-College" casts a wide net and includes children as young as six or seven all the way up to eighteen year olds about to graduate. They come to study various instruments, as well as to be coached in composition, orchestra, chorus, chamber music, and more. When they graduate, many of these once-a-week youngsters will take the stringent entrance exam for the College Division in the hope of becoming full-time students at America's most prestigious music conservatory. Of those who are admitted, a minute number will end up on the concert stages of the world.

Even the least competent of Saturday's children would be regarded as remarkable anywhere else. Entrance to the Juilliard Pre-College Division is based on a competitive performance examination, and as the school catalog makes clear, the program is intended for "talented young people who plan to pursue a career in music and will devote considerable time and seriousness of purpose to their study." Beginners are not even considered.

As the new century begins, the great majority of the children at Juilliard are from the Far East, and the younger they are, the higher the proportion. This is particularly true for the piano and violin students, most of whom are hoping for a solo career. If you sit in the lobby of the school on a Saturday, when Pre-College is in session, you might easily be in China, Japan, or Korea.

When DeLay started teaching at Juilliard in the mid-1940s, virtually all of her students were Jewish. They were children of the great wave of immigrants who fled Russia and Eastern Europe in the early part of the century for either America or what was then Palestine. By the next generation, in the 1960s and 1970s, many of the gifted violinists at Juilliard were Jews coming from Israel, not, like their forebears, as refugees, but as young artists in search of a larger musical canvas. Itzhak Perlman, Pinchas Zukerman, and Shlomo Mintz came to the United States specifically to study with DeLay and Galamian. As these artists became established, the Israeli tide gradually ebbed, and the only major young violinist in that tradition at the turn of the century is the superbly gifted Gil Shaham, who began studying with DeLay in 1980 at the age of nine.

The early 1980s saw the beginning of another cultural shift at Juilliard, as well as at many other educational institutions, as students from the Far East began arriving in the United States in ever-increasing numbers. The occurrence did not go unnoticed in the press. An article by Fox Butterfield in the 3 August 1986 issue of *The New York Times*, entitled "Why Asians Are Going to the Head of the Class," described the parents of these students as being "similar to the Jewish immigrants of the 1930's" because of their emphasis on learning and the importance of the family. The cover story of *Time* magazine on 31 August 1987 was headlined "Those Asian-American Whiz Kids," and described these students as "the most impressive generation of immigrants' children in

A party at the home of the late Sheldon Gold, president of International Creative Management, in 1980. Left to right: Cho-Liang Lin, DeLay, Pinchas Zukerman, Isaac Stern, Itzhak Perlman, and Eugenia Zukerman. Courtesy Dorothy DeLay.

decades." The article estimated the number of Asian and Asian-American children at Juilliard at that time (1987) to be twenty-five percent of the student body. Ten years later it was more than double that number. Sheryl WuDunn, writing about music education in Asia in *The New York Times* on 14 November 1997, said that students from China, Japan, and Korea, "were going in droves to America's prestigious music conservatories," filling up orchestral spots overseas, and accumulating prizes at international music competitions. WuDunn ascribed the development in part to the increasing enthusiasm and admiration for Western classical music in Asian countries.

In 1999, easily two-thirds of DeLay's students alone were from Korea, Japan, or China, in order of numbers. However, William Parrish, assistant director of the Pre-College Division at Juilliard, suggested in a conversation we had in 1998 that another change in the ethnic makeup of the school might be already under way. "The number of Korean and Japanese students may be reaching a saturation point," he said. "The expansion had already begun ten years ago, and today we are starting to see an increase in the number of students coming from Eastern Europe."

In musical matters, America is most certainly the land of opportunity. A country like Israel, for example, is too small to support the career of a soloist. There are not enough different venues or audiences—a musician cannot tour Israel, as he can tour America, and make a living. The reasons why musicians from various parts of the world are eager to come to the United States are easy to understand. What is less clear is why the center of violin talent has shifted from Russia and Eastern Europe to Israel and then to the Far East in the course of the twentieth century. Here is a sociological study begging to be done, and one can only speculate about some possible factors. Is the migration connected with music's ability to leap over the language barrier in a foreign land? With values instilled in the country of birth? Are there changes in the social goals of the second generation that lead them to other, more mainstream, professions? How important is the emergence of a great teacher at a particular time and place—such as a Leopold Auer in St. Petersburg or an Ivan Galamian or Dorothy DeLay in New York—in determining these shifting patterns? Any number of larger political and demographic factors at which one can only guess may be at work behind this phenomenon, but there is no denying its existence or the richness of its contribution to our musical life.

DeLay talked about the problems her Asian students face when they arrive at Juilliard, saying that children from the Pacific Rim who come to the United States have a difficult time because they have been taught to respect learning, hard work, and achievement. "They come here and they find many children who have not developed this respect and many children who are just looking to have a good time. The Asian children have a hard time dealing with that," she said.

> I think, in all honesty, that if a child is going to develop early—and I'm not sure that it is necessary for a child to develop early—but if a child is going to develop early, he has to have at least one parent with him who sees to it that discipline takes place, who sees to it that the work habits are established, that the time is well spent. The Asian families make sure that happens. I admire this push toward learning. I think it's a wonderful thing.

The emphasis on obedience, on respect for one's elders, and hard work, can sometimes be a hindrance as well as a help. Rebellion in any form, even merely expressing an opinion, is simply not an option for some Asian students. On occasion, DeLay does not hesitate to be subversive with these excessively dutiful children when she thinks the time is ripe. She teaches them how to stand up for themselves, sometimes providing them with the necessary dialogue and encouraging them to practice on her. "You will have to learn how to say No," she said to one particularly cowed and unhappy Korean youth, during a lesson. "In Israel, all boys of around fourteen, fifteen, and sixteen automatically say No before they say anything else. It is part of their culture. It may take you a little time, but you can learn," she assured him. "When we get grown up, we have to think 'I am the person who knows about my life,' so there are times you need to be able to say to someone: 'No—Sit Down!'"

After the lesson, DeLay commented that while both the Israeli and Asian students are highly motivated and disciplined, they have to be taught in a different way. "The Asian kids have to be encouraged to be more assertive, and sometimes they find it very difficult," she said. The Israeli boys, DeLay explained, "are taught that if you want to be a man, you have to win the argument, so all little boys want to turn everything into an argument, and say No to everything and prove that you are wrong. In so doing, they prove that they are men." DeLay goes along with this knee-jerk reaction of saying No because she knows that is all it is—a knee-jerk reaction. It will pass, and pass more quickly if it is recognized as simply part of the way these children are taught to deal with the world.

DeLay drew a deep breath and continued in mock self-deprecation:

> Another thing I have become very involved with at this late age is that suddenly the ideas of Women's Lib have hit me. We are having a seminar here at Juilliard on harassment, and I am urging all of my classes to go. I am not going to speak, because I don't know anything about it except what I have lived through, and of course it was very different when I was young from the way it is for the kids today. Some of the students, especially the girls who come from Asia, really need Women's Lib.

I asked her why she thought that there are so many more Asian girls trying to make it at Juilliard today than there had ever been Israeli girls in the past. "Something is hitting the mothers," DeLay replied. "I think the mothers are starting to see the advantages of having a job. They are people for whom marriages have been arranged, and their life depends entirely on the man their parents have chosen. I think they want to see their girl children trained for a profession." It can't hurt that music is a prestigious profession in Asia today.

DeLay's own teacher, Ivan Galamian, may have contributed to the limited number of female students at Juilliard in previous generations. "He never wanted to teach girls—he thought it was a waste of time," DeLay said. "He said it very privately to me. He said that women are not serious." She added that Galamian did in fact teach women, but only when his financial situation required that he take on more students. Rather than teach less-gifted men, "he took on gifted women because they would do well in the schools and would pass the examinations and so forth. He was a very practical person. Times change and styles change, but people don't."

Career possibilities for women musicians have expanded enormously in the last two generations, a development that is particularly noticeable in the chamber music scene. At the time when the Budapest Quartet was in its heyday as the quartet in residence at the Library of Congress, from 1938 to 1962, few professional quartets included women. Women were regarded as more likely to leave than men, and therefore a risk. At the start of the twenty-first century, the presence of women is taken for granted, and a number of distinguished ensembles, including the Colorado Quartet, the Lark Quartet, the Cavani Quartet, the Cassatt Quartet, and the Eroica Trio, are composed only of women. The Da Vinci Quartet in Colorado has been working with a shelter for battered women, to which it gives a proportion of its earnings. The number of women in orchestras has also increased dramatically, although the Vienna Philharmonic remains a holdout in this area. In spite of tremendous criticism, including being picketed when it comes to New York, the Vienna Philharmonic remains the only major European or American orchestra to have no women as formal members as a matter of policy. There was a brief flurry of excitement in 1998 when a change in the rules was announced, but all that it amounted to was giving its female harpist of twenty-eight years token status as an official member.

The waiting area outside DeLay's fifth-floor studio at the Juilliard School is poorly lit and furnished with a beat-up couch, an immovable table, and a few chairs. This is where the Pre-College children and their parents congregate on Saturdays before a lesson. It also serves as a hangout for the older full-time students, and the trash basket nearby usually bears evidence of pizzas past—there are always crumbs on the carpet in spite of regulations and the janitorial staff's best efforts. On Saturdays the atmosphere is electric. Here, some waiting mothers sit and knit, like, as Edward Newhouse has remarked, Madame DeFarge watching the tumbrels pass by during the French Revolution. Probably more people have sat for longer periods in the area outside Room 530 than anywhere else in Juilliard.

The mothers of the Pre-College students are excruciatingly polite to one another, but there is no mistaking the appraising eyes and the savage jealousy. One-upmanship is the order of the day, and satisfaction lies in seeing your opponent discomfited. "The teacher telephoned me at home this week and we had a very good talk." (About what? About what?) "We came in early today to discuss a particular recital possibility with the teacher." (Where? Where? Why didn't I know about it, too?) The children themselves seem pretty carefree as they wait their turn, but being a Juilliard mother or father can be a full-time job.

One does occasionally see unhappy instances of mistreatment on the part of these ambitious families. Eight-year-old Philip's parents, for example, have, much against DeLay's advice, drilled him into learning the Beethoven Violin Concerto, a feat akin to making him memorize the role of Hamlet. The boy is note perfect but now plays like a little automaton and his hoped-for career is unlikely to develop very far in the future. Kristina, a gifted ten year old, is saddled with an aggressive mother who constantly seeks special treatment under the guise of parental concern and affection. "Please arrange for Kristina to have a concert/ get management/meet Isaac Stern/meet Kurt Masur/meet whomever, Miss DeLay, or she will be so unhappy." Kristina's mother is a classic stage parent with a cultivated repertoire of tricks, ranging from the obsequious to the hysterical to the underhanded. While it is probably true that if you scratch any major violinist, you are more than likely to find an ambitious parent in constant attendance in the background, not all of them, mercifully, fit such a destructive profile.

A typical Saturday finds anywhere from four to eight of the Pre-College kids in the studio. Some are there for individual lessons, and some will be participating, as all her students do once a month, in a group class where they learn from each other—and where their parents get to size up the competition. The "star" students also have a private lesson once or twice a week, either with DeLay or one of her associates. The youngest children have been scrupulously brushed and polished, particularly the little Korean girls, and the older ones look more like standard-issue students in jeans and T-shirts.

At the studio, DeLay first has to run the gamut of the waiting parents, each of whom wants some special attention, before getting inside and closing the door in order to chat briefly about the afternoon lineup with the accompanist. On most Saturdays, this is a young man named Evan Solomon, although there are others from time to time. Solomon's role is to play the piano reduction of the orchestral part as accompaniment for the student playing the solo. This is no mean feat in itself. Solomon must not only be able to perform the notes, which often come in great handfuls since they represent all the instruments of the orchestra, but also be ready to stop and jump into the middle of any bar or phrase that DeLay decides needs to be worked on. He has more than forty violin concertos at his fingertips, and uncountable numbers of solo works. He once made a list of these for me, which included seventy-five pieces *plus* "Heifetz: numerous transcriptions," "Kreisler: numerous short pieces," and assorted other collections. Solomon is utterly unflappable. No matter how often a student has to go over and over a particular passage, Solomon is instantly at the ready. I have never seen him run out of patience or be unable to deal with the part that is put before him.

When Solomon and DeLay have finished talking, he goes out to give the nod to the group outside. The sense of tension among the mothers does not dissipate even when they and their children file into DeLay's studio and the lessons start. One quickly gets the sense that every nuance of approval and disapproval from the authority behind the desk has the power of a sledgehammer. Every word she utters is noted and processed with the speed of light. What was the significance of that raised eyebrow, that tap of the pencil on the desk?

DeLay presides over the scene like the prototype of the benevolent mother, greeting the children with eyes that sparkle and a smile that radiates warmth. She is always immaculately coiffed and manicured, and her capacious form is stylishly dressed, down to her trademark neck scarf. No hard edges here to alarm a virtuoso of tender years—to them, DeLay is Lady Bountiful in body, mind, and spirit.

The studio contains a grand piano for the accompanist, several straight-backed chairs, and a coffee table with some books—including *Grey's Anatomy*, Henry Roth's *Violin Virtuosos*, *The Harvard Dictionary of Music*, and Michael Thomas Roeder's *A History of the Concerto*—

in front of a dilapidated couch. What the couch lacks in springs is made up for in stuffed dolls and animals that students of all ages have brought in over the years. Between the windows that look out over Lincoln Center Plaza there is a large framed page of a Bach manuscript affectionately inscribed to DeLay from Isaac Stern and his former wife, Vera, and a set of contact prints, also framed and signed, of Itzhak Perlman. Near the piano, there is a faded color photograph of a wheat field near DeLay's Kansas birthplace.

The most interesting pictures are on the inside doors of two floor-to-ceiling cupboards on the wall opposite the windows. The doors are completely covered with photographs of friends and students past and present. Isaac Stern figures here, too, sometimes with DeLay, sometimes with her students. There are snapshots through the decades of Itzhak Perlman, from boyhood to marriage, to his growing family of five children, and later yet to the weddings of two of them. Pictures of the unknown and the well-known jostle each other in higgledy-piggledy order. Here is seven-year-old Midori, twelve-year-old Nadja Salerno-Sonnenberg, and thirteen-year-old Shlomo Mintz, along with a student who ultimately became a doctor, another who teaches in the Midwest, and several of the current crop who have yet to appear in public. One door is dominated by a dramatic portrait, probably a publicity shot, of Sarah Chang at the age of about twelve, on which she has written an affectionate message of thanks to her teacher in a round childish hand. The signature must have had more practice than the message. It is firm and assertive and the final g ends up with a splendid flourish, paving the way for autographs on concert programs to come in the years ahead.

DeLay sits behind a wooden desk just big enough for the three huge ring-binders in which she keeps track of what her students are doing, a metronome, a vase of flowers, and a copy of the music being played. When someone is in the early stages of studying a new piece, DeLay takes the music and follows along, making rapid notes to indicate problems that need attention, such as bowings, fingerings, and phrasings, for discussion afterward. Instead of heavily underlined injunctions like "Intonation!!!" or "Watch out here!!!" that are the industry standard, DeLay's markings are made very lightly in pencil. Gradually, as the difficulty is dealt with, DeLay erases her notations so completely that no trace is left. There are no nasty reminders of past pitfalls and problems — nothing permanent that might create a stumbling block.

The kaleidoscope of personalities and backgrounds that make up the small universe of DeLay's studio is astonishingly diverse. For the on-looker, it is an endless piece of dramatic theater—everybody's lives seem so intense—with the violin repertoire providing the musical score, as well as the focus for the action. Watching the Pre-College classes, one is constantly aware of how much is at stake for the adults—the financial rewards for the chosen few can be enormous, as can the attendant feelings of family pride or shame, particularly, but not only, where the Asian families are concerned. The following sketches of these children, some real and some fictionalized composites, are drawn from the lessons I watched over the years. Students' and parents' names have been changed unless otherwise noted.

THE LESSONS

Shunsuke Sato (his real name—he was aged about eleven at the time of this lesson) is the center of everyone's attention before the class starts. He has just come from a television studio where he made a commercial for 3M Bandage Strips in which he played the violin with these tapes on a couple of his fingers. The idea was to show that 3M Bandage Strips are so strong, lightweight, and flexible that they don't interfere with the digital dexterity needed for getting around the fingerboard at top speed. Shunsuke played a finger-twisting piece by Paganini like a veteran virtuoso, and in due course people all over the country will become familiar with the commercial of the tremendously gifted little boy who can play the violin while wearing bandages. Shunsuke Sato has fulfilled his early promise, and two years after this class, when he was thirteen, he was taken onto the roster of Young Concert Artists, Inc., and is rapidly making his mark in the larger concert arena. Whether this early exposure helped is unknown, but it certainly did no harm.

Koichiro, who, like Shunsuke Sato, is from Japan, is the first to play in the class. He is about seven years old, three-and-a-half feet tall, and has a perfectly cut bowl of shiny black hair. His mother, who bowed formally to DeLay when they came into the studio, sits down and takes a small tape recorder out of her handbag. When she gets home in the evening, she and her husband and Koichiro will carefully review the taped lesson to make sure that every instruction and nuance of meaning is understood and incorporated into his practice time. Koichiro may have to do a bit of translating for his parents—their English is rudimentary, while his, thanks to total immersion at school, is now fluent. If the mother

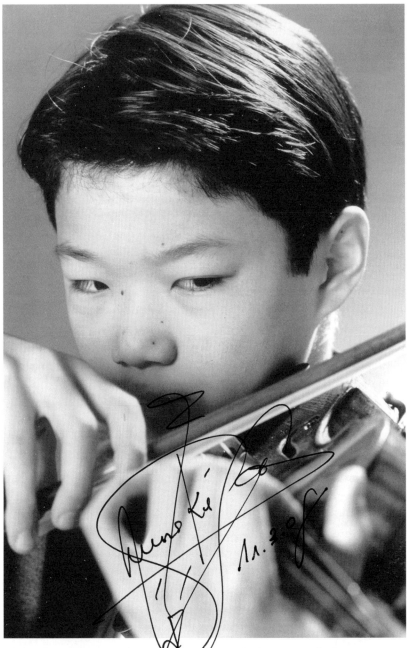

Shunsuke Sato, age twelve, as he began to make his way in the larger musical world. The public first saw him on television, at age eleven, in a commercial for 3M Bandage Strips, playing the violin with a couple of his fingers taped, to demonstrate the product's flexibility and his astonishing virtuosity. Photo: Hashimoto/New York.

wants to say something to DeLay, she first says it to her son, who then says it, presumably correctly, to DeLay.

DeLay once told me about the first Japanese student she ever taught, some twenty-five years ago. This was a little six-year-old girl who arrived with both her parents for each lesson. Of the three, only the father spoke English, and that barely. If DeLay wanted to tell her student something, she would stop the student from playing and explain it to the girl's father. The father would then bow and tell it to the mother, who would bow and relate it to the little girl, who would bow and then play.

In a couple of weeks, Koichiro is scheduled to play a movement of the Mendelssohn Violin Concerto with a community orchestra in New Jersey, and has been practicing the entire three-movement work for his lessons. He gives DeLay a duplicate copy of the music, as well as his quarter-size fiddle for her to tune, since this demands more strength than he as yet has. Koichiro then takes an assured stance halfway between DeLay and the piano. Before he starts, he reaches up and pulls the music stand down to its lowest possible height. He does not really need the notes anymore but still likes to have them nearby for safety. A nod to the accompanist, and the miniature artist, with his miniature instrument, fills the room with sound nearly worthy of an adult. This boy will have no problem being heard with an orchestra.

"Good boy. Mmmm!" says DeLay at the end of the movement, with what I have learned to interpret as a somewhat guarded approval. "There are only two spots where you are not quite sure." The next half hour is spent on the two spots. Different fingerings are found and the phrasing takes clearer shape. Koichiro plays through the third movement with lots of verve, but at the end he says dejectedly, "I can't play fast enough." DeLay laughs. "But you just did," she says, and shows him that she had set the metronome correctly at fifty-four. She tells the boy to drop his elbow a little on the down-bow and to watch himself in the full-length mirror on the wall opposite her desk. She tells his mother to see that he does this properly at home.

"If something feels too fast," DeLay says to the group at large, "remember that the bow will always do it, but if the left hand doesn't want to, just go slower. If you go slowly enough you can play absolutely anything." She pauses for effect. "Repetition makes the brain speed up. It is important never to let your left hand be uncomfortable. A good soloist makes himself comfortable before anything else. Rhythm is in the left hand—not in the bow."

At the end of the lesson DeLay says to Koichiro, "That was Mendelssohn's Second Violin Concerto. Do you know how old he was when he wrote his first concerto?" Koichiro grabs his forehead in an agony of intense thought. "Thirteen," says DeLay, triumphantly. Koichiro looks unimpressed.

Lily, a girl of around fifteen, has been in the United States for a year and is preparing for her end-of-term exams. She is working with one of DeLay's associates, and DeLay hears her from time to time rather than on a regular basis. DeLay told me before the lesson that, much to her annoyance, the examiners have assigned the Sibelius Concerto, which she knows the girl will find too difficult. No hint of this concern is evident at the beginning of the lesson. "I have to know you have the piece thoroughly memorized, and then we'll see if it's in tune," she says after a few minutes of Lily's playing. "Good girl. Good memory. Excellent dynamic. You don't know the orchestra part—you have to memorize that."

It quickly becomes apparent that Lily's difficulty is far more basic than memorization. She cannot get the rhythm. "I know what your problem is," DeLay says. "You've learned it by ear. Let's fix these places." A detailed reworking of the bowings fails to help and she tries another tack. "What are you thinking in your head, baby? Are you counting one-and-two-and, or one-two-three-four?" DeLay herself counts vigorously, her foot taps, her pencil taps, she beams and yells to be heard over the *forte* sound being produced. Lily looks anxious and answers, "Yes, ma'am. Yes, ma'am," whenever she is asked a question. "I like the way you are changing from a spiccato to a *detaché*," DeLay says, marking the music. "This is going to work out, and you are going to play it well. The only thing is whether we can get it ready in time. I don't think we can, and I want you to do well in your exam, so we are going to choose something else you have already worked on." Lily gives an audible sigh of relief and plays a passage again. This time the rhythm, as well as the intonation, is right on target, and the girl, who had been totally without expression until now, is suddenly wide-eyed with surprise.

Most of DeLay's students are indeed very advanced, and I asked her why she took so much time with one who seemed to show comparatively little promise. "I think she has something special," said DeLay during a break after Lily's lesson. "It's not something I sensed in her playing; it's in her person. There is some kind of dignity, some kind of strength behind all that sensitivity and shyness. I want to stay with her."

A little girl named Jin Hi, who must be about nine years old, takes her place in front of DeLay. Her hair is held back with red bobbles that match her red shirt. She has no visible waist, and her denim skirt is held up by suspenders. Jin Hi speaks in a shy whisper and proceeds to belt the daylights out of the violin. She plays Mozart's Violin Concerto in A Major, including an interminable cadenza replete with double stops and other technical difficulties. When she is finished DeLay says, "That's nice, honey. I think we can use this, but not the cadenza — it is a bad one. The [Sam] Franko cadenza is the best," she says, turning to the mother, "and if you have any trouble getting it, let me know." For the first time in the afternoon I felt a thud. The little girl must have put in hours and hours learning the luckless cadenza, and all for naught. Jin Hi, however, displays not a flicker of emotion and launches into Sarasate's Fantasy on Bizet's *Carmen*, a piece that sounds altogether too seductive and sophisticated for this earnest little creature. "Good for you," says De-Lay enthusiastically at the end. "I want you to start finding songs to transcribe for the violin. What do you know about gypsies?" "They don't have jobs," Jin Hi replies in a barely audible whisper. "Well . . . OK," says DeLay cautiously. "But they are also famous for making wonderful music that can sometimes be very wild. See what happens if you try thinking about wild people when you are playing this piece."

"How many hours do you practice?" DeLay asks the next student, Ellen, a stolid, dough-faced child of about ten, who comes in with her father and mother. She reminds me of Mr. Memory in the old Hitch-cock movie *The Thirty-Nine Steps* because she is utterly expressionless and seems to be on automatic pilot.

"Four," replies Ellen, improbably. "One hour on each string, shifting to second position."

"Wow," says DeLay, without a hint of irony. "You will be a fabulous shifter." Ellen is also studying with one of DeLay's associates, in addition to DeLay herself. The child stands foursquare in the middle of the room and starts to play the Dvořák A Minor Violin Concerto, sometimes with her eyes closed. Both parents follow the lesson intently. Ellen's glamorously dressed mother has a little notebook on her lap, ready to jot down notes any time DeLay speaks.

Near the end of the movement, DeLay starts tapping her pencil to keep the child up to tempo. "Very, very nice," she says at the end. "Oistrakh has good fingerings, Galamian has good fingerings. Francescatti's are not good for children, because of their hand size. So I will have to redo these." Ellen, who is totally unselfconscious, jiggles her ankles and sniffs while waiting for DeLay to make the changes on her music. When she is not playing, she looks briefly at her parents, at DeLay, and all around the room. Ellen is definitely a kid. She might be in spelling class, and DeLay could be correcting her composition. "Here, before the letter G in the last section, you are going to want to hear the orchestra," DeLay says. "Your intonation is very good except for a couple of spots. This is a spot." At the end of the lesson, DeLay adds, "Wow! That's great, honey. But keep your bow on the string."

Right after Ellen and her parents leave, a mother comes in with an elaborate explanation about why her child, who was next on the schedule, has to change the time of his lesson and can only come later in the afternoon than had been arranged. Her manner is simultaneously shrill and ingratiating. The change means that another student, who is already waiting, will have to take her son's time slot instead. I am surprised, since I had seen the boy a little while ago sitting in the Juilliard School lobby. DeLay tells me afterward that the mother wants to manipulate the time-table so that the waiting student plays first. The woman has some idea in her head that her son will show off to better advantage if DeLay hears him after, rather than before, that particular child whom the mother regards as his arch-rival. The order makes no difference whatever to DeLay, so she assents and the mother goes off happy.

"OK, sugarplum," signals DeLay to the next student, Julie, who is about ten and has her mother with her. "Have you got your exam program ready? You've got to have a nice piece—in fact, let's do two. You've worked in the Suzuki book. Let's do Fuoco Allegro and the Accolay Concerto." Julie looks impassive but is clearly not thrilled by these choices. "It's better to review old pieces for your exam instead of starting something new," says DeLay, catching the girl's expression. After the class, Julie's mother stays on to talk to DeLay, explaining that she is sick of hearing the Accolay. DeLay tells her that Julie won't get a good grade with works like the Bach or the Mozart that she wants to do, and that the J. B. Accolay Violin Concerto always gets good grades. "If she gets to the stage where she is playing solos a lot, you are going to die, you will hear them so often," DeLay says, adding that Julie is very talented and she would like her to get a nice grade. By now, the word *grade* has been mentioned three times in rapid succession and the point is being taken. What can Julie's mother do but retire with as good grace as possible? After Julie's mother leaves the studio, DeLay remarks that she was not happy because the pieces Julie will be playing will get her through the exam but have no prestige. Suzuki pieces are regarded as déclassé by the parents of this group of children.

The only non-Asian student of the afternoon is a Russian boy of thirteen whose mother, too, is in attendance. The mother moves her chair to be as close to DeLay as she can manage. She is as nervous as a cat and radiates tension throughout the room. The boy's manner, by contrast or self-defense, is sulky and phlegmatic. He seems to have removed himself from the proceedings except for the moment when he starts to play and then everything is suddenly flash and fire. It is as though an electric plug has been put in the socket: swooping down-bows from high off the string, slashing strokes on the double-stops.

The effect is almost funny, like a cartoon study of boy expressing aggression to mother by beating her with instrument and pinioning her with bow. The Kabalevsky work the student is playing fits this spirit, and DeLay seems to be in collusion with him, urging yet more sound. "Be a Cossack," she exhorts. "More bow! The more, the more!" Throughout the boy's playing, his mother swallows continuously in a way that is distressing to watch. It is like a creature gobbling. DeLay tells me later that the first time the mother brought her son to a lesson, when DeLay told the boy his scales were very good, the mother burst into tears, sobbing, "Oh, I've been so worried—so worried." After the Kabalevsky, DeLay takes the boy through a series of exercises, with and without the metronome, in all sorts of rhythmic combinations and with constant checks on intonation. The repetitious patterns seem to take the charge out of the atmosphere and bring things back to what passes for normal for the rest of the lesson.

By this time, DeLay has been teaching nonstop for more than four hours, and except for a supper break, when she and accompanist Evan Solomon send out for Chinese food (but very elegant Chinese food, from the Shun Lee Palace next to Lincoln Center), she will continue for at least another three. Sometimes an Asian parent will bring an elaborate supper for DeLay that has been prepared at home and will heat it up in the microwave at Juilliard. While the motives are undoubtedly generous, the parents are constantly looking for ways to bring their children to the fore, and offering food is a favorite means of calling attention. A couple of the children, invariably female, will present the meal to DeLay with much whispering and giggling.

On this occasion, just when the food from the Shun Lee Palace arrives, a girl of about sixteen comes into the studio and tells DeLay in an apologetic whisper that she has to cancel her lesson because she has hurt her back. "Oh, dear," says DeLay. "You certainly can't play in the school orchestra, then. Tell the conductor that you have extreme pain."

"It's not really extreme pain," says the student, looking anxious. "It's just uncomfortable." DeLay peers at the girl over her glasses for a minute. "I suggest you use the word *pain*," she says firmly. Case closed.

Yura Lee (her real name—she was ten years old at the time of this lesson in 1996) is the next in class to play. She has recently emerged from the cute-little-dress stage and is wearing blue big-boy overalls and a T-shirt. Her hair is in bangs and caught up with a large pink plastic clip. For the past couple of weeks Yura has been working on Bartók's Second Violin Concerto, and already has it memorized. She gives her music to DeLay before starting to play. "Great, sweetie," DeLay says when Yura finishes. "Remember, we were analyzing the structure last time, and here is where we finished." Yura nods and picks up at the spot DeLay is referring to and they start working their way out loud through the thicket of notes.

I had already heard a number of Yura's lessons but I continue to be astonished each time. Everything flows completely naturally. There are subtleties of dynamics that could not possibly be taught—Yura must know by some deep instinct what to say and how to say it. Similarly, there is an inevitability about the phrasing that may be due in part to analyzing the music with DeLay in her lessons, but which must have its basis in Yura's own inner vision. The cadenzas are totally assured, as are the fiendish double-stops and fierce dissonances. Yura seems utterly at home with a musical language that many adults find difficult to grasp. She still keeps a weather eye on DeLay while she plays.

Yura's mother does not follow the pattern of some of the parents already mentioned. She takes no notes, has no tape recorder, and displays no anxiety. She sits poised and serene, sometimes smiling and swaying slightly to the music, through all of Yura's lessons. She behaves, in fact, like a member of the audience rather than an overinvested taskmaster, and seems to enjoy listening to her little girl play. As a result, Yura has not picked up fears the way some children do with a critical parent. Yura's mother is also very beautiful and I love watching her.

"Good girl," says DeLay at the end of the movement. "Your tone, dynamics, and intonation are all much improved. The marks I had to put on your music before are mostly erased, which was a great pleasure."

"The pizzicatos," says Yura. "I still have a problem with them."

"What would happen if you got ready to pull the string a little earlier?" It works! Yura giggles. "I'm so glad I am a musician."

The next time I saw Yura was about eight or nine months later, and she was beginning to look more like a teenager. I was enchanted to see that she had a permanent and was wearing see-through jelly sandals. We talked a bit about school—she goes to the Professional Children's School in New York and was particularly excited to have a couple of friends who were in *Les Miz*. Away from the studio, she was totally caught up in all the ordinary kid stuff—although ordinary only in terms of other kids who are in the performing world—as well as her consuming passion for the violin. At the time of this writing, Yura has become a young woman and is embarked on what may well become a major career.

Every so often, someone waiting outside for the critical moment between lessons will peer around the door into the studio in the hope that DeLay can be interrupted for a few words. Usually it is a student or parent or another teacher, but today's visitor does not fit any of these categories. A formally dressed man of about forty comes in during the break without knocking. He appears oblivious of DeLay's frosty expression and immediately starts talking in a strong—to me, unidentifiable—accent. A conversation, intense on his part, measured on hers, follows, although its actual subject is never mentioned. He had looked surprised to find someone else in the room with her and would clearly prefer that I were not present, but DeLay signals in response to my raised eyebrows that I could stay put if I wished.

The visitor is trying to persuade DeLay to help him in some way that she clearly has no intention of doing. The less she talks, the more he fulminates. "They will ask me what your reasons are," he finally says, in exasperation.

"You can tell them I cannot even consider this without detailed information," DeLay replies.

"What kind of information?"

"We have already discussed this several times."

"I have come all the way over here to get this settled."

"I have given you my answer," DeLay says levelly. "There is nothing else to say." A stony silence ensues. Finally, he flounces out and DeLay explains that the man is something of a charlatan who is trying to set up a questionable business involving recordings and interviews with her students, for which he needs her blessing and her involvement as a lecturer. The statement that he made a special trip for this purpose is totally phony—he has been in the States for months for other reasons, and the "They" to whom he refers are nonexistent.

The break is followed by another phenomenally gifted student—a pretty girl of about twelve, named Helen, who comes in with her mother. Helen will be playing a recital in Merkin Hall in a couple of weeks. She plays the Bruch *Scottish Fantasy*, closing her eyes and concentrating hard during the piano introduction. At the end of the first section, DeLay beams proudly and says, "Thank you, sweetie, that was just beautiful. You need more weight on the bow—when the bow hits the string, you want it to start vibrating. You need a new bow, don't you?" she adds. "But don't commission one—you might not like it. Come back tomorrow afternoon and we'll work on some basics. Now I have to talk to your mother about your dress for your concert in Merkin. You need a fancier one than the one you wore in your first recital."

DeLay is usually the one to decide on proper concert attire for the younger students. They and their parents take over when they get older. "Silver shoes, I think, and flesh-colored stockings, not white," says De-Lay. "A silver top and a big black skirt. A sash with silver dots. A black velvet ribbon for your hair—no barrettes!"

"Too nice, Miss DeLay, too nice!" expostulates Helen's mother in her heavily accented English. "People like to see people dressed up. More red! More gold!"

"You're going to have to start making lots of dresses now," says De-Lay, cheerfully. "Shoes with a little heel. And makeup—a little blush, a lot of eye makeup, and lipstick. Anything that will pick up the light. It doesn't hurt for a girl to be pretty—a man to be poised." Helen looks increasingly miserable during this discussion, and DeLay suggests that she wait outside as she wants to talk to her mother about something else.

After the girl has left the room, DeLay tells the mother that she thinks it is getting to be time to introduce Helen to Isaac Stern. This signals a significant rite of passage. When a student shows particular promise, DeLay makes sure that the top people in the classical music jungle telegraph system are aware of what is happening, for possible future reference.

Later, DeLay gives me Helen's repertoire list, which includes the following concertos: Haydn, No. 1 in C major; Wieniawski, No. 2 in D minor; Bruch, No. 1 in G minor and the *Scottish Fantasy*; Mendelssohn, E minor; Lalo, *Symphonie espagnole*; Vieuxtemps, No. 5 in A minor; Saint-Saëns, No. 3 in B minor and the *Introduction and Rondo capriccioso*; Paganini, No. 1 in D major; Khatchaturian, D minor; Dvořák, A minor; Vivaldi, A minor; Bach, A and E major; Viotti, No. 22 in A minor and No. 23 in G major; Mozart, Nos. 1, 2, 3, and 4 and "Adelaide." After the concerto list are various etudes by Franz Wohlfahrt, Jakob Dont, Ševčík, and Hans Sitt, among others. After that, eleven of Pierre Rode's 24 Caprices and twelve of Paganini's 24 Caprices, and the page concludes with a list of solo pieces by Kreisler, Wieniawski, Saint-Saëns, Paganini, Handel, Mozart, and more.

SUE-CHIN'S STORY

Sue-Chin (not her real name) has been studying with DeLay for three years. Rather than a thumbnail sketch of a lesson, I prefer to tell her story, much of which was told to me by Edward Newhouse. Sue-Chin's story is hardly typical—in many ways it is outlandish—but it depicts the musical development of a child who initially did not even get as far as applying to Juilliard, and the lengths to which DeLay will go on occasion to help a student in need. Sue-Chin and her father came to the United States from Taiwan in 1996 when the girl was eleven, and arrived, unannounced except for a telephone call from Kennedy Airport, on DeLay's doorstep in Nyack. The beautiful little girl and her diminutive father had come to the United States in order for her to take the entrance exam for the Juilliard Pre-College Division, which was to be held the following week. The father had heard about Juilliard but was entirely unaware of the application process. He also knew that DeLay was the most important violin teacher in America, and went straight to the source to ask her to listen to the child and to make the necessary arrangements for Sue-Chin to be admitted to the school. His wife remained in Taiwan since they could not both afford to come. He had, not so incidentally, sold their house in order to pay for the journey.

DeLay listened to Sue-Chin play, and knew within the first few bars that the girl would not be able to get into Juilliard. It had nothing to do with natural ability. The problem was that Sue-Chin played as though she had learned what to do out of a book—a sort of musical paint by numbers. Neither in the way she held the violin nor in the way she played was there any recognizable or workable technique. She was engaged in a kind of three-legged race with herself and the instrument. As Newhouse (who instantly fell in love with her) described it to me, she had been not only badly taught, but miserably taught, and the father was totally deluded about her abilities. He was not alone. Apparently the entire village from which they came was convinced that Sue-Chin was already a star musician.

Whether it was out of sympathy or a recognition of qualities of strength she saw in Sue-Chin, DeLay was determined to see if she could not get her on track and ready to try for Juilliard in a few years. Sue-Chin's father returned to Taiwan to be replaced by her mother, and De-Lay succeeded in arranging some funding from a private source to enable them to eat and to pay the rent. DeLay and her associate, Professor Won Bin Yim, who teaches at both Juilliard and now at the University of Cincinnati College-Conservatory of Music, started working intensively with the bright and lively little girl. The family obviously had no way of paying, and the lessons were given gratis.

All went well for a while until Sue-Chin started to complain of pain in her arm and in her shoulder. This kind of affliction is fairly common among string players. It can result from tension, an incorrect way of holding the instrument, or particularly with violists, playing an instrument slightly too large for a particular physique. Very small distances can create major differences. A cellist who raises the end-pin by an inch, for example, will sit differently and bow differently, and it can take some time to make the adjustment. DeLay arranged for Sue-Chin to see a doctor, who assured the child, her mother, and DeLay that the problem was not muscular, but felt she should see a neurologist.

At this point, DeLay and Newhouse's son, Dr. Jeffrey Newhouse, came into the story. Because of his position as professor of radiology at Columbia Presbyterian, his parents turned to him for advice about finding the right specialist for Sue-Chin. Through him, they were able to contact a distinguished neurologist who was a professor and attending physician at Columbia Presbyterian. After much testing, it emerged that Sue-Chin was suffering from a rare malady known as AVM (arterial venous malformation), for which the only treatment is a procedure known as artificial embolization, which I will not even attempt to describe, except to say that it is extremely delicate, extremely time-consuming as it has to be done over a period of months, and that the doctor to whom DeLay and Newhouse were referred is one of the handful of physicians in the entire country who is able to perform it.

No money changed hands in the course of the successful treatment of Sue-Chin. Both the doctor and Columbia Presbyterian gave their services on a pro-bono basis, and some benefit accrued to the hospital in the form of valuable and well-deserved publicity. CBS News did a story about Sue-Chin and her medical progress on its nightly television news program at intervals during the period of the treatment, and much was made of the generosity and humanitarianism of the hospital and the physician, both of whom earned every ounce of credit they got, and more. The cost of the care Sue-Chin received is beyond imagining, and if all the preceding events had not taken place and Sue-Chin had returned to Taiwan when she was initially unable to get into Juilliard, she would no longer be alive.

DeLay continued to work with Sue-Chin during her lengthy medical treatment whenever it was possible, and again on a regular basis after she was discharged. Two years later, in 1998, when she was thirteen, Sue-Chin went through the normal application process to enter the Juilliard Pre-College Division, which included a performance examination before a jury of the faculty, and she was admitted as a student. Given Sue-Chin's history, both musical and medical, this is a miraculous achievement and a testament to her courage, musicianship, and determination. DeLay has said that as far as she herself was concerned, the two years of helping Sue-Chin to change such deeply ingrained performing habits and absorb new ones was harder than teaching any of the so-called star students, and that nothing had given her more satisfaction.

5 The Upper School Students

Life for the older, full-time Juilliard College students is another story. To be admitted to the school to begin with, they are required, among other things, to pass an audition before a jury composed of members of the faculty. Applicants must present three pieces, only some of which will be listened to, but all of which have to be meticulously prepared, since there is no knowing which section of a work the jury will request. The examination lasts ten excruciatingly long minutes.

Many of the candidates have been told since the age of five that they are the best in the country, and the discovery that they are not even the best among the group that is applying can be terribly painful. Not only are their futures suddenly in doubt, but they face the prospect of having to tell everyone, including their parents, who have often made enormous sacrifices, that Juilliard turned them down.

Those applicants who are hoping to study with DeLay usually audition for her privately, long before the official auditions take place. They come from all over the globe—some arrive in her studio on the basis of recommendations from teachers or other big-wigs in the music world ("I have this marvelous, glorious, unprecedented . . ."), and some who are unable to get to New York will send in a tape for DeLay's opinion, but unless she is already very familiar with the student and his playing, this kind of evidence is obviously too flimsy by itself. It is not unheard of for someone to try and pass a fake—a tape played by some more accomplished musician—in the hope of getting her stamp of approval and squeaking past into the auditions.

DeLay hears about 250 auditions for Juilliard each year and has described that first meeting as being akin to a first conversation since it reveals not only performance ability, but also the crucial aspects of intelligence, humor, and personality. Sometimes the upshot to this whole screening process is that DeLay advises a student to go back and study for another couple of years and try again.

DeLay has her own way of saying No in these instances. One afternoon when I was present, a youth of about seventeen—an American for a change—came into the studio armed with a recommendation from his teacher who felt that he was ready for Juilliard. The student clearly fancied himself and did a little bit of stage business settling the fiddle under his chin before plodding through a movement of a Mozart sonata. When he was finished, DeLay asked him how much he practiced every day. The youth looked a little startled—presumably he had been expecting some praise and a comment on his playing—and he rambled around a bit before saying that he was also studying the piano and that some days he practiced more on the one instrument than the other. The way he put it made clear that he thought this dual interest would be regarded as commendable. DeLay's question about practice time went unanswered. No specific hours were cited. She then asked if he was hoping for a professional career. "Yes," he replied.

"Well," DeLay said, "you will have to decide between the two instruments. You cannot do both. You have to start putting in five hours a day minimum on the basics—scales and passages and repertoire. You've got a way to go." No bruising pronouncements on the quality of his playing, and no closing of the door on other possibilities, such as orchestral work. Kind, but definite and dismissive, DeLay laid out what he had to do if he wanted to get anywhere. "OK, honey, nice to hear you play. Talk to me after you play your exam." The student, trying to take in what DeLay was saying, looked a bit like a stunned ox. He had undoubtedly received an excessive amount of encouragement from his teacher, who in turn must have given him a big build-up to DeLay. "He has got to choose what he is going to do," said DeLay after he left. "That is why I was so tough on him. They are not going to take him." Hmmm, I thought. Talk to me after you play your exam? Don't hold your breath.

Final exams at Juilliard, which include a performance, are another similarly fraught period. Near the end of term, DeLay makes a point of giving her students some rapid-fire, practical advice on how to comport themselves. "Come into the room, go to the piano, and tune your fiddle," she will tell them. "Take your time. There is no need to feel rushed. Make a simple announcement of what you are going to play. Don't be too dressed up. Be sure you have done your history for the concerto." DeLay reminds the examinees that Paul Hall, Juilliard's concert hall, sounds better if one plays very lightly, and that if they fluff, they absolutely have to keep going. It is unthinkable to say "Oops! Can I start again?"

Long before that stage, there is much discussion about the choice of repertoire. "It is easier to start with a piece that begins with the piano," DeLay tells her students. "The Prokofiev Second Concerto starts with the soloist all alone, so there are the possible advantages of playing the Shostakovich or Barber concertos. Everybody thinks they are *soooo* difficult," she laughs. "They must need *soooo* much understanding."

While the audition process at Juilliard and elsewhere is not technically the same as a violin competition in the sense of having preliminaries, finals, and prizes (unless you want to count admission to a conservatory as the prize), it is a close cousin. Edward Newhouse has described coming in second in a competition as akin to coming in second in a duel, and DeLay herself is no great fan of the institution. "Some are blatantly political and should be avoided," she said. "Some are well run and scrupulously honest, but the juries are composed of persons with widely divergent tastes—each thinks he knows exactly how Stravinsky should be played. The jury will only be able to arrive at a consensus about whether the intonation is decent, the sound acceptable, and the playing secure." DeLay rolled her eyes at this process and said, "A kind of lowest common denominator will determine the winner—and the winner may go on to a major international career or oblivion within a matter of months."

It is, nevertheless, true that some of DeLay's students have been helped by winning major competitions. When eighteen-year-old Itzhak Perlman won the Leventritt Award, it marked the turning point in his career, but obviously he would have made his mark sooner or later anyway. Nadja Salerno-Sonnenberg won the Naumburg Competition in 1981 when she was twenty, and Kyoko Takezawa won the Indianapolis Competition in 1986. It is hard to believe they would not have gained fame otherwise, although the importance to Salerno-Sonnenberg, as detailed in chapter 13, was as much a personal triumph as a violinistic one. Midori, Gil Shaham, Shlomo Mintz, Mark Peskanov, Sarah Chang, and Nigel Kennedy all got started without benefit of competitions.

The college-age students who manage to jump through all the hoops, pass over all the hurdles, and gain admittance to Juilliard are obviously very, very good. Once inside, they never know another day's peace, because the competition does not end at that point, it intensifies. Catherine Cho, a member of the Pre-College faculty who also works with DeLay with the older students, says that the latter are harder to teach than the little ones because they have so many pressing issues in their lives beside learning the violin (let's not even mention hormones), most particularly, of course, their concern about the future. The little kids, still free of such worries, tend to be more consistently focused and motivated.

THE GROUP AT WORK

DeLay is much more demanding of her students as they get older, insisting that they become their own magnifying glasses, able to identify problems and begin to deal with them independently. In my conversations with current and former students, the phrase "She taught me how to teach myself" came up time and again.

Once a month, DeLay holds group lessons for her older students in which they play for each other under her guidance. The ground rules require that after a student plays, each member of the group has to give a brief critique of the performance before DeLay herself says anything to, in her words, fill in the gaps.

For those students at the listening end, the knowledge that they will shortly have to articulate their reactions wonderfully focuses the mind. For the student up at bat, it is a chance to learn how his or her playing comes across to different people, and perhaps more important, how to cope with criticism. In this respect, the studio is a far more protected environment than the world that lies in wait outside, since DeLay insists that all comments must be constructive — anything purely derogatory or disparaging is absolutely prohibited.

When DeLay began teaching, she tried this group system with the youngest children because she thought it would be a good idea to make the class like a party. "I had no idea how to control a group of little kids," she said. "I would have class performances, and the little boys in the back row would be making snide remarks, so I thought, How can I keep them from saying terrible things about each other's playing? Aha! Ice cream and cake. But they threw the cake around. Finally, I just had to make a rule that nobody could say, 'This stinks!'" Her master classes for all ages abide by the same principle. If you are going to say something negative, you must also say something positive.

98

There is no such thing as a typical group session in DeLay's studio. Too many variables are at work, such as whether someone is preparing for a concert, or has only just started work on a piece, or needs particular help with a technical problem. One afternoon when I was present, for example, it happened that each of the five students in the class was preparing for a public event. One was about to play a concert at Kaufmann Auditorium at the 92nd Street Y, a prestigious New York recital hall; another was preparing for a debut concert with the Cleveland Orchestra; and the other three, to DeLay's regret because she is not a fan of such events, were entering various competitions. This meant that no major suggestions or criticisms would likely be made at this meeting, since there was not enough time to make use of them, and the upshot might be nothing but some bruised morale.

Before everyone arrived in the studio, DeLay and the violinist heading for the 92nd Street Y spent some time discussing her program. Should she play Stravinsky? Tartini? The length of a program has to be carefully thought out. "My César Franck sounds like the German countryside," the student said soulfully. "The main problem with the Y is the pianist," DeLay said, side-stepping the remark because her chief concern was about the girl's choice of accompanist. "The piano is too big for the hall. A lot depends on who plays with you, and how your styles match. Phone me tonight around eleven. Let me think a bit." After the class, DeLay commented that the girl was too easily swayed by the opinions of others. "Where did she get that bit about Franck?" she sniffed.

By now, the group had gathered and quickly got down to business. One student arrived with a back-pack as well as his fiddle, and asked if he might play first, as he was heading straight to the airport to get to a major international violin competition. He seemed quite prepared to risk missing the plane in order to have DeLay hear the Brahms Concerto he would be playing—as though he had to have the royal blessing before heading into battle.

"I've got a couple of small ideas," DeLay said when he finished. "It is important that those sixteenths don't get too long. If they get longer, they lose energy. The energy is in the rhythm patterns." DeLay rapped out the figure on the table to demonstrate her point. "When you make something heavier, you have two contrasting elements at work: crescendo and slowing up. Slowing up gives a ponderous quality. Do you want that?"

"No," said the student, sounding shocked, as he gathered his belongings and dashed off.

He was followed by a young man who was preparing for the Naumburg Competition in New York. He played the first movement of Prokofiev's Second Violin Concerto in G Minor, and was roundly praised by DeLay and the rest of the group. "You are getting tremendous energy, but I think you can get a bigger sound," said DeLay after the general discussion. "A fast bow will do it—it will give you another dimension of color, but you will have to get used to not staying so near the bridge."

In the general talk among the group that ensued, somebody said he had heard that a particular female violinist was playing much better. "Maybe she has got a man," said the Naumburg hopeful. "Chauvinist!" laughed DeLay. "You are just saying that because you are God's gift to women."

"I wish that were true," he said. "They are not exactly beating down the doors."

"You are never home," DeLay riposted. "It wouldn't do any good."

To digress briefly, the Naumburg student, whom I came to know only after his graduation from Juilliard, was David Kim. Kim was appointed to the distinguished post of concertmaster of the Philadelphia Orchestra in the spring of 1999. His description of DeLay in a talk we had in 1995 was particularly vivid: "Her way of motivating her students is to keep them exploring. You love her to death. She is your favorite aunt that you want to be with and to please." The "aunt" theme recurred, coincidentally, in a story DeLay told about Kim as a young boy at a party she gave at Aspen: "Somebody brought their maiden aunt and plopped her down in a chair off in the corner and just left her there. David—he must have been about fourteen—came into the room and looked around and saw the maiden aunt in the corner. He went and sat down on the floor and talked to her until they left. I thought, I've never seen anything so nice."

The next student was going to play in a minor competition outside New York, which drew DeLay's disapproval. "You are going to that thing? They don't know what they are doing," she said, concerned that it might be to his disadvantage to participate in an event so lacking in prestige. "They want you to play the Bach taking the first repeat and not the second? Why on earth? Find out what they want. Ask 'What is the ruling?' It will sound official."

The student who was making his debut with the Cleveland Orchestra played through the Glazunov Violin Concerto. "Good boy. That's great!" said DeLay enthusiastically. "You will do wonderfully." She rummaged about in her handbag and suddenly sprayed herself with perfume. "This piece needs an orchestral rhythm," she added. "You have to be able to think as a conductor." She turned to the accompanist and said, "I want you to play wrong notes, wrong rhythms. Take all sorts of strange rubatos. You must stay with him," she said to the student. "You never know what the orchestra will do. Let's try it again."

At group lessons when no one is under immediate pressure, the comments—at least DeLay's—are far more detailed. The students for the most part confine themselves to a couple of sentences, although every so often somebody decides to hold forth at length. The following description is drawn from several such sessions, and the names of the participants—Janet, Hsing-Yi, Peter, and Robert—are fictitious, although, thanks to the use of a tape recorder, the quoted material is not.

The piano accompanist on these occasions is frequently Rohan De Silva, whose name is anything but fictitious, since he is a familiar figure on the concert stage. De Silva, who was born in Sri Lanka, is an exceptional musician in his own right, and has served as partner to such artists as Itzhak Perlman, Cho-Liang Lin, Joshua Bell, Gil Shaham, and Midori in concert halls all over the world. He has worked closely with DeLay and her students for years, both at Juilliard, where he is a member of the faculty, and at Aspen in the summers. De Silva is not the only distinguished pianist to serve as accompanist in DeLay's classes. Both Emanuel Ax and Joseph Kalichstein held the job when they were students and were working their way through Juilliard.

"Who wants to start?" said DeLay to the group. After a certain amount of kidding among themselves about the dangers and benefits of being the first, Janet got up and played through a Brahms scherzo on which she had been working for a couple of weeks.

"OK, fine," said DeLay, turning to the rest of the group. "What did all of you think? What direction would you go with it in the next three days?"

"It really sounds very good," Robert, a tall bespectacled youth, said carefully. "But if you want it to be even better, I would work on the vibrato. Also, you should try not to make a face if you make a mistake."

"Well," said Peter, the youngest student present, "I think it sounded very polished. Maybe too polished. I didn't think it was peaceful enough. It sounded like 'Here I am. Look at me.' I think it needed more range."

"I thought it was very clean," said Robert, "but it just didn't get me excited. It seemed kind of humdrum."

DeLay turned to Hsing-Yi, who was clearly reluctant to speak. "I think everybody has already given her plenty to work on," she said in a near whisper. Peter laughed and said, "Chicken," which made Hsing-Yi giggle, but she did not rise to the bait.

"It feels to me much stronger, more muscular, than some of his other scherzos," said DeLay. "There is something of war in it. I think it has the extremes of emotion." She indicated a section where, although there is a big crescendo, the student put too much pressure on the bow. I know you are trying to get a bigger sound, but that is all your violin will do. It's like having a small bank account—it's not there. So you will have to get the intensity some other way. Remember, sound control depends on bow speed, sounding point, and weight. Let's try out a few possibilities."

DeLay pointed to a section in the girl's music on which she had scribbled some ideas. "Here, in this shift, I heard all sorts of machinery coming," DeLay said. "Stop the bow so you can shift silently. Here you need to stay on the string for more sound. Start fast and you won't get any scratch. Try it out at home, and see if it feels comfortable. Here we need to make this drop-off much more dramatic, get away from the bridge."

None of DeLay's suggestions touched on interpretation, even though Robert's "humdrum" was right on the mark. Journalist Barbara Jepson, who watched some lessons in DeLay's studio when preparing an article about her for *The New York Times* ("She Helps Fiddlers Help Themselves," 26 July 1992), once told me about listening to a student play a sonata in a manner notably lacking in intensity and expressiveness. Jepson had expected that DeLay would talk about the character of the piece, rather than the amount of sound, and ask the girl to visualize a story—a means DeLay sometimes uses to trigger an understanding of what the music is saying. Instead, DeLay took a particular passage and asked the girl to shape the dynamics so that the top of the phrase stood out. "At first she just could not do it," said Jepson, "but after a lot of experimenting, it suddenly worked and the whole thing took on the kind of excitement that had been missing. What really struck me was that the difficulty turned out to be a technical problem and not an interpretive one."

Janet's problem was not solved as quickly, there were too many old habits in the way, and she sat down to be replaced by Hsing-Yi, who played through Mozart's Rondo K. 373. There was a general murmur of approval from the group, and DeLay, who had been putting pencil marks on the girl's music while she was playing, said, "Wonderful, sugarplum. You've changed so many things. Your vibrato is getting beautiful."

"It's very difficult for me," said Hsing-Yi.

"Where? Where? Play it for me once more, then tell me which measures are difficult, one or two?" Hsing-Yi pointed to the trouble spots.

"Well," said DeLay. "Given your particular hand, let's change the fingerings for the high notes. It is like trying to wear a man's shoes. These fingerings were made by men with big hands and long fingers. It's fine for them, but no good for us. Look at my hand," she said to the class, holding it up for inspection. "My little finger only comes up to two-thirds of its neighbor—to the first knuckle. This fingering just didn't sound good."

DeLay gave Hsing-Yi back her music and took her fiddle for a moment. "You're going to think I'm crazy, but try *this*," she said, demonstrating her ideas for a different fingering. "Try it out and see what you think." After a number of stumbles, since the old fingerings had become automatic, Hsing-Yi began to get the hang of the new ones.

"I'm going to make a statement" DeLay said, in mock pompous tones, flicking invisible specks of dust off the sleeves of her dress. "There is no correct way to do something. There are many ways, and that includes your fingerings, your hand position, and everything else. That sounded good, honey. How did it feel?"

"Good," said Hsing-Yi.

During the break DeLay remarked to me how much Hsing-Yi's playing had improved over the last year. "That is not my work. That is Miss Tanaka's," she said, with pride. Naoko Tanaka, one of her teaching associates, is on the Juilliard faculty and had also been her student.

Robert, a serious and self-assured youth in his late teens, had been working on the Bartók Second Violin Concerto for about a month, and brought it to the group for the first time. He played through the first movement without interruption, and at the end DeLay said, "That's great! You have done a lot of good work." DeLay smiled. Robert continued to look serious and respectful.

"Let's go over a few things," DeLay said. "You started with your violin sounding very brilliant and very edgy. That is fine for those passages, but we also have to be able to do the opposite. Try going to the fingerboard and floating the bow. You can use lots of bow, but only one hair."

Robert nodded and tried repeatedly to get the desired airy sound, which suddenly clicked in. "Fine," said DeLay. "Now let's talk about bow changes. All your bow changes can be heard. There are two kinds of bow changes—click and no click," she said to the group at large. "Here,

I'll show you." DeLay took Robert's fiddle and demonstrated the difference between an audible and a virtually inaudible sound when the bow changed direction. "Heifetz was click," she said, giving the instrument back. "There is no point beating your brains out. My teacher, Ivan Galamian, always told me you must make a bow change that cannot be heard. I think he loved this idea too much. You are always going to hear something. Heifetz always made clicks."

DeLay smiled and rocked back in her chair for a moment. "You know that old joke about somebody telling Heifetz about a concert he had heard where a young violinist was giving his debut? 'He sounded fabulous,' said this fellow, 'just like Heifetz.' And Heifetz replied, 'Think what it is like to *be* me—I have to come out and sound like Heifetz every single night.'" Robert smiled politely and looked a little puzzled at why everybody else was laughing.

Peter, the last to play, got up and bowed with mock formality to the group before launching into Bruch's *Scottish Fantasy*. There were a number of slips, although he managed to keep going, and he looked abashed when he had finished.

"There is too much happening here for you to feel very good," said DeLay, "because on a French shift you are going to hear the slide, and then the articulation of the finger. If it is a short distance with a slow slide and a finger pop, it could be like a woman wearing jewelry all over her dress, instead of just one piece of jewelry." DeLay paused. "Tell me," she said to Peter, "does that kind of shift bother you? Because you were doing a lot of it." She turned to the class. "Does it bother any of you? Have you ever thought of it specifically? Hearing the shift sound and then the pop of the articulation, instead of hearing the one sound, that would be the Heifetz sound?"

DeLay took Peter's violin and tucked it under her chin. "I think another reason you are having trouble is because the violin is around here," she said, placing the instrument very far forward. "It has pushed your elbow way over here. Whereas, if the violin is over here, where it belongs on you, your elbow drops on the down-bow, yes, and you pull your bow out like this and you are not looking at your music, and you would look spectacular. I think that's something really to work on."

Sometimes this sort of talk in DeLay's classes went right over my head—what is a French shift, for example?—but the language and its intensity have a charm all their own, and for me, at least, those last two paragraphs sounded like poetry. I learned later that a French shift means to move to the "target" note by sliding with the current finger to the new position, and then dropping the appropriate finger on the new note.

At the end of the class, someone raised the question of playing by memory, and what to do if an accompanist objects—a not infrequent source of friction between violinist and pianist. "You know how I feel?" said DeLay. "I think that the pianists who tell you that it is good manners to use your music are people who are too lazy to memorize the stuff themselves. I am going to go on record that you should memorize your part and if your pianist resents that you are not using the music, damn it all, she should memorize hers, too." DeLay clapped her hands for emphasis. "And if she wants to use the music and look like an idiot—let her. You sound much better when you are not looking at the music. And God knows you look better."

"I feel nervous if I don't have the music," said Hsing-Yi. "Well," said DeLay. "What you can do is put the stand up, but instead of having it high, you put it way down to the bottom. Now turn it a little bit so the audience can't see what is on the stand. Now, you play from memory." Hsing-Yi did not look convinced. "I think starting in Aspen this summer I'm going to have all sonatas from memory." The entire group groaned. "OK?" said DeLay. "I mean it."

6 The Aspen Music School: DeLay's Summer Studio

In the winter, the little town of Aspen, Colorado, in the Rocky Mountains is known as the playground of the superrich, who fly down in their private jets, ready to frolic on the ski slopes. Walking down Aspen's main street in summertime, it is hard to visualize that scene. The mountains are green, the hang-gliders soar in the darkening sky before sunset, and about eighty percent of the population seem to be carrying musical-instrument cases. The remaining twenty percent stagger around with armloads of heavy-duty books, which are required reading at the Aspen Institute, the Aspen Center for Environmental Studies, the Aspen Center for Physics, or the Global Change Institute, among other local summer think tanks. Assuming you are not too picky about your arithmetic, this still leaves room for a sizable number of concert-goers and lecture auditors, not to mention the permanent population. Intense study rather than conspicuous consumption are the watchwords at Aspen in the summer.

The Aspen Music Festival grew out of the Goethe Bicentennial Convocation and Music Festival, held in 1949 in celebration of the 200th anniversary of the German poet's birth. The success of the bicentennial led to a continuation of the Aspen Music Festival, and the Aspen Music School officially came into being in 1951. The two institutions are joined at the hip, with faculty and students of the school participating in the festival's many concerts, alongside big-name guest artists from various parts of the globe.

The music school is just out of town in an idyllic setting of aspen trees and trout ponds, and the festival concerts take place in a vast tent in Aspen that seats about 1800 people, as well as in various other locations around town, including year-round Harris Hall. DeLay's headquarters, where she and her associates have their studios, is right on the main street in a series of rooms on the ground floor of St. Mary's Church.

When DeLay crossed the Rockies to join the Aspen faculty in the summer of 1971, it was also the crossing of a personal Rubicon; her long association with Ivan Galamian was at an end. Aspen itself was at a turning point when DeLay decided to accept the invitation of Gordon Hardy, Aspen's president emeritus, and began spending her summers there. Three years earlier, Hardy had started the Aspen Chamber Symphony, a venture that proved so successful that more string players were required on a regular basis, which also enabled Hardy to cast a wider net for fellowships for the participants. DeLay served as a magnet for young violinists from all over the world as well as from Juilliard, and before long the Aspen Music School was bringing not only her, but her Juilliard assistants and some of her students for the entire summer session. Unlike Juilliard, where children in the Pre-College Division attend classes and lessons only on Saturdays, Aspen is a total immersion experience, with music the only spoken language. Some students come straight to Aspen to start studying with DeLay even before entering Juilliard, as did Midori as a child. Sarah Chang was six years old when she first arrived in Aspen with her family. By the end of the 1990s, the entire summer entourage attached to DeLay and her associates consisted of about 150 students from all parts of the world, along with several piano accompanists and assorted parents. Practically a small town.

DeLay's eightieth birthday (which had been celebrated in New York under the aegis of Itzhak Perlman, as described at the start of this book) was marked by the Aspen Music Festival and School by parties and a gala concert in her honor, performed by many of her students, and I flew out for a few days to catch some of the festivities. Aspen does not stint in these matters. They had marked her seventy-fifth birthday over a two-year period with the world premieres of four violin concertos they had commissioned from prominent composers, including Stephen Paulus, Christopher Rouse, Dan Welcher, and David Winkler, as well as a violin sonata by William Bolcom. The soloists for those premiere performances—Robert McDuffie, Cho-Liang Lin, Nadja Salerno-Sonnenberg, Mark Peskanov, and Paul Kantor—were all, not coincidentally, former DeLay students.

"Where else could you drive Dorothy out in a golf cart?" asked

Robert Harth, the ebullient president of the Aspen Music Festival and School, when we met in his office, which looks out on the little islands, ponds, and pathways of the institution. He was describing plans for the eightieth birthday gala, to take place that evening.

> I told her we wanted her on stage, and she said, "Oh, sugar, no! No!" So I knew I had to come up with something that would capture her imagination a little bit. So I said, "I've got a golf cart to bring you on stage," and she just lit up and exclaimed, "You *do?*" and then I knew we had her. I don't think she has ever gone on stage before. She is very stubborn.

Robert Harth succeeded Gordon Hardy as president in 1989. By the time he arrived in Aspen, DeLay was already a legend for having "put the school on the map" (as both men put it) and for creating a string program that served to strengthen all the other departments. "She is indefatigable," Harth said. "She is still making that impact." Even if we make allowances for a certain amount of hyperbole on behalf of the school, Harth came across as someone who deeply admired DeLay and got a kick out of his association with her.

Before taking the job at Aspen, Harth had worked for the redoubtable Ernest Fleischmann for ten years ("I'm the only one who made it that long") as general manager of the Los Angeles Philharmonic, when Fleischmann was the orchestra's managing director. Harth was also managing director of the Hollywood Bowl at the time. Before that, he was with the Ravinia Festival (the Chicago Symphony's summer home), and even before that, when he was very young indeed, he got his first taste of concert production and stage management where he now wielded the power, at the Aspen Music Festival. Harth was a trained violinist, flutist, and composer before turning to administration.

"Dorothy's mind never stops working," Harth continued, after outlining the birthday plans in some detail.

> She is not interested in teaching, she is interested in learning. Because she is interested in learning, she stays young. This is a woman who is a lateral thinker as well as a forward thinker. By lateral, I mean—well, why don't you try this? When you think you have reached a conundrum to which there is no answer, often you cannot move forward or backward, and you need to move laterally. Get around the issue, and then eventually move forward.

Harth shifted in his chair. "Some people who have gotten on in years are rigid: 'This is the way I do it, this is the way I have always done it.' There is just none of that with Dorothy. She has got very strong opinions, don't get me wrong, and yet is very willing to hear other approaches, other solutions."

"What opinions come to mind?" I asked.

Harth laughed and said he was trying to think of one that could safely appear in print. "We are a pretty complicated institution," he continued after a pause. "There are 930 students and 140 faculty members, so we have a lot of programs going on," implying that the numbers gave ample opportunity for personality clashes among the participants. "You are faced with the fact that although we live in a very egalitarian, democratic society, in its purist form the music business is a hierarchy—an aristocracy, if you will. There is a reason why there is a first violin and a concertmaster, why there is a principal oboe, and a second and a third oboe, and it has to do with quality." Harth smiled at his politically incorrect observation.

"Dorothy is very opinionated about quality. She is very opinionated about the needs of the few sometimes outweighing the needs of the many," he said, adding that violin and piano are obviously the two instruments where the most soloists develop. "Dorothy is very strong in her opinion that we need to have our student orchestras accompany our best kids in concerto performances. This is not met with universal joy by our other faculty members. They say, 'Well, if Dorothy's students are getting concerto opportunities, how come my bass players are not getting to play solo bass concertos?'"

"She can dig her heels in," Harth continued. "You see that happen in board meetings and you see that in committee meetings," he said, confirming a report I had heard elsewhere that DeLay could be something of a Lone Ranger—an image in keeping with her Kansas background—when issues about which she cared deeply came up for discussion. "Of course, the most famous opinion where Dorothy weighed in was before my time, when they were looking for a new president after Gordon decided to step down. They learned very late in the day, at the eleventh-and-a-half hour, that the successor had intended to keep his winter job, that this was going to be a part-time thing." Harth rolled his eyes at the thought. "The story has it that there was a big meeting of the corporation, and at this meeting, Dorothy was so upset about what was happening that she took her crutch and started banging it on the floor to get everybody's attention." Harth laughed and then concluded in more sober tones:

> When Dorothy gets upset, which is very rarely, she commands a lot of attention. She always commands mine. I have seen her upset, but she has never been upset with me. She has been upset about things that happen, and she comes in to see me, and we try to resolve them. What I find amazing about her is that—well, I find everything amazing about her—she comes and meets with me about goals and objectives for her program, and ideas that she has about conductors or guest soloists; she comes to meetings on a regular basis, committee and board meetings; she flies out here for our winter meetings with the board of trustees; and she goes to more concerts than any other faculty member. Not just the violin ones.
>
> There she was at the Mahler Ninth yesterday. She had just had the most exhausting day of her life—we had a dinner party celebrating her birthday after that performance, so I know she had a late night—and there she was, asking the father of a violin student why the student was not at the concert. After that she went on to listen to eight auditions. She is about to fly to Tokyo for twelve days with the Aspen Festival in Japan, and we have just called United Airlines to make sure they understand that the Queen of England is going to be on that flight, so that everything is going to be just fine.
>
> I don't spend a lot of time thinking about what we will do without Dorothy. She does not show any signs of not coming back. One does not replace Dorothy DeLay when she finally leaves, one finds a new way of doing things. That is how phenomenal she is.

Some 1800 people filled the festival tent for the evening's concert, which was billed as "An Eightieth Birthday Celebration." The program was a pastiche of movements from various violin concertos, along with a couple of larger chamber works, including Bach's Brandenburg Concerto No. 3 and Mendelssohn's Octet in E-flat Major. Robert McDuffie and Nadja Salerno-Sonnenberg were on hand again as soloists, having flown in from other parts of the world to participate in the concert, as had Sarah Chang. James Conlon, the principal conductor of the Paris Opera and a summertime regular at Aspen and Tanglewood, was the evening's conductor with the Aspen Chamber Symphony. Since the orchestra included a host of her students, between them and the above-named soloists and chamber musicians, DeLay made pretty much of a clean sweep.

Sarah Chang appeared in a pretty and girlish black-and-white dress for the opening chamber music piece, and then the sixteen year old changed into a far more sophisticated flounced number for her solo. Nadja Salerno-Sonnenberg came on stage rubbing her palm across her nose, in a devil-may-care manner, and then gave a little shove to the harp with her foot (startling the harpist) when she reached the front of the orchestra to give herself a bit more room. Robert McDuffie melted everyone with some beautifully played Kreisler bonbons. They all seemed to be having a splendid time. I mention these details of dress and manner because nobody in the hall was there just for the music. How often, after all, does a musician get up in front of an audience knowing that from the first row to the last, he will be listened to without anything remotely like a critical ear? Intonation a bit off? Who cares. Entrance a little late? So what.

At the conclusion, all 1800 or so heads in the audience swiveled to the back of the tent to the spot where DeLay traditionally sits, and started applauding, expecting her to stand up, even though they could not see her. When all the clapping and the shouting kept on going, DeLay finally made her appearance on stage in the promised golf cart, and everyone cheered and swiveled back again. DeLay was helped to the microphone by Robert McDuffie, who first made a little speech about how much beloved she was by everyone in Aspen. DeLay gazed at the audience, looking overwhelmed, and said "I love all of you, too," and headed back for the golf cart. I felt choked up on her behalf. All those years at Aspen, all those students—what an emotional moment this must be for her. McDuffie told me later that she had been fretting all day about having to say something after the concert, and kept asking him what she should do. He said, "Just tell everybody you love them." When she came off stage to find him waiting in the wings, she giggled and said, "Well, I hope you noticed I did exactly as you advised! Was it OK?" I had to laugh out loud myself for having been so wide of the mark when McDuffie reported this to me. "Overwhelmed" may have been my reaction, but it did not seem to have been hers. She was having too good a time.

A couple of days after the concert, I ran into one of DeLay's Juilliard students, a young man named Cornelius Dufallo, outside her studio at St.

Mary's Church in the center of Aspen. We fell into conversation, since we were both Being DeLayed—that is, waiting for her to arrive for a class. Dufallo, a charming and serious young man who was then about seventeen, had been studying with DeLay for six years. He had the job that summer of keeping DeLay's appointment book, which meant that he was responsible for the scheduling and rescheduling of her lessons. I remarked that that must keep him pretty busy, given the number of changes that she and her students make. Dufallo, apparently thinking I was registering a criticism, shrugged his shoulders and said, "When I am in a lesson, I am the only person on her mind. If you don't take it personally, it is not a problem. Some people want someone else to do all the work for them and then they blame the teacher."

With no sign yet of DeLay's arrival, Dufallo and I went on talking. The usual suspects were starting to straggle into the building, mostly teenagers and a couple of little ones. Sarah Chang and her father arrived, and shortly thereafter the pianist, Rohan De Silva. Dufallo told me that he was also studying with DeLay's associate Pyotr Milewski (who subsequently left Juilliard to teach at the University of Cincinnati College-Conservatory of Music). He and Milewski met approximately every other week, alternating lessons with DeLay. "Lessons are basically the same with both of them," said Dufallo. "Mr. Milewski loves to teach, and he has a tendency to tell me everything at once. When I play for Miss DeLay, it's more like a performance. She won't stop me. I'll go through the entire movement, and then she will point out one or two areas she really wants me to focus on so that I can move on."

At my urging, Dufallo then gave a sort of "View from the Bridge," a violin student's portrait of DeLay as a teacher that echoed the accounts of many other students with whom I had spoken over the years.

> When I came to Miss DeLay, I had a lot of feelings about music but not a lot of technique, so we worked mainly on technique, playing in tune. She said to me, "It's great that you have all these feelings— all these ideas—but right now we need to focus on just playing in tune." No one had ever said that to me. So I started working on that, and it got much better, and then we started working on having a clean sound, a nice, clean, beautiful sound. Then we worked on vibrato. After that we worked on analyzing the score and coming up with really good, solid musical ideas. Miss DeLay breaks it all down for you, but it's always one thing at a time with her, it is never overwhelming.

It has helped me with my practicing, because when I practice a piece I say, "Hey, I am going to work on this aspect of it first," then I go back and do another aspect, and that way it is very clear.

She has a very deep understanding of human psychology in that if she sees that a student is having trouble, or a student is not working, she doesn't get angry at all—she doesn't take it personally—but she actually tries to understand what is going on in the student's head. I think that is great, because I know a lot of teachers would take it personally and say, "Why aren't you practicing? You are wasting my time."

"What does Miss DeLay do under those circumstances, when someone is not working?" I asked.

Well, she teaches each student differently. She usually tries to talk to them and wants them to think of her as a friend. I have seen situations where a student is not working and then he will have a long talk with Miss DeLay, and he really changes his attitude. She makes you believe you can do it, and that is what we all want to believe. She can't make somebody believe they can when they really can't —I think she's pretty honest about that. She would not be teaching you if she did not think you would be good. She doesn't say "That's wonderful, sweetie" to everybody.

"There must be times when nothing helps," I said. "How does she handle a student who just isn't getting anywhere?"

If a student really does not improve, usually it is because the student is not working, and then Miss DeLay will say, "I don't want to teach this student anymore." She is really not quick to do that. She is going to try to make a student work. I don't think she would take a student unless she thought there was a lot of potential.

I look forward to every lesson I have. I can remember one time we were working on my sound, and there was this one note I played, and Miss DeLay stopped me and said, "Now *that* is a beautiful sound." It was like, Wow! If I can do it there, I can do it everywhere. She explained that you have got to work on every note so that every note has a beautiful beginning, a beautiful middle, and connects beautifully into the next note. It was such a clear way of thinking about it. You listen to Perlman and others, and think, How am I going to have a beautiful sound? and it is just an overwhelming concept to a student.

By this time, a few more students had congregated in the building. Some were familiar faces from Juilliard, and others were working with DeLay only for the summer. Shortly afterward, DeLay sailed, smiling, into view, and Dufallo picked up his scheduling notebook, nodded good-bye, and went to meet her as the waiting crowd poured into the studio.

I could not help but be struck by Dufallo's initial remark. How could it be that no one had ever suggested that he needed to focus first just on playing in tune? Dufallo had already been studying the violin for a number of years and had gained considerable facility before he came to DeLay, and the idea that it could come as a revelation that he needed to work on something as basic as accurate intonation seemed astonishing. Why had nobody mentioned this before? Was it just too evident to be confronted in simple terms? My guess is that such an obvious problem had been drowned out in the static of too many injunctions and too much information from earlier teachers.

Everyone—at least, everyone that *I* know—is familiar with that unpleasant sensation of paralysis that comes with feeling overwhelmed by difficulties. DeLay's advice has many uses. Simplify (which in the case of learning an instrument often means take things slowly), break the problem down into little steps, do one thing at a time (but make yourself do it), and it will become manageable.

Heidi Castleman, one of the most sought-after viola teachers in the country, is a professor at Juilliard, and also runs an intensive program for violists at Aspen in the summers. She and I have been in touch on and off over the years, and we met for breakfast a few days after my conversation with Dufallo, about which I told her. Castleman nodded agreement about the negative effects of feeling swamped. "Miss DeLay combines that ability to communicate support with very high expectations and exceptionally clear presentation of information," she said over coffee. "Information that works, in terms of how-to—such as how to get a specific sound—information that is ordered in a very sequential way." Dufallo's account of moving step-by-step from working on intonation, to sound quality, to vibrato, to analysis, certainly confirmed Castleman's description, and even if things are not really quite so simple in practice (so to speak), it is an approach that demystifies some technical monsters and brings them down to manageable size.

Castleman is herself a former student of DeLay's. She started taking private lessons with her as an undergraduate at Wellesley College, and she credits DeLay with having been the source of her own decision to become a teacher. "Within one or two weeks of being with her, I knew that that was what I wanted to do with my life. There was simply no question about it," Castleman said. "The decision came about completely as a result of studying with her—the combination of her incredible attention and the ability of her logical mind to break things down into doable sequences. I know those things molded a lot of how I would be with my own students later." She paused for a moment. "You could wake me up at any hour of the day or night and I would choose what I am doing again."

"There may be other studio teachers that spend a lot of time linking what they do to the outside world, but I don't know anybody who spends more time," Castleman continued. "Miss DeLay has really directed her kids very strongly to go into a community and not limit what they do to just performing a concerto with the orchestra, but to find out what is needed and then try to provide it. This is the ultimate in outreach. It did not start right away—how did she figure this out?" Castleman thought for a moment and said, "There is no way that Midori's foundation would exist without Midori having studied with Miss DeLay." The Midori Foundation was established in 1992, and its purpose is to inspire children through music. Midori and other prominent artists spend time in the public schools talking with and performing for the students. "I'm sure there must be a connection. Whatever led Miss DeLay to direct her students this way is what motivates the idea of 'How can we participate?' and not 'What are you going to do for me.' This is a woman who keeps growing by leaps and bounds every year, and she is perpetually interested in new things."

The last afternoon of my stay was again spent sitting in on DeLay's classes in St. Mary's Church. A Korean girl of about nine, whom DeLay had not seen before, came in with her mother, who was dressed in an exquisite floor-length silk coat. The child's regular teacher had asked DeLay to give him an opinion about her playing. DeLay gave some comments and suggestions and spent perhaps twenty minutes with the girl. Before leaving the room, the mother, who spoke hardly any English, came over to DeLay's desk, bowed, and handed her an envelope, which clearly contained money. DeLay smilingly refused, saying that this was not really a lesson, she had just listened to the child at a colleague's request.

DeLay with Midori, age fifteen, in 1986. In addition to her career as a superstar, Midori has established a foundation in her name that brings outstanding musicians, herself included, to work in New York City's public schools. Photo: Charles Abbott.

The mother, uncomprehending, kept proffering the envelope until DeLay managed to bring matters to an end by indicating with a lot of smiling and hand-waving that the interview was over. Some Asian families take for granted that gifts of money, either over or under the table, are expected by people in prominent positions, be they teachers or administrators. Joseph Polisi, Juilliard's president, is said to be regularly offered money by parents who assume that the wheels of Juilliard's admission process need to be greased, and are totally taken aback by the abrupt rejection of the gift.

The final lesson of the afternoon involved a Russian father and his eleven-year-old son. The family was living in Europe but the father wanted to immigrate to the United States with his wife and their son. He had taught violin in Russia, and his already tall, dark-haired son had been his pupil since the boy was three years old.

DeLay had heard the boy—let us call him Gregor—play on a previous occasion, and told me a bit about him, as well as about his father, before the lesson. She thought that Gregor had potential but was hampered by a lot of problems, particularly with his bow arm, as a result of faulty teaching on the father's part. Apparently the father's nose was already out of joint because he had expected DeLay to shower the boy with lavish praise the first time she heard him, which did not happen. DeLay confessed that she found the father very irritating; in spite of a limited command of English, he continuously argued with her, trying to push her into a corner to do what he wanted. DeLay kept a bland demeanor throughout the lesson, but it took only a minute to understand her reaction, and to feel concern for the boy on whom so much aggressive energy was focused.

Gregor dove lickety-split into Sarasate's *Carmen* Fantasy, a work to which DeLay must have listened thousands of times in the course of her career—a considerable affliction, given that it is hardly a great piece of music. In the middle of the movement, the father asked—no, told—the accompanist to slow down; it was the first time I had ever seen a parent intervene directly during a lesson. When the boy finished, DeLay gave him an encouraging smile and said, "You have very good speed. The next thing you have to work on is articulation." Articulation? Father and son looked blank. DeLay tried to explain, "Bow stroke? *Detaché*? *Martelé*?" Finally, she took the boy's instrument and demonstrated. "Ahhh, *Da! Da!*"

DeLay started to pick the piece apart with a series of questions delivered with many gestures. Where are the passages in which the theme is repeated? Should they be played louder the first time, or softer, or the same? "You are going to have to decide," said DeLay. "It is difficult." The boy nodded and tried out a few possibilities, keeping a weather eye on his father.

"Since your bow is so small, you have to keep your thumb farther back," DeLay told him, before turning to the father to say that the boy should have a full-size bow rather than the three-quarter size he was using. The father dismissed this piece of advice with a shake of his head, saying that the bow is OK, the bow is fine. DeLay dropped the subject, which I gather had been met with a similar rejection on their previous meeting, and told Gregor he needed to improve his tone production, and took him through some exercises. "Start by dividing the bow into two: heavy, light, heavy, light. Then divide it into four, and into eight. Then play six notes to a bow, and eight to a bow, and twelve, and sixteen." Gregor started to laugh at the impossibility of this idea, but did his best. "Now do very heavy, long bows so you get to understand the relation between weight, bow speed, and the sounding point," said DeLay. "Go as close to the bridge as you can go without losing the sound. Practice playing to the bridge and to the fingerboard, so that you can feel the difference in speed that the bow needs." Gregor's father became increasingly restless as the boy followed DeLay's instructions, and finally interrupted, saying, "What gives with these exercises? What is the point?" DeLay explained again that Gregor had to learn to make a bigger sound, and that in addition to the exercises, he needed a bigger bow to accomplish this. Oof! The father had been sandbagged. His expression darkened.

Scarcely five minutes later, however, the father switched gears and was fawning over DeLay, explaining that a world-famous artist had recommended that he bring Gregor to her, that nobody else would do, and that she and only she must be Gregor's teacher. DeLay remained expressionless through all this. The father said, "How can we do this? How can we come to Juilliard?" DeLay replied that the first thing was to get a job that would enable him to come to the United States, and offered to get him in touch with an organization that helps Russian immigrant musicians find work in the U.S. The father did not look remotely interested in this suggestion and made no response, although he came up with a barrage of requests at the end of the lesson: "Can Gregor participate in a master class?"

"Yes, of course."

"Can he play in the recital series?"

"Yes, that would be fine. Speak to my secretary and we will arrange it."

After the lesson, DeLay invited me to join her for supper at a restaurant called the Little Nell, where she was greeted by various people, diners and waiters alike, wishing her a happy birthday. She was obviously a favorite of the staff, who cosseted her and arranged a special table outside. Before bringing the menu, the waiter came over with a shawl in case the night air turned chilly. Later, when DeLay wanted to pay, she was told that the restaurant had canceled her dinner bill for the occasion.

During dinner, we talked about the afternoon's events, including Gregor's lesson and his problems with technique. DeLay reiterated that what the boy needed most was to work on his bow arm, and that, yes, over time it was something that could be fixed. She found Gregor very likable, but made no bones about the fact that the father got under her skin.

"He's a schnorrer," she said, to my amusement—the word sounded so startling on her lips. (Among the many definitions of this splendid word given by Leo Rosten in his classic work, *The Joys of Yiddish,* are a cheap-skate, a chiseler, and a moocher. A schnorrer, according to Rosten, does not ask for alms so much as claim them.)

As far as taking Gregor on as a student, DeLay was in a bit of a bind. On the one hand, there was the father, who she felt was trying to manip-ulate her and was plainly angling for her to give him a job as one of her assistants at Juilliard, "which is obviously out of the question," she said. Trying to assist an entire family without work to get established in this country is a major undertaking. On the other hand, she would like to be able to help the boy, who had some promise but was handicapped by the family's financial circumstances.

Later, when we were sitting in the hotel lounge having coffee, one of the staff came to greet her and to return a crutch that she had lent him some weeks before, when he broke his leg—the loan was her idea and not the doctor's. After he left, the conversation revolved around instru-ments, various students, and life and death. It was abruptly interrupted, without apology, by a woman in her fifties wearing an elegant black pantsuit and several heavy gold bracelets, who congratulated DeLay (whom she did not know) in strident tones on her birthday and the pre-vious evening's concert gala. "I was there," she repeated several times, as though she was the one to whom the congratulations should be directed. "I was in the sixth row. When is your next master class?" DeLay told her it would be in a week. "I will be there," said the woman, jangling a ban-gle, and flashing a white-capped smile. "You can count on it." She waited for a moment, presumably for an expression of gratitude, but had to make do with an amiable nod from DeLay, and took herself off.

The last person to join us was a student of DeLay's—a lovely Korean girl of about twenty—who was preparing for a competition. She said that she thought she was the strongest contestant but was worried about choosing the right unassigned piece to play in addition to those that were required.

"Don't let them work you into a corner," said DeLay, figuring out how to call the shots. "You could go in and lose if you haven't had enough time to prepare. What is your strongest piece?"

"Shostakovich."

"Tell them you will play Shostakovich or nothing. Juggle the dates if you can, to give yourself a little more time. You can bargain a bit. They want the competition to have prestige. They want somebody of your ability to win."

After the girl left, DeLay said that the girl had recently played one of the assigned competition pieces for her and had expressed frustration at not being able to play it up to speed.

"How much time have you spent practicing it?" DeLay had asked.

"I've been working on it for a whole week," the girl replied, seeing nothing amiss with the answer.

7   The Emperor's New Clothes? DeLay and Her Critics

Diary entry, 1992:

The more people one talks to about DeLay, the more varied the picture one gets. She certainly does not provoke indifference. Her admirers do not just like her, they adore her. Students and former students in this category regard her as mother as well as mentor and they rely on her for support and advice of all kinds. They, and others of like mind, such as her piano accompanists, who have worked closely with her over the years, search for superlatives in describing her.

DeLay's detractors, who get as worked up as her supporters, claim her reputation is an emperor's-new-clothes story—that nothing is really going on in her classes, no serious teaching is taking place, and that the music establishment is somehow joined in collusion to hide this fact because of DeLay's political clout with conductors and management. According to this view, no one speaks out because they fear possible repercussions and reprisals—that is, that DeLay could discreetly arrange to have them blackballed professionally. Her critics also say that there is no great trick to teaching brilliant students, and that those are the only ones she takes on. Is this sour grapes on their part, or is there some validity to the criticism? Does she teach less talented students? Should she, if she does not? Is it possible that DeLay's reputation as a master pedagogue is without substance and for years we have all been witnesses to a gigantic hoax?

The other familiar criticism, which indeed is based on fact, is that students sometimes sit on the beat-up old couch outside Room 530 for as long as three or four hours, waiting for their lessons. Why does DeLay permit the waiting brigade to waste so much time? Why, at the least, are they not practicing until summoned?

Many months and many classes after that early diary entry, I realized that the answers to some of these questions were not so simple. Yes, as students at the Juilliard School, the children who DeLay teaches are, for the most part, extremely gifted. No, the stars are not the only ones she teaches—they are the only ones the public hears about, and their numbers are extremely limited since there is not a huge market for solo violinists at present. While all DeLay's students are required to have a high level of technical ability before being accepted into her studio, even they can have basic problems from time to time. I have been present at lessons where DeLay has had to teach a student how to count a measure, or how to check that he or she is playing on pitch. I have heard her criticized for putting in valuable time with a student clearly not destined for a big career, at the expense of another who seems more promising. One ex-student, a concert artist, told me that he couldn't understand why DeLay wastes her energy with those who obviously aren't going to make it, by which he meant have a solo career.

Whether one wants to call it favoritism, a pecking order, or a matter of practical judgment, there is no question that not all students are treated equally. DeLay has poured more of her prodigious energy into that handful of students who will be taking center stage in Carnegie Hall and elsewhere. These pupils have had more frequent lessons with her in addition to those they took with her associates. They have studied with her not only at her studio in Juilliard but also at her home in Nyack. They are the ones in whom she has taken a greater personal interest and whose careers she has helped to foster through introductions to influential people in the music world, including managers and conductors. The students who rise to the top of the professional music world get there through a process of natural selection that comprises exceptional talent, imagination, concentration, hard work, luck, and connections. Of these attributes, DeLay can foster the first, and help with the last.

An oft-repeated story about DeLay and her overabundance of students was told to me by Robert Harth of the Aspen Music School, who had heard it from his father, the violinist Sidney Harth, whose name has somehow become linked with the tale. The younger Harth describes it as "probably an urban myth." A student with a violin case gets on a plane and passes by DeLay's seat. "Oh, sweetie," she says, "You study violin. How interesting. Who is your teacher?" The student, looking uncomfortable and perplexed, replies, "You, Miss DeLay."

One may certainly argue that DeLay has taken too many students. At the time I was following her, she had ultimate responsibility for approximately 160 pupils, whom she shared with a group of distinguished associates. Chief among these at Juilliard were Professors Hyo Kang and Masao Kawasaki and the concert artist Cho-Liang ("Jimmy") Lin. All three are faculty members with their own studios, and a great deal of cachet is attached to studying with any of them. Kurt Sassmannshaus, chairman of the string department at the Cincinnati College-Conservatory of Music and a former Juilliard associate, teaches with DeLay at Aspen in the summers. Professor Won Bin Yim teaches at both Juilliard and Cincinnati, and Naoko Tanaka is a professor at the Juilliard School Pre-College Division.

Given the sheer numbers, some students are DeLay's in name only —but this particular name is, of course, the main attraction. To be able to put "Studied with Dorothy DeLay" on one's résumé carries sufficient power to perpetuate the system and to keep one sitting docilely outside her studio for what may turn out to be merely a token lesson. For the young unknown virtuoso, the teaching pedigree is tremendously important. Beyond having won a major competition, a violinist has little else to offer a prospective manager or booking agent to look at, let alone listen to.

The link from performer to manager to concert presenter goes in one direction only. The supply of musicians is so great and the performance opportunities so few that the artists, in spite of all their years of training, are at the bottom of the food chain. They are in a similar spot to newly minted Ph.D.'s looking for slots in academia, except that the musicians are seeking employment not from their elders in the same field but, in some instances, from people whose musical backgrounds may be only sketchy, and whose expertise lies in an understanding of the bottom line and having a nose for what sells. Seeing the name of an important teacher on a musician's résumé raises a flag in the minds of those on the business or booking end of the equation. For this reason, the students who do not yet have management or are not in the top ranks are the very ones who would protest most vigorously if they were struck off the rolls of DeLay's studio.

Is the unsubstantiated use of DeLay's name by a few students a con game or a recognition of the way the world works? However one regards the situation, it can involve a certain amount of fabrication on all sides. A student may fabricate by stretching the truth in identifying himself or herself as DeLay's; DeLay fabricates for the sake of the student, since her imprimatur helps the student to obtain management, not to mention concert engagements; and managements continue the fabrication because they are in the business of making money, as well as fostering careers.

DeLay is well aware of these interlocking factors when it comes to having her name borrowed, and she sensibly—in my view—shrugs her shoulders. I asked her how she felt about having her name used as a sort of "Good Housekeeping Seal." She readily acknowledged that a number of students list her as their teacher—often without her permission—whom she scarcely knows. She may have seen them once or twice in a group setting or for an entrance audition. Granted, these students are misrepresenting the truth, but what would be gained by her telling them to desist and by breaking the circle? And anyway, would they listen? Realistically, there are simply not enough hours in the day to give full time to all the students who want to study with her, and unpopular though the rationale may be, giving more time to those who show the most promise makes a certain amount of sense.

Edward Newhouse, who was present during this conversation, recounted a joke about a beggar sitting outside the Metro in Paris, playing his violin with the case open for contributions. Ravel walks by, stops, and says to him, "That is the worst playing I have ever heard. It is horrendous, simply unspeakable." The next day Ravel again passes by, but this time the beggar has a sign next to the case that reads "Studied with Ravel."

Who are the detractors? Students who didn't make it, for one. For all her motherly warmth, DeLay has been known to drop a hopeful with comparatively little gentle ado—he or she may simply be advised to consider another career. Other critics include some who studied with Ivan Galamian when they were young and acquired a spare-the-rod-and-spoil-the-child attitude from the experience. They had to walk five miles to school in a blizzard every day and endure strict discipline when they were young, and it made men—and a few women—out of them, so why should the next generation have it any easier? Another group, composed largely of teachers and parents not connected to Juilliard, knows somebody who knew somebody whose nephew had to endure all kinds of high-handed or indifferent treatment when he was part of DeLay's studio. There is also the assertion that DeLay's pupils do not receive the kind of rigorous technical training the instrument requires, and that some study behind her back with other unidentified teachers outside the Juilliard orbit in order to get what they need. Again, no specific names of either teachers or students are ever mentioned, so it is hard to know how to deal with the stories. How many students? Over how long a period? At what performance level was the anonymous student? Was there friction of some sort between the student and DeLay, or some other personal factor in his or her life at the time?

DeLay's chronic lateness is referred to by her students as Being DeLayed, and the magnitude of the phenomenon leaves no room for doubt. DeLay's schedule is frequently merely notional, and students sometimes wait hours for their lessons. A student with a two-o'clock lesson will pop his head in the door at the appointed time and be asked to come back at five, for example. Those who throw in the sponge on making any other plans for the day and go off and practice somewhere nearby, such as the spacious fifth-floor bathrooms, don't seem to mind the haphazard timetable. The ones who suffer are those who make the mistake of expecting to be taken on time and then sit and fume and watch the clock.

The explanations for why DeLay sometimes keeps her students cooling their heels for so long at a stretch are remarkably varied. To me, this aspect of DeLay's conduct—the way she handles her schedule—remains an enigma. I suspect that I would fall into the fuming category, but then, I am not a professional violinist, some of whom, I discovered, could not care less. By analogy, most people dislike the not-uncommon experience of spending hours in a doctor's waiting room, although it is less onerous in the company of a book and with no other appointments for the day. The parallels between a doctor's office and DeLay's studio are several. Both patients and students are likely to present problems that are not predictable. For the doctor, a symptom that may have seemed trivial turns out to involve complications, requiring more time and testing than was anticipated. A student may have slipped unawares into a different way of holding the violin, for example, which is causing strain in the shoulder. If left uncorrected too long, it can become a habit that will be far more difficult to undo later on. Crises and emergencies arise that require the doctor/teacher to abbreviate or postpone an appointment in favor of a more urgent situation. For DeLay, this might be an unexpected opportunity to have some influential individual, such as a manager or a conductor, listen to one of her students, or the discovery that she suddenly has a television crew on her doorstep, effectively pitching the day into chaos.

Those who complain most vigorously about DeLay's ever-shifting timetable see it as arrogance on her part and accuse her of using it to assert her power. Equally galling would be to have DeLay interrupt a lesson in favor of an unscheduled student whose needs she regards as more urgent, such as someone preparing for an upcoming debut or recital. "It was pretty annoying to have Nadja [Salerno-Sonnenberg] or Midori waltz in just when you are in the middle of a piece, and to be put on hold because they had a date coming up and you didn't," recalled a student who studied with DeLay in the seventies. A member of a piano trio, who also did not want to be identified, described a time the group stopped in to see DeLay, who had taught the violinist, for a quick greeting just as she was starting a lesson with a young female student.

> Miss DeLay saw us coming and she said to the student, "Sweetie, would you mind leaving the room for a few minutes?" We came in and she talked totally casually, as though it were a Sunday afternoon and there were no appointments until the next day. We began to feel pretty uncomfortable after a few minutes. This was this little girl's lesson, and she had probably practiced her backside off for the past week. We walked in and it was finished.

DeLay's various alleged shortcomings were the basis for a conversation I had in 1998 with someone who was no longer involved with her, but who continued to feel a deep resentment for some real or fancied illtreatment. He had heard that I was writing a book about DeLay and her students, and wanted to put me on the right track. "Nobody will tell you the real truth," he said. "Everybody is afraid of the fact that she has so much power." Ah, I thought. At last, my very own Deep Throat. The fact was that nothing much of DeLay's dark side had swum into my ken, and except for a couple of pro forma stabs, like trolling for students on the internet and interviewing other leads, I had not been interested in seeking it out. The first shocker that my informant brought up was how long DeLay sometimes keeps her students waiting. The second was that, in his estimation, her style is really very cold and impersonal: if a student has difficulties, DeLay makes no effort to discover the cause and is simply dismissive. The third criticism was that she does not always exercise the immense influence she has. She will, on occasion, refuse to help a student, even if it requires no more than making one telephone call to another source of power, presumably a manager or conductor. "There you are," this person concluded, as though I had been made privy to some huge revelation. "Those three examples should tell you what I am talking about."

What an anticlimax! *Of course*, there were situations where DeLay was unwilling to extend herself for a particular student if she thought the request inappropriate. As for being cold and dismissive, the description was so remote from everything I had seen or heard as to be unrecognizable, but I suppose not categorically impossible. Another curious take on DeLay was this critic's interpretation of why she kept her students waiting so long. Having affirmed that DeLay was a highly intelligent woman, he said that she was certainly not doing this by accident. He suggested, somewhat disingenuously, that her purpose in doing so was to prepare her students for the real world, where they will have to put up with similar hard knocks. This sounded like fancy backpedaling to make up for his earlier criticisms. In any event, his explanation had the charm of novelty, and I doubt that DeLay, even in what she would call her goofiest — or most experimental — moments, would have been able to come up with such an interpretation.

Some ex-students to whom I spoke reported that they had not minded Being DeLayed in the least. Virtuoso Robert McDuffie said, "Generally speaking, if she was three hours late, that's when I would get my best practicing done, knowing that I was going to be seeing the greatest teacher there is at the end of that time." Heidi Castleman said that she, too, found the extra time before a lesson more of a blessing than a curse. "At one point I was taking lessons with Miss DeLay at Juilliard instead of at her home, and that's where I learned about the long waits," said Castleman. "I spent more time in the fifth-floor ladies room practicing than I could sometimes manage during the week, because I was so busy. I was actually grateful."

Perhaps because she is a teacher herself, Castleman has a particularly sympathetic view of the vagaries of DeLay's schedule. "You know how there is a kind of tapestry of rich, chaotic stuff that goes on in the mind, and then you pick out what you are going to organize and fit together?" she said. "My happiest existence is when I can just follow those instincts, uninterrupted. I think DeLay is like that. I think she trusts that process and values it, and when she feels she is on to something, she will go with that rather than setting up boundaries and limits." I asked her what she thought about students who wait for hours for a five-minute lesson. "I think that is disrespectful," Castleman replied candidly, "and I think it comes out of an addictive behavior, not something she can control. She has done that for as long as I can remember."

Another ex-student, who studied with DeLay many years ago, shrugged her shoulders about DeLay's lack of punctuality. "If she had only started doing it in the last five years—or even the last ten years—I might say this is a real abuse of power, but she has done it since way back, when she was still working with Galamian, long before she became such a big name. She just has a problem with the time—I don't know what it is." The most appealing explanation was provided by Kikuei Ikeda of the Tokyo Quartet, who had been a DeLay student in the 1970s. Ikeda ascribed DeLay's lateness to her putting in such long hours at night that she sometimes needed extra sleep.

> I don't know about now, but in the days when I was studying with her, she used to go to so many concerts. She never missed a performance of one of her students. Then she would come back at midnight and talk with her husband for a long time about each student. I know, because I have never met Mr. Newhouse, but he knew me. That may be the only time they got to talk, and it probably went on and on until it got so late that it was the next morning.

If DeLay were an unknown teacher with an undistinguished track record, would she be able to get away with such disregard for the clock and the convenience of her students? Obviously not. Students would no more spend hours waiting for a lesson with an indifferent instructor than they, or anyone who had the choice, would hang around indefinitely to see a third-rate doctor. DeLay's students wait for the same reasons that the patients of a top-notch doctor wait, even if the waiting is irritating and inconvenient. Experience counts. DeLay and the physician have seen the problems a thousand times—they know all the signs and symptoms, and they have a history of knowing how to deal with them. If they don't always have an immediate cure, they know how to ask the right questions to approach the difficulty from another angle. Anyone who has reached a position of power is subject to criticism, and while Being

DeLayed may be exasperating, it is not a sin that begins to approach the level of a teacher who is harsh and belittling of his or her students. That is arrogant, destructive, and a real sin.

Part Three

THE WORLD OUTSIDE: ON STAGE AND IN PERFORMANCE

8   Looking for Work

In the spring, the young musician's fancy turns, with increasing anxiety, to thoughts of the future. Those who are about to graduate are acutely aware of the minuscule job market that awaits them, and while Juilliard may have seemed like a competitive pressure cooker, the "real" world will be far tougher. Even though these students are better off than many because of the school's prestige, they pour out of Juilliard into a very small funnel en route to the classical music stream.

Finding a manager ranks near the top of the list of worries, in part because the clock is ticking. According to DeLay, managements have no interest in you if you are over the age of twenty-two. Their view is that if they have not heard of you before then, you are probably not worth their time.

Given that adolescence is the most difficult period for these young artists, it is no wonder that their anxiety levels are high. Some musicians do go it alone and serve as their own managers, but this requires a particular kind of personality as well as hours and hours of time. You may be a wonderful musician but a rotten salesperson, poor at negotiating fees, awkward at making contacts with presenting organizations, and ignorant about how to publicize yourself, to touch on just a few of the hot spots. In addition, having your name on a firm's roster provides a stamp of credibility in itself. Even with a twenty percent cut from your earnings, professional management begins to look like a bargain, and is as important to most musicians as a handler is to a prize-fighter. Soloists who perform abroad have to be able to command substantial fees just to break even: there will be two plane fares (one for the accompanist), two hotel rooms, a twenty percent foreigner's tax, and twenty percent to the agent, so roughly fifty percent of the fee is gone practically before you touch bow to string.

On one particular March day in 1996 near the end of the spring term, DeLay, ever the pragmatist, arranged to have a top music manager give a talk to her students on the nuts-and-bolts of making a career. The speaker was David Foster, president of ICM Artists, Ltd., one of the most prestigious managements in the business, and a division of the global company International Creative Management, whose clients include such movie stars as Arnold Schwarzenegger and Jody Foster, and similar prominent names in theater, television, writing, and sports. David Foster had moved to ICM Artists after some twenty-five years of serving as vice president of the music-industry giant Columbia Artists Management.

Roughly sixty youngsters were crowded into a classroom in Juilliard intended to hold half that number. All the students bore the violinist's trademark or stigmata: a raised, and sometimes raw-looking, red patch just below the left jaw line where the instrument is tucked under the chin. (Some violinists call this "fiddle bite.") The overflow crowd, many with instrument cases, sat on the floor, perched on radiators, and leaned against the wall, eyes channeled on Foster, who was leaning back in his chair at the front of the room chatting with DeLay, seated next to him. One or two Juilliard teachers, including Joel Smirnoff, first violin of the Juilliard Quartet, came in to check out the scene. A star pupil of De-Lay's, Yura Lee, who was at that time ten years old, came in with her father. She had just been taken onto ICM's roster—their youngest musician ever—and before the class began DeLay introduced Foster to his diminutive new artist, whom he had not yet met. Yura looked demure in a pale blue coat with a scalloped collar and a pair of neat, little black suede boots. Her feet did not quite touch the floor when she sat down. She was by far the youngest in the room—most of the other students were in their mid to late teens—but she was already way out in front. She had major management.

"Launching a career after the age of eighteen is becoming more and more difficult," said Foster after a brief introduction by DeLay, shaving four years off her estimate. "You will be increasingly responsible for making your own way. One of the reasons is that arts institutions in the United States have to realize more of their own income than similar organizations in Europe, which receive heavy government subsidies." A faint air of gloom settled over the audience. "Community Concerts doesn't exist anymore as it once did," Foster continued. "It's like talking about the dodo bird." This last remark may have startled a couple of students who were planning to audition for Community Concerts within the next few weeks. Community Concerts had been a division of Columbia Artists for many years, where it had the reputation of being the agency's scrub team, sending artists all over the country to whistle-stop at small venues for low fees but big exposure, in terms of numbers of performances. In later years, Community Concerts' emphasis shifted from classical musicians to booking various forms of entertainment, but it continued to have a number of artists on its roster at the time of this lecture and subsequently. Community Concerts left Columbia Artists officially to become an independent booking agency in 1996, although the process had begun three years earlier.

"You have to learn how to talk to agents," continued Foster. "Part of the process is a delicate give and take." The group perked up—this is what they had come to hear. How do you get an agent, to begin with? What do you do to breach the castle walls? What are the secret handshakes? What does he mean, "delicate give and take"? What are the blunders, the hidden traps, to avoid? Being admitted to the most exclusive club in town is a snap of the fingers by comparison. The ability to talk casually about "my manager" is every aspiring artist's dream. The possibility of living in the purgatory of perpetual hope is their nightmare.

"I've been in this game for more than twenty-five years," said Foster. "It's a good idea to get an agent who has had a lot of experience. You can't possibly get a serious agent by sending in a letter and a tape. I put that kind of thing directly into my waste basket. It has to be done by word of mouth." The nascent purveyors of junk mail stared ahead in silence. A good idea to get an agent with experience? Wow! Finally, a Russian immigrant student put his hand up and asked, in halting English, how to go about finding someone to do the word-of-mouth part. "There is no such thing as a hidden great talent," replied Foster. "Every agent has people they trust who send them recommendations." So clang went that door, and the student sat down. Upstairs, somebody was going over and over a passage on the trumpet without success. DeLay looked at Smirnoff and made a throat-slitting motion at the racket. Otherwise the room was dead quiet.

"Repertoire lists that are too big are another give-away to a manager," Foster continued. "Nobody can have a long list that they are able to play really well—the repertoire is so big that you just cannot do it, and if you think you can, you are not examining your own musical clarity enough." The Russian youth rose again and asked Foster to give him an idea of how big a list should be presented, and what sort of pieces it might include. He was beginning to look like the group's Candide—an inno-cent abroad in his expectations of help from someone in authority. Fos-ter replied that he was reluctant to get into specifics, and the youth, after pressing the question unsuccessfully a couple of times, subsided into his chair, looking baffled.

By now the audience was very glum indeed. This was not the first time they had heard about the harsh realities of life in the classical music market. Juilliard conscientiously does what it can to help its students in this area, and one of its most popular courses is "The Business of Music," which deals with writing résumés, finding a manager, making demo tapes, negotiating contracts, and so forth. The air of gloom was most likely due not to the students' learning something new about the diffi-culties that awaited them, but rather to their getting a glimmer of the paucity of support and encouragement they might expect from the world they were about to enter.

"Everyone is in this for the long haul," said Foster, as though he were addressing a group of young executives. "Your career should be at its maximum for about thirty to thirty-five years. Except for Milstein and Stern, that is about the norm." Foster exhorted the group never to play below their very best, and advised them that if they felt on a given occa-sion that they would not be able to give one hundred percent at a con-cert, they should cancel. Now it was my turn to look baffled. I must have misunderstood what he meant. To look out at the world from the com-parative safety of a manager's roster would be wonderful indeed, but to look out and say "I'm not at my best at the moment—I'm canceling" is something only big-name opera stars can get away with, and then not for long.

Toward the end of the hour, DeLay stepped in and shifted the dis-cussion to questions of programming, and to suggestions of ways in which the students could help their careers themselves. "In the thirties," she said, "the style was all encore pieces. Today it has to be three big sonatas." Foster concurred, saying that critics in major cities could be very tough on "insubstantial" programs. DeLay continued:

> A lot of people are going back to the idea of presenting music in the home. Somebody with a large living-room gets together with, say, twenty other families and they hire an artist for a private concert. It's a wonderful way to get to perform, and you don't have to have a manager to do this. In fact, you have to be your own manager and find ways to make yourself known in a community. Maybe you can

also help some family to start giving concerts at home. If any of you kids are going out to do this kind of performance, I'll arrange a master class. Come and speak to me after class.

So an element of hope was restored, and the meeting wound down. Outside in the hall afterward, no one talked very much.

Discovering the musical needs of a community is a frequent theme of DeLay's in her classes. Since the majority of her students will be concertizing in small cities, she urges them to learn about everything involved in a concert series in those settings—why people come to a performance and what the artist is doing for them. "The students have to understand that it is not a question of standing up on stage and getting a lot of applause, but that they are part of a community effort, and they have got to make a contribution that is not purely musical," she said one afternoon in her studio. "Of course they have to play and they have to play beautifully, but they have to go further. They have to be helpful to that community in keeping the concert series going, in improving it."

While Foster's remarks were geared to achieving a major career as a soloist, probably only one or two of the students present, if that, would make it to the very top. Those who do not will have lesser solo careers, or will choose other paths such as orchestral work, chamber music, or teaching, or often a mix of all three. A former highly placed administrator of the New York Philharmonic once remarked to me that some of DeLay's students who later became members of the Philharmonic had, in his words, "taken poison." He described these ex-students as having been brought up to believe that they would become soloists, with the result that they regarded orchestral life as beneath them. (Never mind that many musicians would die for a job in the New York Philharmonic, whose auditions are about the most competitive in the world.) His remarks about these disgruntled and unhappy orchestra players may well be true, but his implication that DeLay was the one administering the evil dose is misplaced. She has taught the violinists of many of the world's most distinguished string quartets. For these players, chamber music was the first choice. It is the families, and sometimes the early teachers, who make these performers feel that they have failed if they do not make it as soloists. The unspoken threat of being a disappointment to these adults has loomed over them from the beginning and can remain a source of trouble throughout their lives.

"Some students start playing much more than they should," DeLay said about the youngsters who are unable to stay the course once they start concertizing. "It's so hard to keep the lid on a career. For example, a girl who is little and cute and who is getting dates for the wrong reasons. There should be a learning process, but with that much success, the parents and the children don't realize that a lot of it is visual, and does not have anything to do with the future." DeLay shook her head. "So they are not willing to put in the time learning the stuff they are really going to need if they are going to have a top career later. They just want to cash in on it now. It is real exploitation." DeLay conceded that sometimes it is the manager who pushes these children too soon, but said that most frequently it is the parents who are responsible.

Lee Lamont, Foster's immediate predecessor as president of ICM and later its chairman, joined the organization when it was founded in 1976. She had cut her managerial teeth at Hurok Concerts, and subsequently worked for Sarah Caldwell's touring opera company until it was disbanded. In the period before ICM was established, Lamont was Isaac Stern's secretary, and when she went to the new agency, Stern went with her as one of their first clients. Stern's enormous prestige served to lure other top violinists to the organization, and in due course ICM built up the most eminent list of string players among all the managements. Lamont became the first woman to head a major management firm by rising through the ranks.

DeLay and Lamont have known each other for years, and their relationship is a prime example of Foster's observation that "every agent has people they trust who send them recommendations." Lamont's style is very different from DeLay's. She is a hard-driving businesswoman with a brusque manner, but she and DeLay have great respect for each other's expertise and are in close communication about how DeLay's top students are doing, with an eye to future management possibilities. At ICM, there has been a steady progression downward in age where little Asian girls are concerned. Midori was taken on at the age of thirteen, Sarah Chang when she was close to eleven, and Yura Lee when she was all of ten years old. Of the nineteen violinists listed on ICM's 1999–2000 roster, ten are products of DeLay's studio.

A few months after Sarah Chang was signed by ICM in 1992, I spoke to Lee Lamont about the special demands of managing the career of a child. We met in her office on 57th Street, which had an uninterrupted view of a large part of Manhattan and was cluttered with photos and mementos of the great artists she represented, including Yo-Yo Ma, Emanuel Ax, and Isaac Stern. "Everything must be paced properly," said Lamont, talking not only about the number of concerts, but the type of repertoire and the amount of media attention appropriate for Sarah. "That's the difference when you're dealing with someone that young. You want to avoid too much pressure."

"Sarah herself is wonderful and natural about everything," Lamont continued. "If it were only she we were thinking of, I don't think there would be a problem—it's the outside pressures. Within the violin world itself, there are the negative impressions of colleagues that may be formed by a youngster getting too much attention all at once," she said. "And with the major critics, there is always the statement that 'Well, she has wonderful fingers; we'll have to see whether she matures,' and some-times that label hangs on you until you're drowned by it."

"I'll become very commercial with you," Lamont concluded in that early conversation.

> "You don't want to give away the whole basket too soon. There are many places, television as well as papers and magazines, where once they have covered you, that's it. You'll never see it come again. So why blow all the publicity at the age of eleven and leave nothing for the age of twenty-one? You want to keep an ongoing interest for the public. It's a disappointment when something very special hap-pens—say her debut at Carnegie Hall—and it can't get the atten-tion it deserves because you've already given it away.

As a footnote to that talk with Lamont, whether the whole basket had been given away too soon or for some other reason, Sarah Chang's debut recital in Carnegie Hall on 16 November 1997, when she was six-teen, received little attention in *The New York Times* compared to what is usually accorded that kind of milestone, although what was said was highly laudatory. In any event, by the time of her solo debut, Sarah hardly needed promoting—she was already a familiar figure to thou-sands of concertgoers.

In 1996 when ICM took on Korean-born Yura Lee at the age of ten, I again went to see Lamont about her new protégé. Almost from the start of our conversation, I felt as if I were talking to a trial lawyer, where every word is measured and all the participants are on their guard.

"You would be doing everyone a favor not to pursue this," Lamont said. "Yura does not have a career, so there is nothing to talk about. You may be raising false expectations." At the time, I did not think to ask Lamont if signing a contract and taking a ten-year-old onto her roster might not in itself constitute raising expectations, false or otherwise, but I found her response puzzling. Perhaps she was trying to protect Yura and had taken her on to preempt any other firm from doing so, with the intention of putting her on ice, so to speak, until she felt Yura was ready to be out before the public. If so, the ice melted fast. The biographical material sent out by ICM's publicity department dated June 1997, one year later, noted that Yura's engagements had included performances with the Lansing Symphony Orchestra in Michigan, a New Year's Eve debut with the Minnesota Orchestra, and recitals in New York, Chicago, San Diego, and Columbus, Ohio. The list for the 1997–1998 season was over twice as long and included concerts with a number of North American orchestras, including Akron, Albany, Calgary, Columbus, El Paso, Greensboro, and Kansas City, as well as with the Bilbao Symphony in Spain. After listing her schedule for 1998–1999, the press release noted that she had been featured on *The Late Show with David Letterman, Fox on Arts,* WABC-TV in New York, National Public Radio's *Performance Today,* and German Radio Broadcasting. Barring unforeseen twists of fate, Yura's engagements will keep on growing in exponential fashion.

For all the care that Lamont puts into trying to "pace everything properly," keeping the lid on this kind of energy and talent seems to be almost an impossibility. Yura seems happy—she is an extraordinarily balanced and self-possessed child who adores performing and gives the impression that she can't get enough of it—and presumably ICM is happy, too, as their coffers continue to be filled. As time passes, Yura's parents, whose English is limited, may be more bemused than anything. Unlike Sarah Chang's parents, they are strangers to the classical music world. Yura's father is a research doctor, and Mrs. Lee has to take care of Yura's little sister as well as Yura. As DeLay ruefully remarked even before ICM came into the picture, Yura's parents did not have the faintest idea of what they would be in for once her career really gets going.

While ICM has taken on the preponderance of DeLay's most outstanding students, some of the stars go to its chief rival, Columbia Artists Management, and others to smaller firms. Most students, as has been noted, look for management when they are in their later teens—Sarah and Yura are obvious exceptions in having been sought out in their extreme youth. Not all managers are eager to take on the very young. Edna Landau of IMG Management said that she deliberately avoids doing so because of the uncertainties involved, including the possibility of having to spend years advising and educating the parents to understand that, in business terms, they cannot count on anything happening, and that nurturing the child should be the prime concern. "We can only do one at a time," said Landau, "but if somebody extraordinary comes we will make an exception." IMG (which represents Itzhak Perlman, among others) did make such an exception in the case of Hilary Hahn, a brilliant young violinist who studied with Jascha Brodsky at the Curtis Institute of Music and who is about the same age as Sarah Chang. Hahn has already made a considerable name for herself as a soloist.

DeLay's clout in the business arena has rubbed some managements the wrong way. Someone from a prestigious firm, who did not want to be identified, told me that the firm felt strong-armed and insulted by De-Lay, who "threatened to give" a student to a different management if they did not make up their minds on the spot. The head of another organization complained that DeLay "has the arrogance to assume she can just call the shots and we will all be grateful for whatever she sends."

Musicians Corporate Management handles a relatively small number of artists, and specializes in outstanding young chamber music ensembles, some of whose members include ex-students of DeLay's. "If Miss DeLay comes to you and says that there is somebody she would like you to hear, you listen," said Tom Gallant, MCM's director. "She has a tremendous track record, and she really tries to help her kids. I can't tell you what a difference that makes to a manager. There are not many teachers whose reputation gives them that kind of authority and reliability, and of those who could, few actually put in the effort. Once their kids are out of the studio, they generally lose interest."

Young Concert Artists, founded by Susan Wadsworth in 1961, is not technically in the management business at all, but is a nonprofit organization that helps young musicians, selected by audition, get started on making a career. For the recipients, this is no small deal. YCA provides the winners with services that include arranging recitals, recordings, radio and television appearances, and other forms of publicity, for a minimum of three years, all without any fee. Over the years, a number of DeLay's students have been among the beneficiaries. Wadsworth is something of a visionary and gave credit to DeLay for having supported and encouraged her when she came up with the idea for the organization. The YCA auditions have gradually outstripped many other awards because of the substantial prizes involved and the caliber of its judges.

A few days after the class with David Foster, I met DeLay in her studio, and by coincidence, the topic of management surfaced twice in short order in the course of the afternoon.

"I've been on the phone all morning with one of the Mamas," De-Lay said, giving a little spin to the last word. "She thinks it is time for her son to have management, but he doesn't have enough concertos in his repertoire, so no one will want to take him on. I have been telling this to the parents for years and years, but they just did not or would not get it." DeLay went on to say that the mother thinks her son is the be-all and end-all and cannot imagine that a manager is going to turn him down for a little thing like inadequate repertoire. DeLay shrugged at the impossibility of the situation. Dealing with this kind of pressure from parents is a constantly recurring fact of her life, as it presumably is for other top music teachers.

An advanced student arrived for her lesson and told DeLay that she had just been approached by a manager of less-than-stellar reputation. The student wanted her advice. "This guy is a sleazeball," said DeLay firmly, "but sometimes a bad manager is better than none. You want him to get you dates but you don't want to sign a contract with him yet. Don't forget: he's working for you, not the other way around. You are going to be paying him twenty percent." She tapped her pencil on the table. "Try to hold off. Be vague. Discuss arrangements. Ask what they have in mind for the next couple of years. A key question is how many concerts they can get you per year. Tell him your situation is not quite clear." DeLay assumed a distant, demure tone. "Say, 'Your ideas are very interesting, but there are some things I am not free to discuss yet.' At the same time, give them every idea you have got, including any contacts you have, and think about your larger plans. Then—" she smiled broadly and clapped her hands, "bring the contract here. If it is a standard contract, OK. If not, we will have to go to a lawyer."

"Please, Miss DeLay," said the student at the end of the foregoing advice, "Please, couldn't you call him instead of me doing it, and tell him all the things you just said?" Even though they both laughed at the hollowness of the joke, the student did not look exactly happy at the prospect before her.

After the student left, several of the older kids came into the studio for a group lesson. Management was still on DeLay's mind, and she brought up the subject as soon as they settled down. "Getting management does not make a career," she said. "People who know how to arrange things for themselves do have concerts. You must learn how to be missionaries. I have got homework for you. Go into your community and see what is needed. See what has been done. Find out the cost of renting a space, like a school or a church, and the cost of paying union scale, and then make up three different programs."

"Great!" said one of the group, a boy of about seventeen, enthusiastically. "I love everything to do with concerts. I love worrying about the arrangements. I love the excitement of being on stage. I love talking to the old ladies afterward."

The good managers do work very hard for their clients in making contacts, getting bookings, negotiating fees, arranging tours, making travel arrangements, doing publicity, and generally worrying about and cosseting them. The musicians who make it to the top of the profession are there for good reason. They are the best in their field. But occasionally an artist will catch on for a while, and then, for some unpredictable reason, lose favor. And less occasionally, someone who is really an extraordinary musician will inexplicably go unrecognized and not achieve the fame he or she deserves. Samuel Goldwyn had it nailed when he said, "If the public does not want to come, nothing will stop them."

9   Prodigies

In his autobiographical story, *The Awakening*, Isaac
Babel describes being thrust as a child into the notorious prodigy mill in
Odessa at the turn of the century. "All the folk in our circle . . . used to
have their children taught music. Our fathers couldn't see how they
could get ahead in life themselves, so they organized a sweepstakes. They
built it on the bones of little children."

For a child to be accepted by the great Professor Leopold Auer at the
St. Petersburg Conservatory meant deliverance from the harsh life in
the Jewish Pale for the entire family, enabling them to move to that city
under the accepted doctrine of *svoboda*, or "free artist." Without the necessary documents, any Jew caught in St. Petersburg after six o'clock at
night was subject to immediate arrest by the czarist police. *The Awakening* is about Babel's self-discovery as a writer, which was given impetus
by the misery of being forced to learn the violin.

> When a lad was four or five, his mother took the puny creature to
> Zagursky's. Mr. Zagursky ran a factory of infant prodigies. . . . [He]
> charted the first course, then the children were shipped off to Pro-
> fessor Auer in St. Petersburg. . . . My father decided that I should
> emulate them. Although I had, as a matter of fact, passed the age
> limit set for infant prodigies, being now in my fourteenth year, my
> shortness and lack of strength made it possible to pass me off as an
> eight-year-old. Herein lay Father's hope.
>
> I was taken to Zagursky's. . . . The sounds dripped from my fid-
> dle like iron filings, causing even me excruciating agony, but
> Father wouldn't give in. . . . Infant prodigies brought wealth to their
> parents, but though my father could have reconciled himself to
> poverty, fame he must have.

The fourteen-year-old Babel knew perfectly well that he had no bent for the violin, but fear of parental wrath kept him at the music stand, on which he would place books by Turgenev or Dumas, which he devoured while he "deedled away," as he describes it. By day, Babel spun imaginary tales to the children of the neighborhood, and by night he committed the stories to paper. Babel the writer was thus born in secret. He was still dutifully showing up at Zagursky's three times a week, but before long he was seized by an inspiration.

> The first step was difficult. One day I left home laden like a beast of burden with violin case, violin, music, and twelve roubles in cash — payment for a month's tuition. I was going along Nezhin Street; to get to Zagursky's I should have turned into Dvoryanskaya, but instead of that I went up Tiraspolskaya and found myself at the harbor. The allotted time flew past in the part of the port where ships went after quarantine. So began my liberation.

It took three months for Babel's family to catch up with the deception—Zagursky was in no hurry to bring it to their attention, since he was getting paid and was also afraid of the family's fury—and merely a moment for Babel's father's wrath to explode. He had to be physically restrained by other members of the household from attacking the hapless Zagursky and from battering down the door of the lavatory where Babel had taken refuge.

Edward Newhouse once told me a nearly identical story about himself and the birth of his career as a writer when he was a little boy in Hungary. His parents had arranged for violin lessons and assumed he was practicing in order to be in the school orchestra. They paid the teacher for lessons that in fact Newhouse never took. He simply did not show up. The teacher said nothing about the situation to Newhouse's parents, and for a considerable time the deception went undiscovered.

"I hadn't practiced more than twenty minutes—ever," said Newhouse. "In orchestra I played two inches off the string. I knew how to make the right bowing movements." Newhouse cheerfully agreed that, like Isaac Babel, he and his teacher were basically in complicity. The teacher took the money, and he, Newhouse, lied. "What was wonderful was the realization that I could make people believe things that were not true—and then be able to put such things on paper and make money from them! It was a glorious sensation. That's the genesis of every fiction writer who ever lived," Newhouse beamed.

Babel's story is an archetype for the way many people still think about a prodigy: a child on stage performing wonders akin to Dr. Samuel Johnson's "dog dancing on its hinder legs," with the additional implication that the feat has been achieved through adult force and coercion. But just as all Stradivari instruments were once brand-new, all great violinists began when they were tiny, and few of those who succeed do so under severe duress. An unusual gift usually shows itself around the age of three or four. You cannot take up the instrument at twelve or thirteen and hope to make a career as a major soloist.

Popular usage has bent the word *prodigy* out of shape. Musical prodigies who do not perform in public are still prodigies — that is, children with extraordinary ability — and their number has probably been constant through the ages. What sets these children apart is their ability to do something on an adult level — the areas seem to be confined to math, chess, or music — at a very early age, coupled with an enormous drive to master what they are good at. Rather than the child being pushed by the parents, it is often the parents who are running to keep up with the child. In his study *Nature's Gambit: Child Prodigies and the Development of Human Potential*, David Henry Feldman of Tufts University says that to deter such a youngster from his chosen activity is tantamount to cutting off the child's oxygen. "If you have a child who is in this world to play the violin, and you decide this child is not going to learn to play the violin — you have killed that child, if not physically, then certainly emotionally and spiritually." Watching the youngsters in DeLay's studio makes one realize the strength of their desire to excel in this particular field. The parents may provide the initial structure and the setting, but it is clear that the true prodigies would be practicing even if Daddy and Mummy had to go out of town for a week or so. These children would not simply put their instruments in the closet and subside in front of the television set. True, they might opt for more television than usual, but they would be incapable of leaving their violins untouched for any real length of time.

The negative interpretation of prodigy has been kept alive not only through legend but by people within the music world with an ax to grind. Teachers who have not been able to attract, or to train, youngsters of sufficient caliber to appear in public will cluck that it is against their moral principles to subject a child to such unnatural pressure. Managers bent on showing how clean their hands are can be equally pious in insisting that the child's welfare is their overriding concern rather than the degree of success in strictly professional career terms. Journalists can count on tugging a few heartstrings and rousing some self-righteous ire with tales of youngsters haplessly forced onstage by vicious parents and teachers who are in it for the money.

The Wall Street Journal ran an article on 23 July 1996 charging that the classical music world was turning to child prodigies as a way of saving its faltering economy. The headline, more characteristic of a supermarket tabloid than the usually august *Journal*, announced, "Faced With Plunging Sales, Industry Markets Tots; But Are Kids Exploited?" The writer, Louise Lee, came up with a resounding if predictable Yes, since there would be nothing sexy in an article that came up with a No. Most of the article focused on Sarah Chang, then fifteen years old, as the chief example of "the prodigy trend," and talked about the dangers of burnout and overexposure suffered for the sake of cynical and calculated music-industry economics. Even when the article came out, it was difficult to feel very sorry for this particular prodigy, since Sarah was obviously having a whale of a time. Like most successful prodigies, she has loved to play in public since she was the very tiniest of tots, and there was no indication of having her career "crushed by being pushed too early into the limelight," as the article put it, or of suffering burnout.

By contrast to Sarah Chang, the Israeli violinist Gil Shaham, also a product of DeLay's studio, does qualify as a closet prodigy—sort of. He did not make his American debut until the age of eighteen, although he had been playing for small audiences since he was ten and did a number of concerts in Europe. His sister, pianist Orli Shaham, says that neither she nor her brother really knew what being a child prodigy meant when they were growing up. "There was some sense that when you are no longer a child, that was the end of it all," she says. "Gil used to say that you had to go and clean streets or something." To say that Shaham's parents did not pressure him as a child is an understatement—if anything, the roles were reversed. Both parents were scientists and were concerned that what Orli Shaham called "the screech factor" would be disturbing when they were trying to work. Shaham badgered his parents for a violin from the age of four, but had to settle for the piano. They finally capitulated when he went on strike when he was seven, refusing to speak to them until his demand for the instrument was met.

Samuel Goldwyn reputedly once said to an aspiring actor, "Give me two years and I'll make you an overnight star." Shaham did not have to wait that long. His leap into the limelight took place in 1989 when he

Gil Shaham outside the Aspen music tent in 1991. Shaham began studying with DeLay at the age of nine and was twenty when this photograph was taken. Photo: Margaret Durrance.

was sent to London with virtually no notice to substitute for an ailing Itzhak Perlman in a performance of Bruch's Violin Concerto with the London Symphony Orchestra. Shaham was eighteen years old at the time, a senior at the Horace Mann School in New York and a student of DeLay's at the Juilliard School's Pre-College Division. The fable goes that he was reading Chaucer aloud in class when the fateful phone call came, summoning him to drop everything and get on the next plane. According to DeLay, Shaham's teacher refused to excuse him from school, because he would miss several days of classes, and finally caved in under pressure from all sides, grumbling "Well, I certainly hope this sort of thing will not happen too often."

Shaham may not have been known to the American public as he was growing up, but management was well aware of his virtuosic talents, and they must have decided that a young unknown would be a more acceptable substitute for Perlman than any of the available established artists. The London audience went wild with enthusiasm; the conductor, Michael Tilson Thomas, made plans to re-engage him on the spot; the story made headlines in America as well as England; and Shaham became, well, an overnight star.

At any age, the decision of when to appear before the public is fraught with peril. The child star has the advantage of being judged in precisely those terms—as a child. Since the major allure for the public is the precocity itself, when that quality evaporates with the passing of the years and the young adult is appraised on merit alone, the audience, as well as the critics, may be far more harsh than if they had no earlier standard of comparison. ("Amazing technical facility, but he/she was far more free, more spontaneous, more expressive, as a child." Never mind that during those earlier years, the same people were saying, "Remarkable technique for his/her age, but of course only time will tell if this talent will mature into something more free, more spontaneous, and more expressive.") The youngster who has done his growing up offstage does not have to endure the agonizing experience of being picked apart by the critics. On the other hand, the child who has missed the chance of becoming accustomed to performing in public from early on is faced with having to handle the challenge and pressure without any previous experience, and at an age when self-consciousness may make it more difficult.

DeLay has pointed out that children also benefit from absorbing some of the nonmusical aspects of performance as they grow up. They learn how to deal with the public and the press—what to say when and to whom. They learn about the business side of the profession. If they have management, they get to understand how it functions and what they can expect. These are all necessary parts of an artist's education if he or she is going to be able to sustain a career, and rather than trying to take a cram course as an adolescent or an adult, it is far better to get some solid schooling over a period of time.

DeLay takes a somewhat laissez-faire attitude toward public performances by her young students. "Let's say you are planning to go into politics. You join a debating team. It's the way to learn," she said. "Start playing when you can make anybody listen." Her view is that if a low-pressure opportunity comes up, say with a small community orchestra, a student who seems ready to handle such an event should take it for the experience.

It is much, much easier for children to be at ease on stage if they have started early on. The adolescent period is the very difficult one to get through — that is the one everybody holds their breath about, because that is where the breakdowns occur. If a child has been on stage from the time he was, say, six or eight years old, the playing is part of his life. When he gets to adolescence it is not anything strange.

I do think it is possible to start performing in public at the age of twenty-one or twenty-two, with ease, but I do not know anybody who has done that. Everybody plays in public from time to time. *Everybody.* So it is a question of how frequently, and it is a question of the dates, and it is a question of the reaction of the family to these dates. If the family thinks, "Hey, that is great, I like what she did," then that is fine. If the family thinks, "Oh, my God. That was so important and you goofed up," then that is something else entirely.

I don't want them to go out and play so many concerts that they can't continue their education. I would like to keep the number of concerts to a healthy minimum.

What strikes one about the handful of DeLay's young students who are already playing in public is the enjoyment it gives them. "I am always happy when I play," said Yura Lee at the age of ten. "It is second nature. It is like a part of your body that cannot be left alone," said thirteen-year-old Shunsuke Sato. DeLay's prodigies (and she is someone who dislikes the term because of its connotations) are more than eager to get on stage. The appetite seems to go with the territory for these children — they want to strut their stuff at least as much as their parents are anxious to see them do so. I have seen one youngster's face fall in bitter disappointment when he was told that he would be performing with the student, rather than the professional, orchestra in Aspen that summer. DeLay felt that the boy should wait a bit, and he graduated to what he regarded as the big leagues two years later. Public performance seems to hold no anxieties for these children — they just can't wait to get out there and play.

Are any of DeLay's young students the victims of exploitation by parents and others? A few certainly come close, and as a rule they are the ones that do not make it through to a career. These unlucky youngsters do indeed have parents who fit the ugly stereotype of stage mothers and fathers. These adults show up at DeLay's studio at lessons and wheedle and needle for more attention for their children, while mistreating them at home, pushing them to work long hours by using threats and occasionally even physical violence. I remember one frail-looking girl in her teens who told DeLay during a lesson that she could not play for long that day because she had fallen down and hurt her arm. After the girl left, DeLay said that she suspected the bruises were from being pinched—you could see the finger marks—and was sure the girl's mother had been forcing her to practice. DeLay is hard put to deal with this kind of situation directly; any confrontation on her part would result only in absolute denials on the part of both student and parent, and very possibly an escalation of the mistreatment. The mother is not in it for her daughter; she is in it for the money and the status. Every aspect of the situation is reprehensible.

History certainly provides plenty of examples of children who were forced to perform beyond their years—to become little musical breadwinners. Haydn was sent away from a happy home at the age of five, to earn money for the family as a church singer. Mozart was towed around the courts of Europe by his father when he was seven, and often made to perform humiliating musical tricks at the piano. Beethoven's father tried, but did not succeed, in forcing prodigiousness upon him. Paganini's father compelled him to practice ten hours a day by starving him. In the twentieth century, the pianist Ruth Slenczynska stunned the public with a tell-all memoir called *Forbidden Childhood,* an account of her father's treatment of her in her earliest years, when she was being hailed all over the world as one of the greatest wunderkinder ever born. The book was published in 1957 when Slenczynska was thirty-two years old and had recovered from a breakdown, although she was never again able to be a major presence on the concert stage. One prominent critic weighed in with the view that she was "a burned-out candle. . . . The prodigy who blazed for a while and then subsided into mediocrity." Slenczynska described a tortured childhood in which she was forced to practice nine hours a day by her domineering father. "No mistake ever went unpunished," she wrote. "The minute I missed a note, I got a whack across the cheek. If the mistakes were bad enough, I was almost hurled bodily from the piano."

Yehudi Menuhin, the twentieth century's best-known prodigy—apart from Jascha Heifetz, who gave his public debut in Russia in 1906 at the age of five and his legendary New York debut when he was seventeen—came from the other end of the spectrum. Menuhin suffered no such horrors as Slenczynska did as a child, and flourished in the support and affection of his family and his teachers. At the time that Menuhin made his debut at Carnegie Hall in 1927 at the age of eleven, gifted children were out of favor with the critics, if not the public. Olin Downes of *The New York Times* even said, off the record, that Menuhin should not be classified as a child prodigy, but as a great artist who started at an early age. Audiences responded to Menuhin with a frenzy that the music world has not seen since, rushing up to him at the end of the performance, desperate just to touch his garments, as though he were a saint. Only later, after he began to question why he was able to do what came to him so naturally, did Menuhin begin to have problems with his playing.

In his autobiography, *Unfinished Journey*, Menuhin wrote about the painful fight back he had to make as an adult—much of it through the study of Yoga, as is well known—from what he described as a break in sequence. "Between musical vision and its communication, a transition hitherto made intuitively, there occurred—not always, nor predictably, but ever present as a threat—a rupture which brought all to naught. Intuition was no longer to be relied on; the intellect would have to replace it."

Elsewhere in the book, Menuhin wrote about his childhood in roseate terms as a period of absolute innocence and spontaneity, but it, too, must have had its moments of anxiety. By the age of seven, he had already learned a considerable amount of the standard violin literature, about which he wrote, "The lengthening list served less to teach than to graduate me, creating an instant past, a biography-cum-repertoire, which raised me aloft without giving me a sense of stature. I felt like a baby on stilts."

Coming unscathed through the experience of being a child prodigy is difficult but not impossible. DeLay says that one of the first essentials for success is to have at least one person, usually a parent, who loves you and supports you in every possible way. A certain amount of adult pressure and physical presence is essential to establish practice routines and work habits with a young child, but encouragement and approval are the vital ingredients. The really tough problems concern the nonperforming aspects of the artist's life. According to DeLay, "I think there is a crisis period that can happen anywhere from the age of seventeen to the age of thirty. It is a time when, having been put on a track by someone older, we then have to decide whether we want to continue on that track. I think everyone must go through it because it's a transition point."

While some parents and managers will try to maintain the fiction that their budding artist is just like all the other kids on the block, there is really no way that a child can have a "normal" life at the same time that he or she is a serious violin, piano, or, more rarely, cello student. Musical prodigies are pretty well confined to these two instruments since the winds and brasses require too much lung power for those of tender years.

A childhood that includes all the familiar pleasures of regular school, friends, sports, movies, and so on may be possible until the child begins to be known in the outside world—that is, to perform in public—but once that happens the universe shifts on its axis. You miss school because you have a special concert coming up. You miss more school because you are away on tour. Your classmates start seeing your picture in newspapers and magazines, and while your best friends may feel the same about you, your relationships with others are inevitably altered—maybe some of them start to feel jealous. You are already leading a very different life. You are practicing four, five, or six hours a day while your classmates are hanging out at the mall or the movies. Of necessity, school work becomes secondary.

Those parents who insist to the press and public that their prodigy's childhood differs from the ordinary only in having an extra dollop of violin study on top (let us not even think about the possible huge financial rewards) do so for a variety of reasons, which vary from one culture and one family situation to another. The child who can shine as a performer without, apparently, putting in long hours of practice enjoys the same cachet as the "A" student who breezes through exams without cracking a book. It is all the more amazing, and hence all the more publicity worthy. Out of guilt some parents prevaricate about the nature of their child's life. Even when the prodigy is a willing partner, the parents know that the child is missing out on a normal childhood and may end up with a completely lopsided general education—and in some instances, none at all. Parents may be so concerned about possible accusations of exploitation that they will deny playing any role in a child's musical development: "We never pushed," "He was the one who insisted on playing when he was tiny," "The last thing we wanted was for him to have a career," and so on. In other words, the little devil made me do it. For some cultures, particularly in China, Japan, and Korea, learning is so highly prized that for a child to be shortchanged on a proper education because of the demands of an early career can be a source of shame and embarrassment to the family. DeLay has on occasion been at odds with these parents over the balance of school and public performance. She makes no bones about the fact that a prodigy's childhood is different from the usual, and comes down heavily on the side of school, with the view that if a choice must be made between attending classes or going off on tour, then it is the touring that must be curtailed.

Some years ago there was an instance of a family that had taken their gifted youngster out of school because he was already so much in demand on the concert circuit. The family kept up the fiction that the child was leading a "normal" life, complete with the same friends and the same school since first grade. They somehow managed to conceal the truth from the boy's teacher, his manager, the media, and of course, the public. When someone called the school where the child was purported to be a student, it emerged that he had left several years earlier, and the current status of his education was unknown.

This boy was no more a superman than any other child his age. There is a limit to what one person, no matter how remarkable, can do. In purely physical terms, a youngster cannot simultaneously be in a conventional school and also frequently on tour, any more than those legendary mothers can single-handedly raise a family while also serving as CEO of a major corporation. There are no stand-ins for a school-age virtuoso. You cannot hire a substitute to take your exams or play your concerts.

The parents in the instance just cited may have feared that had the music teacher known, he would have put his foot down and insisted that the boy remain in school, running the risk that all those performing opportunities might never present themselves again. They may have worried about being accused of forcing their child to sacrifice so much for the chance of material success, or they may have felt guilty about shortchanging the child of a general education. Whatever the reasons, the incident illustrates the lengths to which some families are prepared to go in pursuit of the prize of a concert career.

A more familiar form of falsifying is the practice of taking a nip here and a tuck there in the child's age to prolong his or her "prodigy" status. The violin virtuoso Joshua Bell, for example, said in the same *Wall Street Journal* article mentioned earlier, "I was fourteen until I was eighteen," and added that as a child he felt like a circus act rather than a true musician. Bell is a happy example of an artist who successfully made the transition from child wonder to mature artist without ever having to go through his early teens onstage. Whatever he may have felt in private, as far as the public was concerned Bell just skipped that stage of life altogether.

In all these instances, the children are asked to shoulder the additional strain of conniving with their parents in promoting the fiction—of living a lie, not to put it too strongly—about who they are and what they are doing. As they reach their teens, the children, and not the parents, are the ones who will have to deal with press interviews and the general public. It is they who will, in due course, be compelled either to rebel or to follow in the pattern laid down by their parents and continue to lie about their age or their schooling. Even if these children are judged to be happy, well-adjusted, and so on, the demand for collusion on the part of their parents, as well as their own acquiescence, must be a huge burden both during childhood and in later life. Yes, there are children who suffer this kind of abuse in the music world, but their numbers, mercifully, are few — at least those about whom we know.

"I don't like the word *normal*," said DeLay when talking about the childhood of those prodigies who go on to the concert stage at an early age. "It implies that the average way is more healthy and the best, and I don't think that is true. I don't think it's possible to live the way the average person does, to go to the usual kind of school and have a career at an early age." In DeLay's view, youngsters who start to perform professionally are much better off in a setting like the Professional Children's School in New York.

The Professional Children's School, which a number of DeLay's students attend, is a unique institution that provides the nearest approximation to an ordinary instructional setting for so-called stage children. Midori and Cho-Liang Lin are among the past musical alumni of the Professional Children's School, as are Emanuel Ax, Lorin Hollander, Eugene Istomin, Ida Kavafian, Pinchas Zukerman, Yo-Yo Ma, and a host of others. To the casual observer, a day at the Professional Children's School seems much the same as at any other school. Kids tear around in the hallways between classes, and teachers write history dates and math symbols on blackboards, or lecture and hold discussions groups in all the standard subjects.

But there is also a room where the students can check out a laptop computer for use while away on tour so that they can do their homework and fax it back to the teacher. The school's "guided study" program is structured to accommodate the complicated professional schedules of its students to allow them to keep up with their classes. When the students return from their travels, the school provides intensive extra help on a one-to-one basis if needed.

Perhaps the most important thing the Professional Children's School does for its students, who are often the only children in an adult world, is give them a community of their peers in which to feel at home and make friends. All these children are in the same boat. There is nothing remarkable about being unusually talented, or being in the public eye, or making money at an early age. There is also nothing remarkable about being very driven and having high expectations of oneself. For these children, feeling comfortably one of the crowd provides tremendous reassurance.

According to DeLay, children make friendships far more easily in a place like PCS because they share each other's interests and live under similar pressures. "If you get a very gifted, very intelligent child and put him into the usual schools, he is totally isolated because he looks at the other kids and finds them quite stupid. Learning to spend your time being responsible for and kind to people who are not as intelligent as you is a very hard thing to grasp."

The students range from musicians, ballet dancers, and actors to professional models and sports prodigies such as ice skaters and golf players. The education these children receive is far from a superficial smattering; the Professional Children's School is a college preparatory institution that makes heavy academic demands. About seventy percent of the students go on to college immediately after graduating, and others do so later when their work schedules permit.

Among these youngsters, the musicians have the longest uninterrupted professional life; the others capitulate much sooner to the ravages of time. Dancers and athletes succumb to aging muscles, child models change shape, boys in Broadway musicals have their voices change, and child actors, while they may continue acting, grow up and out of their roles. Musicians can be very long-lived. Joseph Fuchs was playing the violin until his death at the age of ninety-seven, for example, and conductors, perhaps because of all that vigorous upper-body exercise, sometimes go on to a very advanced age.

Burn-out, like prodigy, is a label that often turns up in conversations about gifted children and the supposed torments to which they are subjected. Youngsters who showed great promise when they were little and then do not continue to pursue the expected career path are assumed to be suffering from burn-out. The general perception of this condition (my own image is of a piece of charred toast or a dead Roman candle) is that the pressure to succeed, from parents, teachers, and the world at large, has become so overwhelming that the system just shuts down, and the student never wants to touch the instrument again.

This does happen. I have known one such person, a brilliant young pianist who won all sorts of prizes and studied with one of the most eminent—and most destructive—teachers of this century; after a great deal of emotional suffering she ultimately made another very successful career in a completely different area. She never touched the piano again; if she tried to, she would throw up. But such stories are actually very rare. Most children who opt out of a career in music as they get older are not suffering from burn-out. They have simply changed their minds about what they want to do. Rather than sitting alone and brooding in a room with the blinds drawn—or running away—they are busy with their futures, following some other more absorbing occupation.

"I think people's lives don't always go in a straight line," DeLay said one afternoon in her studio. "Last year, we had a very, very gifted girl who was going out and playing some concerts for Community Concerts, and she was doing nicely, but she decided that she really wanted to be in medicine. She had had a double interest in medicine and music all during high school, and when it came time to go to college, she decided for medicine and went to Yale to do her premed training. I wouldn't call that burn-out," DeLay said firmly, "I would call that developing another powerful interest. This year, we had a really first-class little girl who was playing beautifully—she was one of the best we had—who decided after a long time to pursue another interest, and that interest was economics. So she is going to University. I don't call that burn-out, either."

As to why the idea of burn-out is so popular, DeLay believes that people who are not geniuses do not like the idea of somebody being able to do so much more than they can, and feel satisfaction at the thought that such gifts bear the seeds of their own destruction.

"In terms of human potential, the really, really bright kids are as different from the average as the average kids are from tremendously handicapped people. The intelligence is there, and the gifts are there, and since they are there, it seems to me we have got to find the healthiest ways to develop them," DeLay said. "There are certain things they learn so much faster. I don't think they learn emotionally necessarily faster, but they can learn some things—mathematics, chess, and of course, music—much faster than average. We have to go with the things that they want, the same way we go with other children who are not as gifted."

Martina Navratilova had a wonderful analogy for the kind of dedication required to become a world-class tennis player. "Think of a plate of ham and eggs," she said. "The hen is involved. The pig is committed." To become a world-class musician is at least as demanding, and for most prodigies, while they need tremendous support in reaching their goals, the motivation to succeed springs from within.

10   Sarah Chang's Story: How to Get to Carnegie Hall

Sarah Chang made her first big career move at the age of eight, when she played with the New York Philharmonic under the baton of conductor Zubin Mehta. In the years that followed, a constellation of handlers, including parents, teachers, managers, and publicists, formed around this young virtuoso to help protect as well as propel her in her journey to the top. No other child violinist since the eleven-year-old Menuhin had captured so much public attention — not even Midori, who will forever be remembered for the concert of the broken strings with Leonard Bernstein at Tanglewood when she was fourteen.

I first heard Sarah Chang in 1987 when she was six years old. She was in a class of about five children at the Juilliard School that DeLay had taken over for the afternoon for an assistant who was out sick. Sarah arrived in DeLay's studio accompanied by her father, Min Soo Chang, who is a professional violinist, teacher, and a former student of DeLay's. Sarah was wearing a white party dress, white stockings, and white patent shoes, and had her hair tied back with a pink satin bow. She was tiny and totally charming. Her first move was to check inside the door of DeLay's cupboard to make sure that the snapshot of herself and her family was still there with the rest of the students, a standard ritual. Everything was in order. Sarah caught DeLay's eye, giggled, and sat down with the other children to wait for her turn to play.

Ten years later, by the time of her glamorous solo recital debut in Carnegie Hall, Sarah had already appeared with most of the world's great orchestras, including the Big Five (the New York Philharmonic, the Philadelphia Orchestra, the Chicago Symphony, the Boston Symphony, and the Cleveland Orchestra), the Berlin Philharmonic, the Leipzig

Gewandhaus Orchestra, and the principal London orchestras. She had been the youngest recipient ever of an Avery Fisher Career Grant Award, and she had seven recordings, all for EMI Classics, to her credit. What follows is a partial account of Sarah Chang's life in the decade between that early lesson in DeLay's studio and the milestone of her New York debut.

Back in DeLay's studio on that afternoon in 1987, when it was six-year-old Sarah's turn to play for the class, she handed her quarter-size fiddle to her papa so he could tune it since she did not yet have the necessary strength to turn the pegs. She then tore into Wieniawski's D Minor Concerto with aplomb. She was totally assured, and impassive through occasional slips. Min Soo Chang nodded along encouragingly through all the finger-twisting double stops. Sarah had worked on the piece for two weeks and played it from memory. It sounded simply terrific. It sounded unbelievable. Nobody paid any particular attention. Some of the attendant parents may have felt uneasy, but Sarah was just one of the class as far as the other children were concerned. Several youngsters in the group, which was almost entirely Asian, had exceptional technical facility. Sarah had an important something undefinable in addition, but she had not yet broken away from the pack.

After the class was over, DeLay talked about Sarah's musical development, and noted that Min Soo Chang wanted his daughter to play for her every couple of weeks. Sarah had already been studying privately with DeLay for about a year, and was taking regular lessons with DeLay's associate, Professor Hyo Kang, who is himself a former DeLay student. Kang, founder and music director of the Seoul Chamber Ensemble and the Sejong Soloists, is a distinguished teacher and musician who since 1978 has been on the faculty at Juilliard where he has his own studio and commands universal respect. A number of gifted students study with both him and DeLay, and in Sarah's instance this arrangement continued to a greater or lesser degree throughout her time at Juilliard.

"I hesitate to put my two cents in with Sarah because the process with Hyo Kang is working so well," DeLay said after that early lesson.

> I don't want to unbalance it. Once in a while I will see something that perhaps should be done, so I'll say something. The real effort is put out by her father and by Hyo Kang. I'm sure Professor Kang is much closer to knowing how that development goes than I. Both

Sarah Chang at the age of six, playing a one-eighth size violin. Photo: Charles Abbott.

he and Min Soo Chang are Korean, and they have known each other for years. Like all cultures, there are particular Korean family customs and ways of communication about which I have no clue.

I asked her what she thought would be likely to happen with the careers of Sarah and another particularly remarkable youngster who had played in the course of the afternoon. "Oh, gosh, I don't have any idea," DeLay answered.

> I don't know either family well enough. I know the families would love to have them have big solo careers. It depends partly on how many young kids are in the managements at that point; what's happened to the business; who they meet that takes a liking to them and starts to promote them. Long before it is a full-fledged concert career, you are going to have years and years in which you have only a few concerts, and long before that, you're going to have years in which children meet established musicians, and the established musicians start to be aware of these kids as possible future artists.

"What would I like to see happen with these two children?" DeLay rocked back in her chair and was silent for a moment.

> Well, I would like to see their development continue, and when a chance to play in public comes, that they will do it. If they just keep learning the repertoire and keep playing, then they will keep growing—I hope. I don't see why a child shouldn't play in public. I wouldn't put them up in front of the New York Philharmonic, but out in our county [in Nyack] we have an amateur symphony, and if they need a solo player, fine. I am not a person who thinks that that is going to spoil anybody's taste. Some people have a theory that if children read bad literature, they'll get bad taste in literature. My kids read everything from the cereal box to cartoons, and they have excellent taste in literature.

It would be another two years before Sarah got up in front of the New York Philharmonic. At the ripe old age of eight, she was invited to be the soloist for a children's concert conducted by Zubin Mehta. A different soloist had been scheduled, but at the last minute Mehta decided to have a young person. DeLay had taken Sarah to meet Mehta and to play for him a few days before that concert, with nothing in mind except to introduce him to a very promising student. DeLay, who is a long-range thinker and planner, makes a point of seeing that people at the center of power, such as Isaac Stern, Mehta, and others, are kept informed about the development of possible concert artists of the future.

"Zubin couldn't believe what he was hearing," DeLay told me one afternoon at her house in Nyack. "I was pleased that he liked her, and when he said, 'Well, I want to work with her.' I thought, Fine, in a few years this will be a nice relationship. That was maybe on Tuesday."

Newhouse joined the conversation at this point and picked up the story.

> Zubin called Dottie two days later, on Thursday, and said, "Can you bring Sarah across the Plaza [from the Juilliard School to Avery Fisher Hall] this afternoon?" After she played he said, "Do you know any concertos?"
>
> "Oh, yes. Tchaikovsky, Paganini —"
>
> "Could you play the Tchaikovsky on Saturday?"
>
> Sarah is an obedient Korean child and she said "Yes, sir." She came out to Nyack to work on it on Friday. The child was also running off the impossible [Sauret] cadenza for the Paganini. You can count the people who can do that on one hand.
>
> At four o'clock that afternoon, Dottie calls Zubin to touch base. Zubin says, "Do you think she could play the Paganini?" Dottie, feeling as though she was talking under water, said "Sure" — because you don't turn down that kind of offer — "Can we have a run-through around twelve o'clock on Saturday?" Zubin said he would do a piano rehearsal with Sarah, and after that she would come out and play with the orchestra. He had told the orchestra that the soloist would be young, but not how young.

Newhouse grinned at the recollection, and said, "You should have seen the faces of the cellists." The violin section, of course, had their backs to Sarah as she came into the hall, and only saw her just when she was reaching the front of the stage. "There was no rehearsal," said Newhouse. "She played the Paganini with the insane cadenza beautifully. The people in the last row of Avery Fisher Hall heard her as well as the people in the first. The orchestra leapt to its feet at the conclusion, and Missy bowed to everyone." Not to belabor Newhouse's point, but when you think about it, what happened was mind-blowing. A little eight-year-old girl got up in front of a packed audience at Avery Fisher Hall and played, with no rehearsal, a piece of legendary technical difficulty with the New York Philharmonic on less than one day's notice, and did it beautifully. Lots of us might have difficulty reading aloud from the telephone book under such circumstances. Who took the bigger chance, Sarah or Mehta? Perhaps risk-taking did not enter into the picture, since neither of them seemed to think for a moment that everything would not go perfectly smoothly.

At about the same time as Sarah's concert with the New York Philharmonic, a friend of Norman Carol, concertmaster of the Philadelphia Orchestra, told him about this phenomenal young player, and Carol reluctantly agreed to listen to her to see if there was any point in introducing her to then-conductor Ricardo Muti. "Norman flipped out," said DeLay, who went along with Sarah to the informal hearing. "There were tears in his eyes, and he said, 'I have never, ever, asked Muti to listen to anybody, but I am glad to ask Muti to listen to her.'" Muti did listen to Sarah and *he* flipped out, and she was immediately invited to play the following year at the annual Gala Concert with the Philadelphia Orchestra.

Looking back on those eventful performances some eight years later, Sarah said that while the New York Philharmonic concert was a big thing, the concert with the Philadelphia Orchestra, which took place a year after the audition with Muti, was a huge thing. "All these people come backstage and I have no idea who they are," she recalled. "Everybody is in white tie and tails, and everybody looks gorgeous. I was an itty-bitty nine year old, so everybody looks very tall." Among this glittering crew were several powers in the music world, including Lee Lamont, then president of ICM Artists; Anthony Coronia, vice-president of EMI Classics; and Elizabeth Ostrow, an independent record producer, all of whom "happened" to be present at the concert, and all of whom were friends of DeLay's. Sarah was being checked out with an eye to her—and their—future.

ENTER THE MANAGERS

Lee Lamont moved swiftly and decisively, and Sarah became the youngest soloist that ICM Artists had ever taken onto its roster. An aristocrat among music managements, ICM handles only top-of-the-line orchestras, conductors, and artists. At the time ICM started representing Sarah, she joined artists that included Yo-Yo Ma, Isaac Stern, Emanuel Ax, and Wynton Marsalis.

Getting major management happened not a moment too soon as far as Min Soo Chang and his wife, Myung, were concerned. Orchestras interested in engaging Sarah for concerts had been calling the Chang household directly for some time, since there was no other option, but after the New York Philharmonic debut, the trickle became a flood. Sarah said that at the beginning her mother had no idea how to handle these calls, and if Min Soo Chang was not home, she would either just hang up or tell them to call back later and then not answer the phone.

Lamont was concerned that her new artist not feel under pressure from too many engagements, and for a while Lamont was able to carry out her intentions. Sarah did very few concerts and was still able to lead a life that included movies, sleepovers, and friends. She was aided by DeLay who placed top priority on Sarah sticking to her school schedule. If there were a choice between doing a concert or attending classes, then the classes must prevail. Once Sarah's career got under way, however, the conflicting demands of her life as a concert artist frequently on tour in the United States and abroad, and her life at school became much more difficult to manage, and ultimately it was the stage that won out.

At the time that ten-year-old Sarah went to ICM Artists, DeLay talked about the advantages of having a father who was himself a professional violinist.

> The advantage to Sarah is that not only does he understand music and is a wonderful musician, and that he helps her and they have a wonderful relationship, but he understands the managerial business as well. Since he has been a performer himself, he knows how the business side of music works. Not that there is anything very complicated about it—there isn't—but if you don't come at it from that kind of background, there is a lot to deal with. You have to learn about the budget, including the hall rental, printing the tickets, advertising, and so on, and you have to have a presenter who takes care of arranging all the details about the hall. If the concert is with orchestra, you have to have a manager to deal with all the organizational aspects.
>
> Min Soo already knows how all this works because of his own background. He understands what the managements do—the mailing of materials, what the salesmen do, and so on. Someone coming from another kind of background would have no idea. Long before Sarah went with ICM, she was playing a lot, and Min Soo was handling all the things that would normally be handled by a management.

As Sarah's career took off, she had not only the advantage of her savvy father, but also of DeLay, who, in addition to their regular lessons, put in hours of intensive work helping the girl to prepare repertoire for particular engagements. DeLay often traveled with her and either Min Soo Chang or his wife, Myung, when Sarah went on tour. Sarah was not the only youngster on the concert circuit at the time, although she was certainly the youngest, and DeLay traveled with the other children as well, when she could.

During a conversation with her and Newhouse in Nyack around that time, I asked her what she actually did in her role as travel companion and mentor to these young virtuosos when they were on the road. "I listen to the rehearsals and make any suggestions I think necessary. There are never very many," DeLay said. "To tell the truth, I think I am a glorified rabbit's foot. The parents just think that if I am there and anything should start to go wrong, we can pick it up and it will be taken care of. But—nothing goes wrong."

Newhouse gave DeLay's role somewhat more weight. "Whenever one of the little ones plays, she has to be there," he said. "The Mamas go, of course, but Dottie has to go to run interference between the kid and the conductor, or to confer with the manager, for example. Dottie usually knows the conductors and smoothes things out for the child. You can't send a kid out on a big orchestra date on his own." Newhouse smiled and raised his eyebrows at the very idea.

> You have to teach a child how to behave in the Green Room, for example. When Sarah was eight years old and played with the New York Philharmonic, Dottie was busy in another part of the hall, and I had to stand with Sarah in the Green Room. You have to learn to handle the barrage of "How much did your violin cost?" "Were you nervous?" etc., etc. Sarah's response was, "I don't know. No, I was not nervous. I was excited." She also learned the other correct responses: "How kind of you to come. Thank you."

"Sarah absorbed something terribly nice from the Korean background," DeLay added.

> Korean women are always very helpful. They come into a situation, they see what is needed, and they immediately become helpful, and Sarah has that quality. On a casual level she will do things like opening doors for older people, she will carry things for them, she will look at a situation and see what little thing she can do to help. She is learning from her father what things are necessary to do out of respect to older people.

Sarah, at age eleven, was beginning to lose some of her diffidence in talking with grown-ups, and one afternoon after a lesson, she surprised me by rattling along like an old pro at being interviewed, with an energetic account of the life of the touring artist.

> It's very different playing with an accompanist than with an orchestra. I always talk to the conductor before a concert. Miss DeLay comes when I travel, and we are met wherever I go to play. She listens to rehearsals and advises me about the balance with the orchestra. She goes all over the hall to see how the sound is carrying. When I was little, say four or five, concerts were just for fun. I went onstage, bowed, played, bowed, and went offstage. It was just like acting a part in a play. I didn't know what it was all about, I was just doing it because I wanted to. It was fun. Now I know what it's all about, and it's still fun. Some of my friends get jealous because they think I travel so much. They say, "You're so lucky, you get vacations, and everything." Well, I don't call it a vacation. It's fun but it's work!

At this stage, DeLay was still trying to put on the brakes to prevent Sarah from doing too many concerts. "She needs time for practice, school, movies, friends—she needs big blocks of time, and she can still do the important concerts," she said. Sarah continued going from her home in Philadelphia to Juilliard on Saturdays, and Nyack on occasional Sundays, working with DeLay and Hyo Kang.

A LESSON, CREAM CAKES, AND A VIDEO

One Sunday in January 1992, I went out to Nyack to see a rough cut of a video of a trip Sarah had made to England the previous summer when she was ten years old. I was also planning to sit in on part of the lesson Sarah would be having in the morning.

Newhouse had told me a bit about the video a couple of weeks earlier. "She played for the Royal Family, and Yehudi Menuhin comes on at the very beginning, saying, 'I thought Sarah was the most wonderful, perfect, ideal violinist I have ever heard.'" Newhouse paused. "Of course, he has a particular claim to authority on the subject of being prodigious," he said dryly. "It is such an extreme statement that one hesitates to use it in any way for publicity purposes. It sounds too strong. But—he said it. Of course, it is true that Menuhin has a reputation for extreme generosity. If you have studied the violin for four months, he refers to you as his colleague. Baby is on screen for a large part of the time, and of course, Dottie is there, too."

Sarah and her father, Min Soo Chang, drove up from Philadelphia, nearly a three-hour journey, as they did on most Sundays at this stage of Sarah's career. Neither Sarah nor her father had yet seen the video, and the idea was that we would all watch at the end of the lesson.

The house in Nyack is one in which it is exceedingly easy to feel at home. DeLay and her husband have lived there almost since they were married, and it is comfortable, unpretentious, and feels vaguely from an earlier era. The living room includes a piano they bought for two hundred dollars at the time they married, which is pressed into use when a student needs an accompanist during a lesson. Newhouse's sanctuary upstairs is a bibliophile's paradise: the shelves are crammed with books from floor to ceiling, spilling over onto his desk and other bits of furniture. Three or four huge dictionaries are placed next to his armchair — a chair that Newhouse, with customary gallantry, insists on having his visitor use, rather than himself. In recent years DeLay and Newhouse have added another wing downstairs, as well as an elevator to the second floor, as her difficulties in walking became more severe.

DeLay usually teaches in the dining room, seated behind the highly polished table. Above the nearby sideboard hangs a large portrait by Wayman Adams, painter of American presidents as well as prominent musicians, of a lovely young woman in a white dress playing the violin. The portrait is of DeLay aged thirty-two, and it had come into her possession only recently, due to a serendipitous occurrence in the life of conductor and violinist Peter Oundjian, who is one of her former students. A nonmusician acquaintance of Oundjian's had shown him the catalog of a forthcoming art auction because it included a number of Wayman Adams's musicians, including portraits of Gregor Piatigorsky, Raya Garbousova, and Ivan Galamian. Oundjian, leafing through the catalog, realized instantly who the beautiful young woman violinist must be, and called DeLay to ask if she had ever sat for Wayman Adams. Indeed she had, and had no idea what had happened to the painting after its completion more than fifty years ago. She excitedly asked Oundjian to buy it on her behalf at the auction since he was thinking of bidding on one or two other works himself. Even so, it nearly didn't happen. Oundjian was in Europe on the day of the sale, and in spite of detailed international telephone and timing arrangements made beforehand with the auctioneer, there was a mix-up with another bidder that had to be resolved before the painting found its way to DeLay and Newhouse's dining room.

When I arrived, DeLay and Sarah were already hard at work. DeLay was settled at the head of the dining room table with the violin score of the Sibelius Concerto in front of her, and Sarah was standing opposite. Sarah was a good deal taller than the last time I had watched a lesson of hers a couple of years earlier, and one could begin to see the young woman in the little girl.

The day turned out to be a somewhat scattered one in the household. DeLay's telephone goes constantly, but calls during lessons are usually fielded by her housekeeper, Susan, or sometimes by her husband. Neither was in evidence on this particular occasion; Susan was out, and Newhouse was upstairs with a bad case of the flu. The telephone kept ringing, sometimes with pieces of advice from friends and students about how to take care of Eddie and his flu, and DeLay answered the calls for a while, but later turned the chore over to Sarah, since Min Soo Chang did not feel sufficiently secure in his English to handle the situation.

"Why don't you tell them I'm not home," DeLay said to Sarah at the third interruption in fifteen minutes. "Tell them I've left. Tell them I'm getting my hair done." While Sarah was answering the phone in the kitchen, Min Soo Chang told me that Sarah had already done almost all the major concertos with DeLay two years ago, including the Sibelius, which they were picking up again today because Sarah would be playing it in a few weeks with the California Symphony in San Francisco. "Bartók, Bruch, Mendelssohn, Berg, Prokofiev, Paganini, Tchaikovsky . . ." Min Soo Chang trailed off and looked to DeLay who confirmed that indeed Sarah now had all the major repertoire but the Walton Concerto. I started to ask Min Soo Chang, who had also studied with DeLay, about his own background as a violinist, but he turned this aside, saying, "Miss DeLay and Sarah are the important people; I am only the father."

Miraculously, the phone was still for a while, and Sarah and DeLay settled back into working on the Sibelius. Sarah played through the first movement while DeLay scribbled notes lightly on the score with a pencil and periodically hummed, whistled, and rapped the pencil on the table when the tempo lagged. Sarah, of course, played from memory.

"Good, baby," said DeLay at the end of the movement. "The rhythm in general is an awful lot better. The area that we have to work on now includes what you are doing with the bow, and also includes the vibrato."

Sarah came and stood next to DeLay so she could see the notations on the score. "Once I do what she wants," Sarah explained to me after the lesson, "she removes the marks. The circles with the crosses in them are to show the sequences. She always likes me to find the sequences so I know where they are and what I want to do with them. It's a simple system and very good."

The rest of the morning proceeded in a kind of rapid-fire shorthand, with DeLay pointing out phrases that needed more study, and Sarah working on the trouble spots. Occasionally, DeLay would take the fiddle from her and demonstrate the effect she wanted. Sarah remained totally concentrated on what was being said throughout the lesson.

"OK," said DeLay, "Let's go from the beginning. This spot is a rhythmic thing. I think I would make these notes broad [DeLay sang the phrase] so that they are very powerful—really strong. Even though it's very loud, it could be slower here and here." Sarah tried out the new tempo. "I like that better," DeLay said. "How do you feel about it?" Sarah shrugged diffidently and tried the same spot again. "Good, sugarplum. I thought that was great. It sounds so strong," said DeLay, picking up the score once more. "Now here's another spot where the rhythm isn't clear. I heard Evgeny Kissen do a piano recital recently, and the rhythm was not to be believed, it was so beautiful. You can pick up character from the dynamic, and you can also pick up all kinds of character from the rhythm, which is maybe even more important."

Sarah nodded respectfully. "OK, those are the two spots," said DeLay. "Let's talk about vibrato and tone here." Sarah played the indicated passage and DeLay took her violin. "That's pretty nice, but I wonder if this would work better," she said. "Try playing the vibrato fast forward and slow back." DeLay's perfectly manicured fingers demonstrated what she was after. "When you practice it, honey, don't go back from the G to the F-sharp; go from G only halfway back to the F-sharp. I wouldn't get it too fast. There! You've got it! That's fabulous." Sarah lit up and smiled from ear to ear. "OK. I'm sure you will find other rhythmic patterns that you like also, but I think those two ideas are the most important thing for us to do right now."

DeLay went piecemeal through the rest of her notations on the first movement while Sarah kept pace, trying out the suggestions.

Here we want to make sure that the F-sharp and C-sharp are good. . . . On this stroke, your bow is starting to do this [DeLay demonstrates]. . . . Here's your *detaché*. . . . I'd give myself time to grab the *martelé* and give myself time to shift. . . . Good. This time you did something very good here—you did the shift and you shifted into a balanced position so you could vibrate. . . . These stroke ends sound a bit lumpy and the reason is the bow speed [she demonstrates]. On this stroke, I would drop the bow. . . . How are we going to take this note? We need to make sure the bow is heavy on both strings. . . . You should be looking at your sounding point and making sure your bow is parallel to the bridge. Let's go back over that business of keeping the bow straight—that's going to be your life.

DeLay stopped for a moment and turned to me. "It's not a natural motion, bowing. It's like ballet dancing," she said.

Every one of my kids who goes out to play concerts comes back with his bow crooked. They don't have time to watch it, so they have to straighten it out again. You know how ballet dancers walk like ducks? They have their feet turned out? The ballet master is not the choreographer. The ballet master keeps telling the dancers, "keep your toes out, keep your toes out," because it's not natural to walk like a duck. Bowing is unnatural, too, so we have to keep watching it because our arms just don't want to do it.

Another call during this brief break, and DeLay picked up the portable phone in the dining room. "I don't know what I'm going to do yet," she said to the caller. "If he's not feeling a lot better, I'm not going to come in. Pepto-Bismol??" She hung up, rolled her eyes, and got back to business.

"You have to see what your orchestra does," DeLay said to Sarah. "You might like a slide here. When are you playing? Three weeks? We could learn a slide by then." Sarah nodded solemnly, and DeLay went back into high gear. "Let's take a three here and a three there," she said, marking the fingerings on the score. "Up here you need a vibrato, and I was glad you did the crescendo here because most people forget. Here, you've got wonderful bow changes, but these could pop more when you drop the fingers. I would pop the half-steps. That will give you a real lot of energy."

"What about the character of this chord? You can accent the top, you can accent the bottom, you can play it quickly or slowly." DeLay demonstrated and Sarah started to giggle at all the possibilities. "You're going to have to figure out what kind of chord you want here. What about the character of the whole phrase? Your bow changes got a little bit not clear here," she said, marking the score. "But your timing was excellent." The lesson, which has lasted most of the morning, came to an end.

DeLay, Sarah, and I repaired to an upstairs bedroom to watch the partially edited video of Sarah's visit to London, which later became an hour-long television program for PBS and received wide distribution. Min Soo Chang went to the kitchen to warm up in the microwave some soup they had brought from Philadelphia. "Don't blow it up," Sarah giggled as he left.

The rich soup was just the beginning. Min Soo Chang, obviously familiar with DeLay's fondness for confectionery, had brought all sorts of sweetmeats for "lunch," including two boxes of croissants and cream cakes with various fillings—all probably bought at the best shop in Philadelphia, and clearly part of the ritual. "That's just beautiful!" said DeLay enthusiastically, offering them around as she settled herself on the bed, propped up against the headboard. Sarah perched on the edge of the bed, ready to deal with the video machine, Min Soo Chang stood at attention throughout the video, and I sat in an armchair. DeLay talked a bit about the background of the video while we had the soup.

Initially, the purpose of the trip to England was for Sarah to play a benefit concert for an organization called Live Music Now, a charity founded by Yehudi Menuhin and an investment banker in London named Ian Stoutzker. Live Music Now gives young artists a chance to perform in homes for handicapped children, as well as in prisons and hospitals. Stoutzker, a passionate music lover, had graduated from the Royal College of Music, wanting to become a concert violinist. Having later come to the conclusion that this was not going to happen and that he was not interested in an orchestral career, Stoutzker went to the London School of Economics and then embarked on a highly successful business career. His deep interest in music continued unabated and in addition to serving as chairman of Live Music Now, Stoutzker has helped a number of promising musicians in their careers and is a close friend of many major concert artists of our time.

Stoutzker had heard Sarah play in the United States in 1991 and had, in DeLay's words, "flipped out," settling on the spot that he wanted her to play for Live Music Now's benefit concert in London. He proceeded to make all the arrangements, and became so enthusiastic about

Sarah and her playing that he decided to organize some additional concerts and to make a video of her first trip to London, for which he was the producer and narrator.

The remains of lunch were cleared up by Min Soo Chang, and Sarah started the tape. It was the first time she had seen the video and for the most part she watched with expressionless concentration. Menuhin came on the screen, as promised by Newhouse, with the words, "I thought Sarah was the most beautiful, the most ideal," and so forth, after which Sarah played a piece by Fritz Kreisler. DeLay and Min Soo Chang were then introduced by the narrator of the video, which developed as a sort of collage. The video shows Sarah enjoying the standard sights and sounds of London—visiting the Tower, London Bridge, and so on—like any other young tourist. It also shows her performance at the Live Music Now benefit that was held in St. James's Palace in the presence of the Duchess of Kent, as well as a concert she played at the Royal College of Music for an audience of youngsters from the college's junior school, many of whom were violinists. Sarah's performances, as well as her travels around London, are interspersed with some general thoughts about child prodigies from Menuhin, DeLay, and Stoutzker.

"I find it quite remarkable that children, who may be otherwise inhibited and not be able to say what they want, will take to the violin and express what adults would like to think are adult emotions—but I say they are universal emotions peculiar to the child—very personal and very deep," said Menuhin. "A child's emotions are at least as intense as an adult's. An adult has learned to formulate, to curb them, to perhaps allow some to rub off and wear off. The child's emotions are absolutely pristine. They are powerful and overwhelming."

"I don't like the concept of prodigy," said DeLay, following up on Menuhin's remarks. "I think of Sarah as an extraordinary person, and I think she should be given the same chance to perform as any other person who plays well should be given. Performing is part of learning, a large part of learning. There are things that cannot be told to a young person—he has to experience it—and I think a limited amount of performing for a child that age is actually educationally necessary."

Stoutzker had witnessed Sarah's rehearsal in the room earlier in the week with her parents and DeLay:

I could not really believe what I heard, particularly when they repeated sections, because she played with such spontaneity. Every time she played something it was slightly different, it was completely free and completely natural. One always assumes with these highly gifted acrobats on an instrument that they have been so programmed they can only do it one way. Marvelous though it is, it tends to be mechanical so often, and the interesting thing with Sarah is that she played with such spontaneity and such musical insight.

A couple of times while watching herself on the screen—particularly in Sarasate's Fantasy on *Carmen*, which she played with the flash and fire of a seasoned virtuoso—Sarah shook her head with mild annoyance and said, "Oh, I played that so slowly."

"I think it sounds terrific—plenty fast enough," said DeLay, who had been bouncing up and down on the bed with the beat of the music from time to time. To my mind, there was no way that the *Carmen* Fantasy could possibly be played any faster, and I was, in addition, totally floored by this ten-year-old's interpretation of a woman who had, in Newhouse's words, been around the block a few times. Where on earth did all that passion and sophistication come from the moment that Sarah started to play, and to what remote place did it disappear as soon as she put down her bow? Surely not from the Germantown Friends School in Philadelphia that Sarah then attended, and equally surely not from her life at home with her father, mother, and little brother.

From Sarah's point of view, she was not doing anything out of the ordinary in her performance. As Stoutzker remarked in the video, she was behaving perfectly naturally—doing something that to her was as spontaneous as speaking or walking or any other activity of which a child is capable. Which still does not solve the puzzle of the nature and origin of this kind of extraordinary gift.

Professor Kang

A few days after this lesson in Nyack, I got in touch with Professor Hyo Kang, with whom, as mentioned earlier, Sarah had also been studying almost from the time she first arrived at Juilliard. Professor Kang was originally hesitant about talking with me and letting me sit in on his lessons with Sarah at that period of her life, and asked if I would submit my questions in writing, as he did not feel entirely comfortable with his grasp of English. I was reminded, as on other occasions, of how protective almost all the grown-ups are of these gifted children in their care.

Kang responded thoughtfully, also in writing, noting that "it is very fortunate that she has the combination of talent and innate discipline," and described Sarah as having a high level of awareness and an ability to grasp and understand musical ideas at an adult level. His answer to a query about her strengths and her weaknesses provided the following vignette of her at the age of about nine:

> Sarah feels very responsible to her family, self, teachers, and school. I remember being very touched by the sight of her taking care of her baby brother a couple of years ago. She was trying to let him sleep in surroundings not familiar to them, and she was tired herself because the family had been traveling. but she stayed up, more like guarding, so her brother's sleep wouldn't be disrupted. It was a very special and warm atmosphere.

After our written exchange, Kang agreed to let me come to his studio as an observer one weekday afternoon. A slight, elegant man, dressed in a neat business suit and tie, Kang arrived for the lesson precisely at the appointed time, a considerable contrast to DeLay's legendary lateness. He placed his violin on the table in front of him, ready for use if he wanted to demonstrate something, and placed the music score and a pad and pencil nearby. Sarah, by this age, was wearing the same kind of clothes—tights and a T-shirt—that rendered her indistinguishable from any other school kid, in Juilliard or out. She was about four-foot-nine and had glittering braces on her teeth.

I had run into Sarah's mother, Myung Chang, and her little brother, Michael—who was then about four years old—outside the studio before the lesson, both in very high spirits. He was running down the hall, giggling, and Myung Chang was chasing him. I remembered hearing stories from DeLay about his chewing on Sarah's violin bridge as a baby, and later putting her metronome in the toilet.

Sarah was still working on the Sibelius Concerto, as she had been at her lesson with DeLay in Nyack, in preparation for her performance with the California Symphony, and it was already sounding more polished. She played through the entire work. "Bravo. It's beautiful," said Kang at the conclusion. "Is there anything you would like to run through again?" Sarah shrugged politely, and Kang proceeded to take her through some of the sections in detail. The content of what he said was similar to DeLay's lessons with Sarah—there was the same emphasis on how to achieve a sense of energy through the use of the bow, and on the importance of knowing exactly where a particular phrase was going—but the style was in sharp contrast. Kang is gentle, fastidious, and precise, whereas DeLay, generally the essence of clarity, can also be quite earthy and vague (she would say "goofy") on occasion. It is hard to imagine Kang in that state.

"The second movement got too fast," said Kang. Sarah nodded in understanding. "Unless you really mean it, watch your shifting—sometimes it sounds as though you are sliding. Good. Now you have got it. Play the beginning louder but with a faraway mood." Kang conducted with his pencil. "More, more! Which note does this phrase go to? In the third movement you can get a lot of energy from the rhythms. You get more energy by not rushing. Make sure you feel the beat. Rhythmic clarity is very important."

For her part, Sarah did not utter a peep throughout the entire lesson, except for giving soft, monosyllabic answers to direct questions. I wondered if this was typical of her behavior at that age during a lesson with Kang, or whether she might have been uncomfortable at the idea of talking when there was an outsider in the studio.

After the lesson, Kang told me that his classes with Sarah are usually seventy-five percent in English and twenty-five percent in Korean, confirming my sense that my presence had altered the usual dynamic between them. He added that Sarah's being a full-time student at school in Philadelphia was becoming a bit of a problem. Kang is a man of charm and twinkle. He described himself as having been at Juilliard since the subway fare was fifteen cents.

FAMILY MATTERS

Min Soo Chang came to the United States from Seoul in 1979. He holds two Master's degrees, one from Temple University in Philadelphia—where he also earned a Ph.D.—and the other from Juilliard. His wife, Myung Chang, is a pianist and has a Ph.D. in composition from the University of Pennsylvania, where she studied with George Crumb. The family includes Sarah's brother, Michael, seven years her junior.

"When Sarah was two years old, she would hear a melody on the radio, and then pick it out with one finger on the piano," Min Soo Chang told me in an interview around the time of Sarah's famous debut concert with the New York Philharmonic.

At two and a half, Sarah wanted to play my violin when we were in Aspen, and I realized she had perfect pitch. I have never wanted to push, and as long as she wants to play, I'm happy. At this age [eight] she practices between two and three hours a day, more during the summer at Aspen. She watches TV and does her homework after school. If she did nothing but study the violin, she would be in trouble later on. If she wants to become good, she has to grow up emotionally as well.

DeLay noted that both parents, from the time Sarah was a baby, were involved in helping her to learn. "They were not interested in just playing with her and shaking a rattle in front of her face," she said "They were teaching her things and spending a great deal of time with her." At the age of three, Sarah began going to a special school in Philadelphia that provided advanced teaching for gifted young children. By the time she was ready for grade school, it had already been clear for some time that she possessed an exceptional musical ability, and at this point, Min Soo and Myung Chang, hoping to give Sarah as normal a childhood as possible, sent her to the Germantown Friends School in the middle-class Philadelphia suburb where they lived.

Because of the danger of hurting her hands, some physical activities at school had to be curtailed. Sarah's first public appearance had been not as a violinist, but as a participant in a gymnastic demonstration on BBC television when she was four years old, but that activity, as well as her other favorite sport, volleyball, were ruled out. Swimming, roller-blading, and horseback riding were deemed less perilous, but fate caught up anyway one summer when Sarah was about eleven. She slipped and strained her wrist while chasing her little brother around the swimming pool, forcing her to cancel a couple of important concerts. When I heard the reason for her misfortune, I couldn't help grinning and mentally cheering her on for behaving like a kid without a care in the world.

To the outside eye at least, the atmosphere within the family as Sarah was growing up seems to have been particularly serene. For all her strong-mindedness and independence, Sarah's manner with her parents, as well as with DeLay, was one of affection and deference, even when it came to such important matters as clothes—her preference for miniskirts as a young teenager was not shared by her parents, nor was her fondness for rock music. Generational disagreements such as these seem not to have escalated into issues—both parties apparently accepted the other's position with a certain humor. Sarah's parents knew that their authority would not be flouted by actual behavior, and Sarah, just as surely, knew that her time to be her own mistress would come.

Standard female prodigy attire has not changed much over the years. Puffed sleeves, frilly skirts, and black patent Mary Janes are still de rigueur for the little ones, and they comprised Sarah's concert wardrobe through much of her childhood. At that early stage of her life, one or both of her parents, as well as DeLay, would be on hand to take care of her and to help her get dressed before a performance. She always brought three or four dresses and tried them up against the stage to see how they looked. "It's theater," DeLay explained, "and for a woman it's very important what people see." By the time Sarah was ten, she was doing her own makeup before a concert because she found everyone else too slow. "I like to take a nap, so I'd rather do it myself," she said, matter-of-factly. "The Tchaikovsky is very long, for instance—it's forty-five minutes—and you get very tired, so I know I have to rest before." Performance anxiety? Apparently it plays no part in her young life.

Because Sarah adhered to the conventional style of dress throughout her early teens, her entirely new persona at a concert with the New York Philharmonic in Avery Fisher Hall when she was fifteen was all the more startling. She was the soloist in Lalo's *Symphonie espagnole*, and came on stage in a sleeveless, rather daring red gown that brought an astonished gasp from the audience. Sarah, totally self-possessed, acknowledged the reaction with the hint of a smile. "Good Lord, she has grown up," said a music critic who was sitting behind me, and the tone was not entirely complimentary. Afterward people seemed annoyed that yesterday's child prodigy had been transformed overnight into today's full-fledged artist without either their awareness or any intervening transition.

I gathered later that the dress was chosen by Sarah and her mother, DeLay having long since ceased to give advice in matters of taste. After the concert, DeLay expressed some concern that the grown-up dress might deprive Sarah of several protected years, since people's expectations would inevitably alter and she would now be judged as an adult performer rather than as a child. A Korean friend suggested to me that the riveting red dress might be subject to very different cultural interpretations: those in the Carnegie Hall audience who gasped probably saw the gown as a bold statement of entering adulthood, whereas in Korea and elsewhere in the Far East, clothing for a celebratory occasion is expected to be very bright. Red in particular is regarded as an auspicious color and is traditionally worn for major events, for which a concert with the New York Philharmonic would certainly qualify.

For her solo debut in Carnegie Hall in November 1997, shortly before she turned seventeen, Sarah looked splendid in a fuchsia gown with a gold bodice that somehow lacked the shock value of the earlier outfit. She played a solid program of Mozart, Richard Strauss, Prokofiev, Chopin, and Sarasate with elegance and fire, and whether she might have tripped herself up by appearing as a grown-up too early no longer seemed to be a question worth asking. Unlike some wunderkinder, Sarah had gained a poise and self-assurance as a child that remained intact as she developed into an adult. The critic Shirley Fleming, writing about this debut concert in the *New York Post*, noted that many young musicians must view the rite of passage of a solo recital with some apprehension. "Chances are, however, that this particular ex-prodigy never turned a hair at the prospect. . . . She is sailing swiftly and smoothly into a major career."

A few months before Sarah's solo debut at Carnegie Hall, when I was in Aspen for DeLay's eightieth birthday celebrations, I was sitting outside the festival tent talking with Masao Kawasaki. Kawasaki, like Hyo Kang, is a distinguished professor of violin at Juilliard where he has his own studio and shares in teaching some of DeLay's students. In addition, Kawasaki, who is much sought after as a performer, heads the string department at Brooklyn College and is on the faculty of the Aspen Music School. A young woman, bubbling over with vitality, came over and greeted both of us enthusiastically. Kawasaki responded with a hug, but I could not place her, and wondered privately if she had me confused with someone else. "I'm Sarah," she said, laughing at my blank expression. "We haven't seen each other for a couple of years." I was dumbfounded. I could not connect this bustling, extroverted young woman with the "don't speak until you are spoken to" child I had come to know. Sixteen-year-old Sarah, whose careful eye makeup emphasized the new contours of her face, seemed so much bigger in every way. She was probably only a little taller, but it was her manner that had changed. Her shoulders were thrown back, she was ready to meet the world, and everything about her expressed self-assurance and an enjoyment of life.

We arranged to meet the next day at the inn where I was staying. Sarah arrived with her father, Min Soo Chang, who had driven her over, as at age sixteen she was still too young to get a driver's license. Min Soo

Sarah Chang at age sixteen—a publicity shot used for her debut recital in Carnegie Hall in November 1997. She had appeared there regularly with orchestra since the age of eight, but the Carnegie debut is a major milestone in any young virtuoso's life. Photo: Christian Steiner.

Chang made a show of leaving us alone together ("Now that she is grown up!") but settled himself on a couch quite literally at my elbow. When I listened to the tape recording of our interview later on, Sarah's voice and Min Soo Chang's came in at the same volume.

It became clear early on that the dynamic between father and daughter had indeed shifted. The days of the deferential, obedient little girl were past, and Min Soo Chang, accustomed to his position as authority and adviser, was having trouble grasping his new role as bystander. DeLay, too, must feel some pangs as her students gradually move on to the great world of the concert stage, but for the teacher, like Peter Pan, there is always a new generation waiting in the wings. Sarah, eager to assert her independence, was determined to speak for herself, and when her father broke in, as happened with some frequency, they simply talked through each other until one of them prevailed. Often, but not always, it was Sarah.

As we talked, Min Soo Chang took on the additional roles of spin doctor and explicator, determined to communicate his particular portrayal of Sarah and her childhood. One subtext was to make sure I did not think she had been in any way pressured by her parents, and another was to drive home the point of her extreme precocity from the very beginning.

"When I first went to Miss DeLay—" Sarah started.

"I just took her to Miss DeLay to see what she thought," Min Soo Chang interjected. "I thought it would be nice, as a parent, to show her. Miss DeLay asked Sarah to come to Juilliard immediately, when she was five, but you can't just stop school in the middle of the semester. I really didn't have the idea to send my kid—five years old—to Juilliard. I just wanted to show her to Miss DeLay because she was my teacher. That was all. Very simple."

Parents of prodigies are routinely accused of forcing their children to work against their will, but Min Soo Chang's "very simple" description of Sarah's introduction to DeLay seemed a bit disingenuous. Not that the Changs had in anyway pressured their gifted daughter—I am sure they did not—but they had, as noted, sent Sarah to a school for specially gifted children when she was three years old, so they were obviously concerned about helping her development. Min Soo Chang knew that he had something special on his hands at that time, as well as when he decided to show his teacher what his little girl was up to at the age of five. Sarah may have been ready to settle for a general remark about "When I went to Miss DeLay," but Min Soo Chang was concerned with making it clear that the meeting was almost by chance, and that the initiative to start lessons came from DeLay and not from him. He reiterated at this meeting what he had said on previous occasions—that he had never wanted a professional career for his daughter, that he did not like the idea of raising his daughter as a musician, and that his own experience had taught him the difficulties of such a life.

"When I was six," Sarah continued, "the people I hung around with at Juilliard were well into their teens."

"For the first three or four years, there was nobody her age," Min Soo Chang elaborated.

"School friends are my best friends—those are the ones I call when I am on tour," said Sarah. "There are some music friends from Juilliard and other places, but they did not feel like her own friends because they were older," said Min Soo Chang.

"There was also a very big break when I was fourteen and fifteen at Juilliard, when most of the friends I had grown up with went to college." said Sarah.

"That is because they were three or four years older than Sarah from the beginning," said her father, drilling his point home.

As for the "age factor" to which Sarah's father kept returning, much of the message seemed to be concerned with the groundbreaking role played by her extreme youth when she began to perform in public— Min Soo Chang's point being that they had trod where none had trod before, that they were, in fact, pioneers without a compass in unknown terrain. I found this theme somewhat poignant. First, Min Soo Chang's view was not quite accurate; even if the comparison applied only for that particular point in time, there were several children making it on the concert stage, perhaps not as notably as Sarah, but still she hardly qualified as a lone trailblazer. Second, Sarah's extreme precocity as a child, once a source of amazement, no longer plays a part in her attraction for the listening public. By this time she was out there with the big guys, being judged by what she did last night, last week, and last month—not on being a child phenomenon.

After catching up on Sarah's recent performing and recording activities, which were bountiful, I asked her about her perception of DeLay as a teacher over the years since she had begun studying with her.

When I was six, Miss DeLay was more like a third grandmother. I would go in for lessons and just feel so relaxed. I could tell her anything and know that she would understand. That changed after a while when she started to become more of a mentor. When you play a concert when you are very, very young — say seven or eight — she will let you enjoy it for a week before saying anything. Then, when I was about thirteen or fourteen, all of a sudden, after a concert she would go over everything, basically because the following week you had another performance with the same concerto, or you were going to record that concerto, so there was no time to be careful or nice. You had to get things done.

There is a point where things change, and you realize that everything is not so rosy or nice, and you need to think for yourself — and she helps you to do that. After a while, she does not do it for you. She does not say, "Play this forte, play this soft"; she says, "What do you want this phrase to say?" Or, "What do you want it to build up to?" Or, "What is this whole second phrase meant to mean?" The transition to making me think for myself was very gradual — it probably came at the point I started to record a lot, when I was around eleven or twelve.

At this point in Sarah's life, she is on tour a great deal of the time, and no longer taking lessons. She continues to keep in touch with DeLay, either by telephone from the other side of the world, just to say hello, or in person, when she will check in at DeLay's studio when she is in New York.

When I see Miss DeLay in her studio at Juilliard, we order enough food from Shun Lee for ten people, and we just sit and eat and talk. I don't necessarily have to play anything. If I have a recording coming up, or a big concert coming up, I'll bring some material and we'll go over it together. If I am back from a long tour, like an Asian tour, she'll ask me what it was like, and what I'd like to do the next time. Very long-term stuff. Everything we talk about now is two or three years in advance.

She has been in many roles in my life and she has always been great. First and foremost as a teacher, but there is so much more to her, so much more to learn from her, because she has made such a success of her life in every way.

Our talk began to wind down, and Min Soo Chang came in for the wrap-up:

What we can say is that Sarah is now sixteen, but she has studied with Miss DeLay since she was six. She played with the New York

Philharmonic at eight, and by fifteen she had played with the Berlin Philharmonic, the Vienna Philharmonic, the Amsterdam Concertgebouw, and the London orchestras. All the majors.

If we had somebody who had done these things before, we would have had some examples. There were no examples ahead of us who had played with every major orchestra so young, so whenever we had to make any of the important decisions, we talked to Miss DeLay. We followed her advice all the time. Miss DeLay was a great teacher, was a great helper, was a great adviser to Sarah, who gave Sarah all the confidence in the world.

The Sarah who presented her solo recital in Carnegie Hall at the age of sixteen did great honor to her parents and her teacher, not the least for gently shaking free of them as she found her own way. She gives not the slightest hint of feeling regret at a "lost" childhood, nor any sign of having been subjected to unusual pressure by her parents, or anyone else, in order to force her on stage. Perhaps there is still a rebellion or even an about-face in favor of some other career in Sarah's future — she is still only in her teens, after all. For now, she is where she wants to be.

11 Itzhak Perlman's Story: Bringing Out the Best

Itzhak Perlman, undoubtedly the finest violinist of his generation, and Dorothy DeLay go back a very long way. He was thirteen years old when she came into his life, and the meeting, which took place in a dismal hotel room in midtown Manhattan in 1958, was not auspicious. DeLay had been asked to audition the young Perlman for Juilliard, and she found him in a furious mood. He was glued to the television set and scarcely looked up when she came in. Mrs. Perlman hovered in the background.

The boy had won a major violin competition in Israel, and he and his mother had been flown to New York to appear on *The Ed Sullivan Show*, which was then at the height of its popularity. The Sunday-night television program was a variety show that featured such acts as circus performers, dancers, trained animals, comedians, and musicians. Sullivan, whose bumbling and wooden manner endeared him to his fans, had an astonishing ability to recognize undiscovered talent with audience appeal. His programs did feature big-name artists, such as Bob Hope, Humphrey Bogart, and Maria Callas, but his greatest coups resulted from introducing American audiences to previously unknowns, including the Beatles and Elvis Presley.

"Mrs. Perlman had no English, and he had virtually none," DeLay recalled of their early meeting.

> We communicated with sign language as best we could. It was a dark and rainy day in the middle of winter, and the whole scene was pretty depressing. You could see that Itzhak was fed up and disgusted with being yanked out of school and away from his friends. He made clear that he had zero interest in meeting me. He played

the Mendelssohn Violin Concerto faster than I had ever heard it before—probably to get it over with. I couldn't believe my ears.

In spite of the rocky beginning, DeLay was to have a tremendous influence on Perlman all through his adolescence, and in later years a deep and lasting friendship developed between the two. Perlman's appearance on *The Ed Sullivan Show* was followed by a three-month tour across the country with Sullivan's "Cavalcade of Stars," at the conclusion of which it was decided that, rather than return to Israel, Perlman and his mother would stay in New York, where he would attend the Juilliard School and study with Ivan Galamian and his assistant, Dorothy DeLay.

Perhaps it required the balance of these two powerful personalities, Galamian and DeLay, to produce a Perlman. "I studied with both Miss DeLay and Mr. Galamian from the age of thirteen until I was twenty-one or twenty-two," Perlman said in an interview in 1995 at the time of his fiftieth birthday. "They had different approaches to teaching, but similar systems technically speaking, especially with the bow and the way it works. The goals of the two were basically similar—certainly technically they were."

DeLay's tutelage of the thirteen-year-old Perlman, newly transplanted to New York City and to a totally unfamiliar life at the Juilliard School, extended far beyond the studio. The boy had left his school friends behind in Israel, spoke little English, and had to cope with the crippling disability that resulted from contracting polio at the age of four. Among the first things DeLay did was to help him gain independence by arranging for him to travel to Juilliard on his own. Perlman greeted the idea with enthusiasm, and despite some initial apprehension on the part of his mother, she put him in a taxi on the mornings of his days at Juilliard, and fellow students helped carry his books and hail a cab so that he could return home by himself in the evenings. Perlman's autonomy was completed a couple of months later when DeLay contrived to get him a lightweight instrument case that he could carry along with his crutches. The experiment was a splendid success—before long, Perlman, gregarious by nature, found friends at Juilliard and was able to enjoy a normal social life. Perlman is not the only student for whom DeLay went far beyond the call. She extends herself for the students with whom she works closely in any number of ways, from helping them to get concerts, to getting along with (or sometimes without) their parents, to teaching them to balance a checkbook. But Perlman's courage in dealing with his disability affected her deeply, and she went all-out to help him become as independent and self-reliant as possible. She had precisely the qualities of imagination and practicality needed for the task.

When Perlman reached his teens, DeLay taught him how to drive, first in her own car, and later in one equipped with hand controls. Most children gain a sense of how to steer when they learn to ride a tricycle or bicycle, an advantage obviously denied to Perlman. DeLay would pick him up in her car and the two would head for some remote, traffic-free spot where she would let him steer while she remained in the driver's seat. Later, hard as this is to credit, she got him used to the feel of the accelerator by letting him operate it with his crutch. (She, too, had a lot of courage.)

Some of the driving lessons took place at Meadowmount in the summer when DeLay was teaching there and Perlman was a student. He was initially accompanied by his mother, who always kept a kosher household, and finding the proper butcher in the area proved to be an impossibility. As a result, every couple of weeks DeLay would drive Mrs. Perlman and her son, sometimes with Itzhak at the wheel, all the way to New York and back in her DeSoto to get the necessary supplies.

Even when it came to his marriage, DeLay played a significant part in Perlman's life. Perlman and his wife-to-be, Toby Friedlander, met as students at Meadowmount, where she was also studying with DeLay. Teacher and student became good friends, and as DeLay tells it, Toby decided almost the moment she was introduced to Itzhak that she was going to marry him. After that first summer, it took nearly three years, during which DeLay served as mother confessor and confidante on an almost constant basis, before both parties came to the same conclusion at the same time and tied the knot.

During our interview, Perlman said that DeLay's matter-of-fact conviction in his ability to surmount the challenges he faced, regardless of skepticism from some powerful forces in the concert business in the early days, played a major part in the development of his career. "There was a time when my parents and Miss DeLay were the only people in the world who believed I could have a concert career," he said. "The fact that I was disabled—a lot of people thought it would be out of the question, but she never had the least doubt."

DeLay has described Perlman as the most gallant of fighters whose life stands for the courage to overcome a severe handicap. Recalling how

Perlman as a child hated mention of his disability, DeLay pointed out that he later used it to the advantage of so many others through his on-going efforts to require equal access to all public institutions, including concert auditoriums across the country. "I had had enough of spending my backstage life in the freight elevators of America's concert halls," Perlman said. Carnegie Hall used to have no facilities for the disabled, and installed chairlifts as a result of his efforts.

It is perhaps not generally known that Perlman taught master classes at Brooklyn College for nearly twenty years. In an interview we had in 1996, he talked about his students there, and it was evident that his own teaching style was drawn from his studies with DeLay rather than Galamian. "I try to look for the positive things a student does, and point out when it works." he said. "After a student tries something again and again, and finally gets it, I say 'Stop! Did you hear that? That was a great sound. Did you hear the difference? That's what I want. It sounded wonderful.' You have to give support as well as be instructive—the support part is so important."

Like DeLay, Perlman tries to see things from the student's perspective rather than teach by edict.

> Every so often, I just cannot imagine why this person cannot get what I am trying to say. So what I do is take the violin in my right hand, and I take the bow in my left, and I try to make a sound—and I cannot do it. Then I think, Now I can understand. It's so frustrating. Here I am. I'm in a situation where I know how it works. It's not that I'm a novice—I know how it works, and I can't play it with my left hand. No matter what my background is, and my knowledge, my hand does not want to do what I am asking. It's always very sobering. It makes you gain a lot of patience. Every new individual I teach is a totally new ball game.

In 1995 Toby Perlman's interest in music education led her to found the Perlman Music Program, a summer camp in East Hampton, Long Island. Her idea was to provide "a noncompetitive, creative, and supportive environment"—principles she said she learned from Miss DeLay—for youngsters aged ten to eighteen who are budding soloists. Itzhak Perlman was to do some occasional coaching, and to conduct the orchestra at the end of the season, but as it turned out, his involvement expanded far beyond what had initially been planned. He discovered that he got a tremendous kick out of teaching the gifted young kids the camp attracted, and over the next few years, the summer program grew into a vital part of Perlman's life.

At the end of the interview, I asked him if there was anything he would like to add to what he had already said. He thought for a moment and then said emphatically, "Yes. The thing that I think is crucial in teaching is the ability to give instructions and suggestions and ideas and advice to students without making them feel that they are no good, or that it is hopeless, or whatever." He stopped for a moment, and continued in milder tones.

> I believe in being kind. I think that I have to do my job and I have to do it in a kind way and a constructive way. Even though the basic message is the same, the way it is presented is what is really important. You can tell somebody the same thing in two, three, or four different ways. One way, they can listen to you and feel terrible, and another way they can listen to you and feel wonderful.

Toby and Itzhak Perlman on their wedding day in 1967. Both the Perlmans were students of DeLay's when they were in their teens, and DeLay served as confidante throughout their courtship. They became, and continue to be, among her closest friends. Courtesy Dorothy DeLay.

12   Toby Perlman's Story: Another Perspective

Toby and Itzhak Perlman's Manhattan townhouse is a place rich in sound and color. The long double living room on the ground floor is filled with overstuffed couches in vivid colors and patterns and a mix of chairs, tables, chests, art objects, and books, none of which is lined up in formal fashion and all of which look inviting. The element of sound on the particular day when I went to speak to Toby Perlman was provided not by music but by the Perlmans' two dogs, wheaten terriers named Latke and Yontif. (In Yiddish, the word *latke* means potato pancake, and *yontif* means holiday.) The dogs had just been shorn of their winter coats and seemed to be having an identity crisis. Only their great shaggy heads had been left untouched, and they rushed around the room trying to get comfortable with themselves again. Toby Perlman, petite and animated, was dressed in overalls and a T-shirt. She had just brought Latke and Yontif back from the vet, and suspended the conversation from time to time to soothe and calm them.

Toby Perlman moves with energy, she speaks with energy—you can practically hear her think with energy. When I first met her, I was so bewitched by her way of talking that I nearly lost the thread of the content. There are no shades of gray in her delivery; everything is imbued with a kind of spontaneous drama. An oscilloscope would zingingly vibrate and register extremes of high and low in every sentence. When Toby Perlman wants to make a particular point, her voice will sometimes drop to a barely audible whisper; at other times she will turn up the volume and repeat a phrase for emphasis: "No! No! It was never like that! It was never like that!" All the varied dynamics are expressed in classic New Yorkese—"Whaddo*I*know?" and "No *problem*." She is so refreshingly open and direct about what she thinks that one gets the sense of someone for whom honesty and lack of pretension are moral imperatives.

> I realized, when I thought about this interview, that the problem for me in talking about Dorothy DeLay is that it is all larger than life. Miss DeLay is the smartest woman I ever met. In addition to being the smartest woman I ever met, which is quite a statement in itself, she is extraordinary beyond being extraordinary, so that anything that I can say is kind of too much and too big and too good to be true. So maybe I would like to have you ask me some questions, and then I can focus on specifically what you want to know.

I asked about her own early training as a violinist, which, like her husband's, had been with both DeLay and Ivan Galamian. Toby Perlman had also previously studied with Oscar Shumsky.

> I came to them [DeLay and Galamian] late. I was old—I was already nineteen—so my experience was entirely different from that of a child who did not know how to make any kind of evaluation. I found Mr. Galamian and Miss DeLay to be very different, and very complementary to one another. I never had a problem in studying with both of them. I was just a student, I did not know if they got along, or if they did not get along. Miss DeLay was always very respectful of Mr. Galamian. I think that she was crazy about him and that she was in awe of him. He was a great teacher—a great teacher. He didn't have the breadth in many ways that she has, but every kid got the same—you got your sixty minutes of undivided attention. Her style was very different.
>
> I worked very hard. I am very conscientious, and I played better for her because I wanted so desperately to please her. I did not care so much about pleasing Mr. Galamian—he was huffing and puffing but I was not impressed. My husband had exactly the opposite experience. Fear was the great motivator and still is, in his life. He was so terrified of Mr. Galamian that he did much better playing for him than for Miss DeLay, because he was so afraid of Mr. Galamian. He prepared more seriously, and then he would play better in the lesson because he was so scared. A lot of people are not that way, they do not do well under fear, but for my husband fear is a great motivator—he is still that way today. He would lose weight if any of the doctors would scare him badly enough—he would just do it—but now they are all afraid of him.

Toby Perlman sat back and fell silent for a moment. "Miss DeLay—where is the greatness?" she said, starting a new train of thought. "The greatness has to do with seeing the whole picture."

I think that my husband, and the way she handled him, was a perfect example. Many people might disagree. You could argue, "Oh, that is ridiculous. He was so good. He was so advanced when he came to her." But the fact is that she had to completely redo his bow arm—she and Mr. Galamian together. This is when he first came to America at the age of thirteen. He was a baby at thirteen, and she had to have a vision of the future and know how to choreograph things to make it possible for him to have a shot. Nobody was willing to give him a chance.

Ed Sullivan brought him over as a freak in a freak show. That is basically how he got here. Nobody who came to Israel and heard him play would consider it; everybody thought he was great, but nobody would bring him to America. Absolutely not! Disabled child? They wouldn't touch it! Ed Sullivan came and did not know how great he was, but he saw that Isaac was disabled and that he could play the violin, so Ed Sullivan knew it would be terrific on television.

I asked how Ed Sullivan had come to her husband to begin with, since I had been under the impression that Isaac Stern had been instrumental in Perlman's being "discovered."

No. That is a myth that has been perpetrated, but that is not the truth. We try to unperpetrate it whenever we get the chance. There was the Ed Sullivan "Cavalcade of Stars," and he was holding auditions in Israel—he was bringing a whole Israeli show, and he was searching for talent. He was bringing a magician and a hand-shadow artist, which was my husband's favorite, and my husband auditioned for him, and Ed Sullivan brought him to America. Then all these Israelis went on a whole tour with the "Cavalcade of Stars" and made money. When the tour was over, my husband came back to New York to study with Miss DeLay and Mr. Galamian.

"No! Don't *do* that!!" Toby Perlman stops for a moment to rebuke Latke and Yontif, who are starting to wrestle. A lot of stroking and patting, and order is restored, followed by another period of silence as Mrs. Perlman collects her thoughts before picking up the conversation. When she speaks again, she does so in emphatic—almost oratorical—tones.

Who was the force? Who was the person we have to thank? Who was responsible? Miss DeLay took this boy and she gave the world a gift. She presented him as a whole human being. By the time she was finished, he was a whole human being. How did she do it? Well, she did it as a teacher—scales and so on—but she also did it, most important, as a human being. She nurtured his interests, encouraged his interest in art, got his parents to get him an art tutor so that he could paint and draw. Took him to museums herself, took him to concerts herself, encouraged his interest in baseball—all the things that normal children are encouraged to do, all that came from her.

She knew that eventually his art would be a reflection of his life. Therefore, he'd better have a life! It all sounds easy—of course she did this and of course she did that—but it's not so, because other teachers do not do that. She saw the whole boy, the whole child, the whole situation, and she supported it. Everybody needs support, everybody needs a helping hand. She wasn't just in there for the lesson time. One of the things that she did—the most remarkable thing—was that she recognized that his disability was going to be a real problem in the eyes of the public. *She* knew that it was no problem at all—it was just no problem—but she saw the way people responded, and she understood that half the battle was going to be convincing the powers that be that this was a boy who could do anything, and she set about doing that.

She set up situations where my husband would appear alone, where people would see him by himself. The thing is that she knew—by that time I was in the picture—that of course he could be alone, what was the big deal? But there were people in our business who were very powerful, whose support he needed and he was not going to get. When I came into his life he was seventeen, almost eighteen, and in a way, I was the answer to her prayers. I don't know whether she approved of me as a mate for him—I think she did—but I was the answer, because here was this boy, this disabled boy who was just turning eighteen, who had a girl, and that was just the perfect kind of thing—for him to have a girlfriend.

What I have been saying is a skeleton of what happened. I'm trying to give you a kind of umbrella for what it was like for him.

"What were some of the ways in which DeLay made it clear to the music world your husband's physical difficulties would be no barrier to a professional career?" I asked.

She would see to it that he would go to concerts where she knew some of these people would be, and she made him go by himself, or he would go with me. It was not actually that she set up anything different than what he would have ordinarily done, but she made sure it happened in situations where people in the business—where Mr. Hurok, let's say—would look for Isaac [as Toby Perlman calls her husband] and his mother, and would see only Isaac, or Isaac and me. Miss DeLay made sure that that happened, so that by the time he went to the competition, it was kind of common knowledge that this was a pretty independent kid. I think before the Leventritt competition there was still real concern about whether or not he could do it, and in that situation, Isaac Stern was helpful. I don't know, because I wasn't there, but that's the scuttlebutt, that Isaac Stern said, "He can do it. He deserves the prize and he can do it." Isaac Stern was very helpful then, and in the years after that he was also very helpful. For example, he went giving concerts around the world and would say to the conductors, "Hey, have you heard Perlman? You should engage him." By that time it was over—being accepted was no problem, because she had seen to it that it would not be.

"What was Galamian's attitude about your husband being able to make a career when he was starting out?" I asked. "Did Galamian believe he could manage independently?"

"Are you kidding?" Mrs. Perlman responded with some asperity. "I don't think my husband ever had a conversation with him in his life. He had nothing to do with it."

"What if he had never gone to Galamian and had had only Miss DeLay as a teacher?"

"Who knows?" she shrugged. "I feel very clear that she was the motivating force in his life, that she was the most important person in his life, and that she still is."

I don't know how much in touch with Isaac she is, but I do know that the few times she has been ill nothing else exists for him—he is just on total alert. I don't know if he sees that in himself. When he sees her, all he does is yell at her. He picks on her mercilessly. It is like a child with a parent, a child who never came to grips with the parent as being imperfect. He is scowling all the time at her. "Why are you doing that and why are you doing this and why did you order that? That's a bad pasta, that's the wrong pasta. Don't get that, get this."

She broke into laughter at her impersonation of her husband. "You know, this is a very complicated relationship," she said, followed by a long silence. I asked whether she might be wary of my writing about it. Lacking a taste for the jugular, I had told her at the beginning of the interview that I would be glad to turn off my tape recorder, or to delete anything she did not want to appear in print—an offer that in fact she never took up.

She answered my question thoughtfully.

No, I am not wary about your writing about it, but I don't want to speak for him. That's the thing. If you quote me, I would absolutely be happily quoted as saying, "She is the motivating force, the most important person—if you had to pick one—that would be it, in my view." But that is only my view. Isaac is so intensely involved with her in a way that I am sure he never looked at. He doesn't examine things that way, men don't do that. If I said to him, "I think you are terribly concerned with Miss DeLay, I think you need to think about it," he would say, "Don't be silly, I'm not at all worried about Miss DeLay. I just saw her the other day. She is fine. She is just fine." It is very childish in a way, defensive and the way a child is with a parent. And it is touching, it is very touching. I think it's OK to write about it. I think it is the truth.

You see, I am not talking about how much she knows as a violin teacher. Although, let me tell you, this woman knows *soooo much.* [Her voice drops to an intense whisper as she says the last two words.] She comes to a concert of my husband's and I get a list at the end of what is wrong. Not just what is wrong, because that's silly, I know what is wrong. She says, "You know, sugarplum, the violin is a little low—I don't like the position, I think he should move it over a little bit."

"And does he listen to that?" I asked.

Yes. If *she* says it. If I wait for the right moment and say, "You know, Miss DeLay mentioned to me—," he'll always say to me, "Did she like it? Did she like it? Did she like it? Was she happy? Did she think it was good?" Or, "What do you mean, she didn't come? What do you mean, she wasn't there?" The questions are of paramount importance. I might say, a week or so later, "You know, Miss DeLay mentioned something to me about your position."

"She did? What did she say?" He is very open. If she said it directly, he'd probably be very defended. "Well, she doesn't know anything. Blaaah"—you know. That is why she tells it to me.

The other thing about Miss DeLay is she has the most incredible mind. Her mind is the mind of youth. Searching all the time. Never thinking she knows everything. Wondering and questioning and listening. She is so interested in everything. I think it comes from being with young people. It keeps her so young. When I talk to her, I feel she's younger than I am. I think it comes from this joyful aspect of her.

Toby Perlman's use of the word "joyful" reminded me of a passage in Ian Frazier's book *The Great Plains*, a history and personal account of the part of America where DeLay grew up. "A person can be amazingly happy on the Great Plains," Frazier wrote. "Joy seems to be a product of the geography, just as deserts can produce mystical ecstasy, and English moors produce gloom. Once happiness gets rolling in this open place, not much stops it." Was DeLay's joy begotten in Medicine Lodge, along with her "limitless sense of the possible" that her husband attributes to being brought up in those great open spaces?

I return to the hypothetical question about Itzhak Perlman and his two teachers. "If the query were switched and your husband had had only Galamian, do you think he would have gained the independence and self-confidence you spoke of?"

No! Absolutely not! No way that would have been OK! Without her, forget it! This exuberance that I was talking about, her quest for knowledge, all of that, she has it within herself, in her daily life, in the way she approaches her teaching—but she made that essential to him. She gave it to him as a gift. Be inquisitive, enjoy everything, learn everything, do everything. She gave him a kind of taste for life and a zest for things. I don't want to say that—that's not fair—it's not fair to say she gave that to him. I think he had that, but she encouraged it. When he would say, "Oh, I really want to go to a baseball game," "Well. Let's go!" Or if she couldn't go, "Well why don't you call up Artie or why don't you call up Paul, sugar?" Or maybe she would plant the seed later with Paul Rosenthal or another one of those guys: "Listen, Itzhak really wants to go to that ball game, and I know you are a Yankee fan."

The defining moment in Itzhak Perlman's career came in 1964, when he won the Leventritt Award, which brought a fairly modest sum of money and a great deal of important exposure in the form of appearances with the leading orchestras. Itzhak Perlman was eighteen years old, and he and Toby had just recently married.

"We went from being students into the world of the rich and famous overnight," she said.

It was unbelievable. We lived in a dream. I found myself at dinner with Jascha Heifetz, and I had to pinch myself. We would be invited to Artur Rubinstein's house. Unbelievable things. You went from having no work to being in tremendous demand. Nobody would engage Isaac before the Leventritt—the only concerts he got were concerts Miss DeLay got for him. She would talk to odd conductors of little orchestras. Nobody would engage him, nobody was interested.

"Because of his disability?" I asked.

Well, sure. What else would it have been! He won the Leventritt and he began to play, and right away he got management. Overnight he was embraced by everyone in the music world. Now, it was a world that musically we were both ready for. I had no problem musically, but in every other way, there were so many issues. In the early years of my marriage, I saw Miss DeLay all the time. She was a constant source, a constant resource, because I needed advice all the time. I was always on the phone or in her studio getting instructions about how to deal with this unfamiliar life. I could not have done it without her. Little things—"Do I write a thank-you note to so-and-so?" "No, sugar, you write a thank-you note to this one but not to that one." Isaac would be away and I would have dinner with Miss DeLay, I would have lunch with her. This was totally away from the violin, this was as a friend, as an adviser, and still as the lady who was in charge. I felt she was in charge, very much so.

Toby Perlman laughed. "I kind of still feel she is in charge."

Toby Perlman herself is passionately involved in music education, and is director of the Perlman Music Program.

The school itself is a reflection of Miss DeLay and of what she believes in. I've never said that to her, but it's the truth. I am very opinionated and rigid, and I have very strong ideas about my school and about teaching and about children. They come from her. They come from the experience of being a student who had no self-confidence—I didn't play very well, I didn't believe in myself—but in her studio, I felt competent. I learned from her that no student needs to feel incompetent. I'm not talking about the student who is unprepared, I am talking about the student who works hard, and who comes in and maybe it's not so good. That student shouldn't feel badly. That student should feel that they've done a fine job—they have done the best they can, and now they are going to do it better. The teacher is going to help them do it better, but they are OK. From her I learned that it is just not necessary to demean a kid, frighten a kid. Not at all. To try to be honest, yes. If it is out of tune, it is not in tune!

At the school, we talk about nerves. Miss DeLay is a teacher who doesn't keep that type of stuff in the closet. She addresses the psyche. "Oh, you're shaking, dear. Aha. Well, I'd be shaking too, if I had to do that. Of course you are shaking. Let's think about it, let's look at it—yes, I think that's normal." Shaking is a terrible feeling. You know what most teachers say to their kids who are nervous? "Oh, you're nervous? That's OK. Everybody is nervous." Well, you know what? It's not OK. It's normal. That is saying something else. You know what? Being nervous is really normal and we need to look at it, and we need to look at how to get the feeling of having power over it. The whole concept of visualizing and preparing for a concert I learned from her. This is all accepted psychological thought now, but at the time, thirty-five years ago when she did it, it was new stuff, and she taught us all how to do it. In our school we are trying very, very hard to put all these ideas into play, into practice. It is all because of her.

I want to add one thing. I think that each teacher in the world gets one tenth of one percent of an Itzhak Perlman in a lifetime. And she got the whole thing, but I don't believe that she gave him more than she gave me. I was the middle of her class, I wasn't a star in any way. I was just quite ordinary as a violinist and as a talent. I got from her every bit as much as he did, if not more, and I believe that I am just one of many, many such people to whom she gave such devotion. I got more time, I got more attention, I think because I needed more.

This is a real example of somebody who did not have an agenda. I think her motivation was human kindness and lack of agenda. If I had to pick one thing, it would be that, the fact that the middle of the class got as much as my husband did. I never remember a lesson where there was ever a harsh word. I don't remember ever feeling stupid in her class. I don't remember ever feeling anything bad. It's true I worked very hard, but it's quite something to be able to say that.

I got up to leave, which occasioned another rush of activity from the dogs, who decided it was time to go out as well. Toby Perlman held out the palms of her hands and said, "Well, you see, that is why I thought about what I was going to say. I can't think of anything to say that is not complimentary. It sounds ridiculous. Nobody is so perfect. But you know—well—there it is."

Toby and Itzhak Perlman with DeLay and her husband, Edward Newhouse, backstage at Juilliard after Perlman conducted the Juilliard Orchestra at a gala benefit in 1998. Photo: Peter Schaaf.

13   Enormous Changes at the Last Minute

In the 1950s, Groucho Marx had a television program called *You Bet Your Life*. It was a quiz show that included one bit of inspired nonsense involving a secret word that was told only to the audience at the beginning of the program. "Say the magic word," Groucho would intone, waggling his eyebrows and leering amiably at the contestant if a female, "and you'll win fifty dollars." If a participant inadvertently used the word, a papier-mâché duck descended from the ceiling, bringing the program to a standstill. Everybody loved that moment.

Success on *You Bet Your Life* was entirely fortuitous, but Groucho's announcement of "Down comes the duck" became a catchphrase for that instant of excitement and revelation when something we have been trying to learn, such as riding a bicycle, suddenly clicks into place, often just at the moment it seemed impossible. We spend weeks wobbling along the path and driving into the bushes, and then in a glorious flash we find ourselves sailing smoothly down the straightaway as if we had been doing it all our lives. Children know about this better than anybody. What can match the thrill of discovering that you can walk, or later that you can read?

The following stories about four virtuoso violinists, Mark Peskanov, Robert McDuffie, Nadja Salerno-Sonnenberg, and Peter Oundjian, chronicle a few moments of truth in their student days with DeLay, when something that had seemed insurmountable or foreign suddenly became a part of them.

Mark Peskanov, like Midori and Sarah Chang, had his first taste of lessons with DeLay in Aspen, before going on to Juilliard. He arrived there from Odessa, Russia, in the summer of 1973, at the age of fifteen, shortly after his family had emigrated to the United States, and he might as well have reached another planet. In Odessa, the Peskanovs had lived on the fifth floor of a ten-story walkup, in a block that was famous because Pushkin had lived there. There were roughly twenty other families on their floor, all of whom shared a communal telephone in the hall. The apartment was so small that the young Peskanov had to practice his violin in the corridor.

"I thought it was great," he said in an interview in 1992, which took place in my apartment. The kitchen timer went off with a loud ping! while Peskanov was in midsentence, and he stopped barely long enough to say "F-sharp" before continuing with his story: "because I started to play for audiences—the other tenants—when I was very young. It was like a commune. Neighbors, friends of my grandmother, would come in and tell her ridiculous tales of what I had been up to, good and bad. If there was a fight, everybody would get into it. But I was a peaceful little boy," he grinned broadly. "I didn't fight."

To be dropped out of the sky from this bubbling pot into a tiny town in the Rocky Mountains, where you lived in a single-story dormitory with youngsters from all over the world and where private practice rooms were taken for granted, must have been staggering for the boy. From DeLay's description, Peskanov was already slightly larger than life, even at the age of fifteen. I met him only as an adult, and from the first found his height, his barrel chest, his smile, his appetite for music, food, and people to have a Rabelaisian quality. He seems to want to grab the world and hug it—to show it how to have as good a time as he is having. He is a positive thinker if ever there was one, and any cynicism melts in the face of such overwhelming enthusiasm and energy. The deep voice and heavy Russian accent, punctuated with much laughter—"No, no, I am just *keeeding!*"—nearly blow you away.

"Mark couldn't speak English when he first came to Aspen, so I kind of waved my hands a lot," DeLay recalled.

> Everything was new and different for him. The kids had to practice scales from eight to nine o'clock in the morning, and Mark didn't like that. His roommate was compulsively neat, and he didn't like that either. The poor roommate was the kind of person who would line up pencils just so, on his desk, and Mark—his stuff was all over the place. The roommate came to me and said that Mark was just not neat, and Mark came to me and said the roommate was driving

Mark Peskanov giving his former teacher a Russian bear hug at her seventieth birthday party in 1987. Peskanov came to the United States from Odessa at the age of fifteen to study with DeLay and has since made a major career here and abroad. Photo: Peter Schaaf.

him crazy. "I want three girls, instead," he would say to tease me, trying to make me shocked. He was really like a big teddy bear. He would sit on the couch and all the little kids would come and cuddle under him.

In Odessa, Peskanov had studied with Boris Brant at the Stoliarsky School during a period when it was officially against the law for such institutions to admit Jews, although one or two were always chosen from the hundred or so applicants for thirty-five places. There is a bitter irony here. The Stoliarsky School was named for the same Piotr Stoliarsky who founded the so-called Russian prodigy mill in the early twentieth century. In Stoliarsky's time, the school achieved fame as a training ground for the most gifted Jewish students, such as Jascha Heifetz and Mischa Elman, rather than as a fortress against them, as when Peskanov was a student. When Peskanov was among the few Jews admitted to the Stoliarsky School in the late 1960s and early 1970s, the only way to get out of Russia was to have the designation "Jew" on one's passport, so eager was the Soviet Union to see Jews leave. On the other hand, all the students at the Stoliarsky School, Jewish or not, were guaranteed a job on graduation. "But let's not get too excited," Peskanov said. "It could have been in northern Siberia."

Boris Brant, Peskanov's teacher in Russia, also emigrated to the United States a few years after the Peskanov family came. Brant died in 1986. "After I grew up, our relationship went from my being like a little puppy to becoming really great friends," Peskanov said of Brant, "but in the beginning he was the one who told me, this is the neck, this is the scroll, this is the pad, this is the hair, and so on. He was very handsome. Everybody was crazy about him. He was also enormously strong and could be very tough and demanding. The only time he would be sweet and nice was when I would play in public. Then he would come and hug me and kiss me. Any other occasion," Peskanov waved his arm, as though he were obliterating an insect, "forget it! When I was ten years old, I played my first public recital—I was playing a Mozart rondo or a Kreisler piece or something. I heard a big crash in the concert hall during rehearsal, and I saw he had broken the seat. He was displeased with something." Peskanov laughed uproariously at the memory.

The transition from this fire-eater to DeLay's nonauthoritarian style required a far greater leap than mere geography had imposed on the fifteen year old when he went to Aspen. "It was *verrry* different," he said, rolling his eyes along with his Russian *r*'s.

> First, she was a woman teacher—a big difference for me. It was wonderful right away. She was so sweet to me, and I needed it after having been a little roughed up. She knows how to bring out whatever is in the person. I didn't have to worry about communicating with Dorothy DeLay. She just looked at me with those eyes of hers, and I looked at her, she smiled and I smiled, she started to laugh, I started to laugh, and then she would go to the piano and play with me—one concerto after another—and show me what to do.

"I just felt a great freedom with DeLay," Peskanov continued, talking about his first months in America. "I would come to her studio and feel that I was more than at home. There was strong guidance there, too. Slowly but surely, while she called me Mark Sweetie," Peskanov gave a menacing giggle and made a gesture like wrenching a piece of iron, "she helped me to change—even my bow grip." Brant had struggled unsuccessfully with Peskanov over the years to change his deeply ingrained habit of holding the bow very deep, in the old Russian school style. DeLay's technique, which was based on Galamian's, was closer to the Franco-Belgian school of the late nineteenth century, as opposed to Auer's stiff-fingered grip to which Peskanov was accustomed. Peskanov said that Brant would literally scream at him not to hold the bow that way, but he just could not make the adjustment. Neither Peskanov nor DeLay had any explanation for how the bow change came about, but Peskanov described it as having been a fantastic liberation. When he played for Brant with the new grip, Brant was overjoyed, and bellowed, "How did she do that? Just for that, I have to bow to her." Peskanov told him, "I don't know how it happened. We were just playing, just having fun."

DeLay's explanation of the change was that the time was right and Peskanov was ready to listen, making it all sound easy as pie. But why did the breakthrough not happen with Brant? Why does Groucho's duck descend so often with DeLay's students?

Robert McDuffie, tall, beetle-browed, and handsome, is another larger-than-life virtuoso, but where Peskanov's manner is all boisterous Russian, McDuffie comes across as one hundred percent laid-back American. Laid-back not in his playing, certainly, which is fiery and intense, but in his easygoing personality. McDuffie comes from Macon, Georgia, and has those classic Southern qualities of charm and wit in abundance. McDuffie studied with DeLay for about five years in the late seventies, and described his particular moment of illumination in an article that he wrote on the occasion of her eightieth birthday in the July/August 1997 issue of the *American Record Guide*, which read in part:

> There was one lesson with Dorothy DeLay that I know I will never forget. It took place at midnight a few hours after my freshman recital. I had a positive feeling about the way I had performed. The audience (mostly friends and family) gave me a standing ovation, and I was ready to celebrate. Miss DeLay came backstage, gave me a hug and said, "Congratulations, sweetie. Come to my studio at midnight, and bring the tape of the recital." I was a little curious why she wanted to see me that soon, but because I was on a high, I didn't give it a second thought.
>
> I arrived at her studio, just as she was finishing her final lesson of the day. She called me in and said, "Hi, sugarplum. Let's listen

Robert McDuffie was a member of the DeLay Brat Pack at the Juilliard School from 1976 to 1981. Others in that distinguished class included Nigel Kennedy, Cho-Liang Lin, Shlomo Mintz, Joseph Swensen, and Nadja Salerno-Sonnenberg. Photo: J. Henry Fair.

to Chausson's *Poème*." I started the tape, sat next to her, and wondered what in the world she was going to say. We listened to the first note, a B-flat. She immediately told me to stop the tape. "Hear that first note?" she asked.

"Yes, Ma'am."

"That's the only note you played in tune the entire evening."

I sobered up immediately. That was the lesson that put me on the path to a solo career, because I began to learn how to listen. DeLay pointed me in the right direction by advising me when and how to adjust my pitch. She even sent me to an ear-training teacher for private tutoring. She knew exactly how I would react to her calculated criticism. I was stunned, but not crushed. Her sense of timing was impeccable.

Before that eventful freshman year, McDuffie had been studying with Margaret Pardee, an eminent violin pedagogue and Galamian disciple who has been at Juilliard since 1942—even longer than DeLay. "Why did you change teachers?" I asked, in a meeting in his apartment in 1990.

McDuffie replied that Margaret Pardee was a great teacher; her style was more disciplined than DeLay's, and she adhered strictly to Galamian's ideas on technique. "She went right by the book, and that's about as good a book as you can get. That is where I got the facility. I switched to Miss DeLay because things were happening in her class—there was this magic. I was part of a large migration that abandoned perfectly wonderful teachers for the DeLay camp." McDuffie added that DeLay was certainly not stealing students; he had to get permission from the dean, Gideon Waldrop at that time, and go through all the Juilliard red tape.

"All of us who moved were looking at the big picture—our long-term careers," McDuffie continued. "I knew that Miss DeLay was setting up auditions with conductors. Some of us, very naively, thought that she could just wave a magic wand and, poof!, we would have a career." McDuffie laughed. "Miss DeLay knew that, too. She knew that some people thought that she was the panacea."

McDuffie went on to describe the way in which DeLay developed relationships with people who ran the business outside of school, meaning the managements, the managers of orchestras, the conductors of orchestras, and others in a position of influence. According to McDuffie, DeLay was alone among the major teachers to concern herself actively about what happened to her students in the larger musical world outside the confines of her studio, and that concern was, of course, part of the so-called magic. The other teachers did not regard that kind of involvement as part of their job.

"I was so nervous the first two years with DeLay because every piece I played for her in my lesson, I knew that she had heard it better—and it had freaked me out," said McDuffie. "You've got Itzhak Perlman's face plastered all over the damn wall in her studio, and also you think about all the other greats she has taught."

McDuffie studied with DeLay from 1976 to 1981 and was part of a dazzling group of students known as the DeLay Brat Pack, whose other members included Nigel Kennedy, Cho-Liang Lin, Nadja Salerno-Sonnenberg, Shlomo Mintz, and Joseph Swensen. In addition to their private lessons with DeLay, the Brat Pack met with her as a class on Thursdays to critique each other's playing, and McDuffie says it was the give and take within the group that made him start to feel comfortable with himself.

"Her ideas are not always right," he said. "But she knows exactly when things are not working and tries something else. She is a woman of theories—she is constantly analyzing the situation from every angle." McDuffie added that as a result of DeLay's training with Galamian, she adhered to many of his techniques, and that some of McDuffie's best lessons took place when he would bring in a standard warhorse, memorized, and hand her the music, which she would mark, often with the basic bowings and fingerings from Galamian, along with talking about bow speed and sound. "She's got the goods," he said. "That's why I call her a full-service teacher. She is the entire package."

Long after McDuffie graduated from Juilliard and embarked on a career that has taken him all over the world, he continued to play for DeLay from time to time. "I think if you ever decide you've got it licked, you're in trouble," he said. "Sometimes she doesn't even need to say anything. You know that you are playing at a higher level. You've been in the trenches together. You're going to reach down and pull out something you didn't know you had because somebody is there that you respect."

"She is an enigma," McDuffie concluded. "She looks like everybody's Granny, until you see the way she drives her Lincoln Continental around in Aspen."

Nadja Salerno-Sonnenberg's moment of revelation involved a problem totally different from that of either Peskanov or McDuffie, and she, too, committed her experience with DeLay to paper in a book intended for teenagers called *Nadja On My Way*.

Salerno-Sonnenberg was by all accounts, including her own, a rebel from early on, and in teaching her, DeLay had to remain rock steady in the presence of sometimes gale-force winds. Salerno-Sonnenberg, who made her debut in 1971 at the age of ten with the Philadelphia Orchestra, arrived at DeLay's studio in Juilliard a few years later with a tremendous talent and a host of technical problems. She had been studying at the Curtis Institute in Philadelphia, and her refusal to take directions from her teacher resulted in the development of some terrible habits as she struggled to find her own way of doing things. By the time she got to DeLay, Salerno-Sonnenberg, by her own description, was like someone who has forced herself to be able to walk with the left foot in the right shoe, and vice versa. It hurt, but she had figured out how to make it work and did not want anyone, including DeLay, telling her that it was wrong and she had to do something about it. She remained as stubborn at Juilliard as she had been at Curtis, clinging to her own technique—if one can call it that—and turning a deaf ear to DeLay's weekly suggestions about fingerings and bowings, in spite of the fact that her playing was suffering.

"She could have just thrown me out of her class," wrote Salerno-Sonnenberg. "I would have gone and that would have been the end. But she stayed with me. At the end of each lesson she would say, 'Sugarplum, you have to change that position.' I would say, 'Uh-huh.' Next week I would do the same thing." This went on for three years, after which it gradually dawned on Salerno-Sonnenberg, while listening to some of her fellow students ("Holy cow, listen to that guy!"), that there was a reason they were so good. They had the right position.

Instead of regarding Salerno-Sonnenberg as obstinate and intractable when she was a student, DeLay saw her as someone with enormous perseverance. "Nadja has tremendous powers of concentration," DeLay said to me one afternoon. "If she starts thinking about something, she is just with it—and that is all there is to that. So that if she were playing wrong and you wanted her to start thinking in a different direction, it was just not possible to get her to do it. She was going her own way, and you could see the determination that she is going to do the particular thing she had in mind."

DeLay paused for a moment to think. "At the age of fourteen, for example, Nadja came to me and said she had to play the Mendelssohn Concerto somewhere. So she brought it the next week, and she was play-

Nadja Salerno-Sonnenberg at the age of five. Courtesy Dorothy DeLay.

Nadja Salerno-Sonnenberg, the only female member of the famous DeLay Brat Pack of the late 1970s, has since made a brilliant solo career. DeLay once threatened to throw her out of her class. Photo: J. Henry Fair.

ing it with two fingers." My eyebrows shot up in an astonished query, and DeLay sang a particular theme and ran the fingers of her left hand up and down her right forearm to demonstrate how Salerno-Sonnenberg achieved this, adding that she was very skillful at the maneuver.

I said, "Well Nadja, we're going to have to fix those fingerings because you can't possibly do that, they are getting you into trouble with phrases," and so forth and so forth. The next week she came for a lesson and said, "Miss DeLay, I have to play the Saint-Saëns *Intro-*

duction and Rondo capriccioso at my next concert. Can you hear it?" OK, so I listened to that, and the next time she brought me the Saint-Saëns again. In the meantime, the public performance of the Mendelssohn had come and gone. She played it but she just never brought it back.

DeLay laughed. "She was not going to change those fingerings. But she was tactful—she didn't want to say, Miss DeLay, I think your ideas are for the birds—she just tactfully didn't bring the controversial subject up again."

In her book, Salerno-Sonnenberg described how, by constantly questioning particular phrases, DeLay taught her and her fellow students to listen to themselves. Why did a passage sound wrong? To answer "I don't know" or "I am not sure" only increased DeLay's insistence that the passage be repeated until the student could analyze precisely what was awry.

Miss DeLay would say, "Play it again. Really listen. What is wrong?"

"Well," someone might say, "I think the B-flat is out of tune."

"Are you sure that note is out of tune? Play it again. Play it again."

"Yes, that note is out of tune."

"Why is it out of tune?"

Sometimes I'd get so mad I'd yell, "I don't know! Why are you getting paid? What is this, I'm teaching myself?"

"I was right," Salerno-Sonnenberg added in hindsight. "She was teaching me to teach myself—and that's why she is a great teacher."

Sometime in her late teens, Salerno-Sonnenberg suffered a crisis of confidence that stopped her from playing the violin for seven tortured months—she describes it as the worst period of her life. She had started her freshman year at Juilliard in the company of other violin students whom she saw as vastly more advanced. Increasingly, she found herself wondering whether she was good enough to make a career. Some of the technically demanding show pieces that she had played since she was a child suddenly seemed impossible—pieces that she had played easily when she didn't know how hard they were. Having been accustomed to being seen as a wunderkind all her life, she started to feel like a failure. By the time she was nineteen, she could not play a G-major scale in tune, and her self-confidence had hit bottom.

Adolescence, with all its self-doubts and uncertainties, is a classic time for this kind of nightmare to hit a young virtuoso, and DeLay speaks from much experience with her students when she says that enormous amounts of support are needed to help someone through the difficulties. Salerno-Sonnenberg started leaving her violin at home when she went for a lesson, and she and DeLay would spend the time talking about music, life, and her problems—in particular her fear of trying and failing. The possibility that even if she went flat out and worked as hard as she could, she might still fail, gnawed at her relentlessly. The pattern of showing up in DeLay's studio without her instrument went on for some months, and from Salerno-Sonnenberg's brief description, the meetings must have been more like psychotherapy sessions than violin lessons.

"Not long after I turned twenty," wrote Salerno-Sonnenberg, "one week, like every week, I went to see Miss DeLay. This time, Miss DeLay looked at me and said, 'Listen, if you don't bring your violin next week, I'm throwing you out of my class.'" Salerno-Sonnenberg listened and laughed. She thought that she and DeLay had become such good friends that DeLay could not possibly mean what she was saying. "Miss DeLay rose from the couch and, in a very calm way, said, 'I'm not kidding. If you are going to waste your talent, I don't want to be a part of it. This has gone on long enough.' Then she walked out of the room."

Salerno-Sonnenberg said that her initial reaction was total shock, and then terror that she might lose DeLay as teacher and friend. She turned to a close friend who had been with her at Curtis, the pianist Cecile Licad, for advice about what to do. Licad gave a three-word answer, which also seems to have been the right counsel at the right time: "Don't give up."

At this point, Salerno-Sonnenberg wrote, she realized she wanted to live—even as an honest failure—and she decided to take a ridiculous chance and sign up for the 1981 Naumburg Competition, which was just two months away. Not having touched the instrument for over half a year, she was in absolutely no shape to play; she said her fingers felt like linguini. If she had sounded bad before, now she sounded absolutely terrible. Her wildest dream was to make it to the finals of the competition, which would in itself be a miracle.

For those two months, Salerno-Sonnenberg was completely obsessed. She worked as only someone with that capacity for concentration can, practicing thirteen hours a day. She dropped out of sight and told nobody but DeLay what she was doing. She persuaded DeLay to teach her at night, in order not to blow her cover. The story, of course, has a brilliantly happy ending. In spite of various disasters that seem somehow in keeping with her tempestuous nature, including accidentally setting her apartment on fire and having her moped blow up on the day of the semifinals, Salerno-Sonnenberg not only made it through the finals, but won the competition. The first thing she did was to tear off to Juilliard to give DeLay the news.

While Salerno-Sonnenberg's musical gift is so great that it would unquestionably have found an outlet at some point in spite of that period of emotional turmoil, its re-emergence might have taken a very long time. Certainly, she would never have even entered the Naumburg Competition those many years ago had it not been for the unconventional help she received in surmounting her terrors and restoring her self-confidence.

Conductor and violinist Peter Oundjian's story, derived from conversations we have had over the years, gives a more general picture of DeLay's gift for enabling someone to look at familiar situations and suddenly see them quite differently.

Oundjian's sixteen-year tenure as first violinist with the Tokyo String Quartet was brought to a close in 1995 when he started developing problems with his left hand that made it increasingly difficult for him to play. The Tokyo had been celebrating its twenty-fifth season by presenting the complete Beethoven cycle in Carnegie and Avery Fisher Halls. The concerts were an enormous success, but toward the end of the series some listeners became aware that the quartet's first violinist was not sounding his usual self. Only after Oundjian's official withdrawal from the group was it made public that he was suffering from focal distonia, a condition of uncertain origin that in his instance affected the small muscles of the left hand.

Many months and many medical diagnoses later, Oundjian was forced to make the decision to change careers, and determined to try to establish himself as a conductor. Because of his brilliant musicianship, public persona, and connections in the music world, the metamorphosis was achieved in rapid order. Within a year, he made his conducting debut at the Caramoor Festival's fiftieth anniversary celebration with the Orchestra of St. Luke's, substituting for an ailing André Previn at Previn's request. *The New York Times* critic gave him a rave review, and Caramoor was so delighted with his performance that they immediately

Peter Oundjian, conductor and violinist, studied with Ivan Galamian, Itzhak Perlman, and DeLay, in that order. Before his career as a conductor, Oundjian played first violin with the Tokyo Quartet from 1981 to 1995. Photo: Peter Kloos.

invited him back for two additional concerts, and two seasons later named him to the post of artistic director. With his title as conductor now on the map, Oundjian found himself busier than ever in his new career as other engagements in the United States and abroad followed.

Oundjian, who was brought up in England, came to America at the age of nineteen and spent three years studying with Ivan Galamian, followed by a year with Itzhak Perlman and two years with DeLay. He and DeLay have remained close since those early days, and he describes her with affection as one of the world's great psychologists, both as a teacher and as a diplomat in the sometimes treacherous shoals of the music business. DeLay, in turn, has always had a particular fondness and admiration for Oundjian.

217

Shortly after Oundjian left the Tokyo Quartet and was in the process of deciding what to do, a prestigious East Coast music organization approached him with what seemed like a very attractive job offer. It was an important opportunity that he found hard to assess, and he went to DeLay, as he had done at other critical points in his career, to discuss his dilemma.

"Let me tell you her response when I asked her about this position," Oundjian said.

> She said, "Is there anything you could think of that anybody else in your position could gain by having this job? If that is the case, then you might consider taking it, to prevent anybody else from taking advantage of it." It was an interesting observation, and at the same time it gave me an insight into how she thinks. It is a very competitive attitude, and perhaps very political. It was also very helpful. I immediately thought, Well, so-and-so wouldn't want this job, and it suddenly clarified things for me.

Looking back to the time when he switched from Galamian to Perlman, Oundjian said, "I think I needed a little more open communication between student and teacher at that point. He [Galamian] was delighted that I went to Itzhak. He was very happy—he had great admiration for Itzhak. I think the truth is also that he was relieved I wasn't going to Miss DeLay." Oundjian added that the year he spent studying with Perlman was wonderful in every way—that Perlman had been enormously inspiring and had freed him up in his playing. While with Perlman, Oundjian also had some lessons with Robert Mann, the founding first violinist of the Juilliard Quartet and long-time Juilliard faculty member. "Bobby Mann had a gift to make people think—to really make them examine what they are doing, and why they make certain choices," said Oundjian. "He is a great and fascinating musician. He challenges your mind." Oundjian added that while one does not have to agree with everything that Mann says, he fires up the imagination of his students because he is so full of ideas.

"When I went into DeLay's class at Juilliard, she taught me a lot, but she also put my mind in a place where I could understand everything I'd ever been taught more clearly," said Oundjian. "Dorothy is so organized—she really knows exactly what she wants to do with every student. Teaching is what she does; she has committed her whole life to it. I don't know what it was she did," he smiled, "but all those things that people, including Galamian, had been trying to tell me for the past several years, I was suddenly able to put into practice."

Oundjian was silent for a moment and then spoke without a pause, as though the words had long been in his mind:

> That is part of Miss DeLay's genius—to put people in the frame of mind where they can do their best. Nobody can do better than their best. Nobody can teach you to play better than God intended. Very few teachers can actually get you to your ultimate potential. Miss DeLay has that gift. She challenges you at the same time that you feel you are being nurtured. You are being told that if you are calm and if you believe in yourself and if you allow your own natural gifts and natural passions to control and lead your musical instincts, then you'll grow and you'll develop in a natural way. It is like putting a plant with just the right amount of light and the right amount of water with the right amount of frequency. If you put it in the sun all day long, it burns out. Maybe other teachers overfeed you with too much information, too much nurturing, too much water, or whatever, but she understands precisely what each student needs, and when. At the end of those two years with Miss DeLay, I believed that I could stand up and play the Brahms Concerto in front of an orchestra anywhere in the world.

"Dorothy" and "Kansas" inevitably bring to mind the story of the little girl who followed the yellow brick road to the Emerald City, and how she and her friends, after many adventures and difficulties, sought out the Wizard of Oz to grant their innermost wishes. Over a period of time, I came to the conclusion that DeLay is not her young namesake, but the Wonderful Wizard himself. At the end of the story, you will recall, the Wizard emerges as a kind and gentle soul—an ordinary human being with the extraordinary ability to enable others to make their dreams real. The Tin Woodsman gets his heart, the Scarecrow his brain, the Lion his courage, and Dorothy finds her "self" in discovering there is no place like home. Without fanfare, the Wizard has done it all. Dorothy DeLay, too, has that extraordinary ability. Her students learn how to realize at least some of their aspirations by discovering their capacities, and gaining the courage and freedom to use them.

14   Postscript

At this writing, it is the spring of 1999, and DeLay has just celebrated her eighty-second birthday. She continues to teach full-time and to plan for the future while concentrating on the present. In recent months, several important events have occurred—the most immediately evident being the presence of a new teacher in her studio. In December 1998, Itzhak Perlman joined the faculty of the Juilliard School and he and DeLay began jointly teaching a handful of her most advanced students. Perlman's interest in pedagogy is hardly new. In addition to the many years he taught at Brooklyn College, he works with the students at the Perlman Program, the summer school on Long Island established by his wife, Toby.

Fascinated by the new development in DeLay's teaching life, I went to watch a lesson with the dynamic duo, as Perlman cheerfully refers to himself and DeLay, on a cold December day in 1998. Room 530 at Juilliard had undergone a face-lift while DeLay was in Aspen the previous summer. There was new bottle-green carpeting, and the beat-up old couch had been replaced by a smart new yellow one, which nevertheless housed the familiar collection of stuffed dolls and animals. Also new to the room was the presence of a motorized scooter—a hand-me-down from Perlman—which enabled DeLay to negotiate the hallways of Juilliard at much greater speed than she could manage on crutches. DeLay was thrilled with this new piece of machinery and had earlier described to me on the telephone how she and Perlman had barreled around the studio like a couple of jockeys on bumper cars, each on his own scooter, when he was teaching her how to handle it.

I arrived in the studio a few minutes before Perlman, and had a chance to chat briefly with DeLay about the shared teaching venture. The arrangement was still very new, only two or three lessons had as yet taken place, and both she and Perlman were feeling their way. The general plan was that DeLay would continue her regular schedule, and that Perlman would join her as often as his own timetable would allow. DeLay was totally delighted with the turn of events. "Itzhak has a wonderful ear," she said. "He knows exactly what the kids need. He has not had the experience of consecutive teaching before, and seems to want me to be around. Of course I'll be there as long as he wants me." DeLay smiled, obviously happy that now, some forty years later, she was still working with her favorite student.

That same month, December 1998, DeLay, who has given master classes in Japan for many years and has taught many distinguished Japanese artists—Midori, for example—received a significant honor from the Japanese government. She was awarded the Order of the Sacred Treasure with Gold Rays and Neck Ribbon. Other musicians who had been so honored include Herbert von Karajan and Isaac Stern. The event was marked in New York with a reception for a small invited audience at the official residence of the Consul General of Japan, Ambassador Seiichiro Otsuka. Juilliard's president, Joseph Polisi, spoke at the ceremony, after which Ambassador Otsuka presented DeLay with a proclamation signed by the Emperor, and an exceedingly handsome brooch that represented the Order of the Sacred Treasure, complete with Gold Rays and Neck Ribbon. The surprise turn of the afternoon was provided by Ambassador Otsuka himself, who entertained his guests with a rendition of "The High Road to Gairloch" and "Brown-haired Maiden," later bowing to popular demand by playing "Amazing Grace" as an encore, on, of all things, the bagpipes. When the applause was over, Perlman brought a huge smile to the ambassador's face by saying to the honoree, "So, Miss DeLay, what do you think—a little more finger pressure? A little more vibrato?"

Beginning in the autumn of 1999, a cherished project of DeLay's will take a giant leap forward. Since the early 1990s, she has been deeply involved in the creation of a center the purpose of which is to train future artist-teachers in her approach. She envisions a program that would be a resource not only for conservatories, like Juilliard, but for schools across the country where music is simply a part of the curriculum. The program was initiated in 1994 with the appointment of two teaching fellows, Catherine Cho and Robert Chen, who worked under DeLay's

In December 1998, Ambassador Seiichiro Otsuka, Consul General of Japan, presented DeLay with the Order of the Sacred Treasure with Gold Rays and Neck Ribbon, on behalf of the Japanese government. After the ceremony, the ambassador entertained his guests with an expert performance on the bagpipes. Photo: Peter Schaaf.

Joseph Polisi, president of the Juilliard School, with DeLay at the Japanese government's conferment of the Order of the Sacred Treasure. Photo: Peter Schaaf.

supervision and whose stipends were funded by the Starling Foundation. Catherine Cho is a concert artist and a member of Juilliard's Pre-College faculty; Robert Chen is now the concertmaster of the Chicago Symphony.

The Starling Foundation, named for Dorothy Richard Starling, has been a benefactor of many of DeLay's activities for years. Dorothy Richard Starling had been a violin student at the Cincinnati College-Conservatory of Music in the 1920s, and later had some lessons with Leopold Auer. She died at an early age, and her husband, a wealthy oil man, established the foundation in her memory. Starling's representatives later asked Jack Watson, then the dean at the Cincinnati College-Conservatory, to find a teacher "of the stature of Leopold Auer," as the request was worded, for an endowed chair at his wife's alma mater. Dean Watson proposed the name of Dorothy DeLay. DeLay has held the Starling Chair at the Cincinnati College-Conservatory since 1974 and the Starling Chair at the Juilliard School since 1987. Starling funds have been augmented a number of times and continue to flow to her students at Aspen and in Cincinnati, as well as at Juilliard, in the form of scholarships and performing opportunities.

In April 1999 the Starling Foundation announced a major financial commitment, with matching funds to be raised by Juilliard, to establish an endowment for the Starling-DeLay Institute at the Juilliard School. The income from the endowment is to support the institute's fellows, who are defined as "Young concert artists who have a serious interest in becoming artist-teachers at the highest level." Now, at the start of the twenty-first century, the Starling-DeLay Institute is firmly in place, preparing the next generation of dedicated musicians to carry on DeLay's, and Juilliard's, tradition of excellence. The selection of the institute's fellows is up to DeLay, who not only supervises the program but is an active participant in its activities.

I asked DeLay how in the long term—years from now—the likely candidates for Starling Fellowships at the Dorothy DeLay Institute would be decided upon. "Oh, I'll continue to select them, of course," she replied, sunnily.

A Partial List of Dorothy DeLay's Students

This list of students and former students of Dorothy DeLay as of mid-1999 has been compiled from a number of sources. In spite of efforts to make it comprehensive, the list has undoubtedly, and wholly inadvertently, omitted the names of some outstanding musicians, to whom apologies are extended. The list represents only those students with professional management and those who are teaching at a college or conservatory. Because of their number, it does not include the many private teachers and orchestra members who received their training in Dorothy DeLay's studio.

Ahn, Angella: Ahn Trio
Almond, Frank W.: Concertmaster, Milwaukee Symphony
    Orchestra; Professor, Texas Christian University
Altenburger, Christian: Professor, University of Hannover, Germany
Anthony, Adele: First prize, Nielsen Competition
Antokoletz, Elliott M.: Professor, University of Texas, Austin
Antonello, Cara Mia: Principal Second Violin, St. Louis Symphony
Armstrong, Vahn: Concertmaster, Virginia Symphony
Azoitei, Remus: Concert Artist
Badea, Christian: Conductor, Columbus Symphony; Conductor,
    Metropolitan Opera
Bae, Ik Wan: Concert Artist
Balanescu, Alexander: Concert Artist
Barachovsky, Anton: Concert Artist
Baty, Janice: Faculty, University of Delaware
Beilman, Douglas: New Zealand String Quartet
Berg, Darrell M: Visiting Associate Professor, Indiana University
Berlinsky, Dmitry: Concert Artist

Berman, Pavel: Concert Artist; First prize, Indianapolis Competition

Berofsky, Aaron C.: Chester String Quartet

Beukes, Regina A.: Principal Second Violin, London Philharmonic Orchestra

Bjornkjaer, Lars: Concertmaster, Royal Danish Orchestra

Blacher, Kolya: Concertmaster, Berlin Philharmonic Orchestra

Blekh, Mark: Concertmaster, Oudkirk Symphony, Holland

Burgdorf, Barbara: Second Concertmaster, Bayerische Staatsoper, Munich

Carney, Laurie: American String Quartet; Professor, Manhattan School of Music

Castleman, Heidi: Professor, Juilliard School

Cepinskas, Vilhelmas: Concert Artist

Chai, Liang: Concert Artist

Chan, David: Concert Artist

Chang, Min Soo: Professor, Temple University; Aspen Music School

Chang, Sarah: Concert Artist

Chao, Evelina S.: Assistant Principal Viola, St. Paul Chamber Orchestra

Chastain, Nora: Professor, Lübeck Conservatory

Chay, Min-Jae: Associate Professor, Chungang University, China

Chee-Yun: Concert Artist

Chen, David: Associate Professor, Rubin Academy of Music, Jerusalem, Israel

Chen, Robert: Concertmaster, Chicago Symphony

Chiba, Junko: Concert Artist

Cho, Catherine: Concert Artist; Faculty, Juilliard School, Pre-College Division

Choi, Anna Jee Hee: Professor, Southwestern University

Clapp, Stephen: Dean, Juilliard School

Deglans, Wilfredo: Associate Concertmaster, Rochester Philharmonic

Del Castillo, Anabel G.: Concertmaster, Málaga Symphony Orchestra, Spain

Dembow, Brian: Angeles Quartet

Dexter, John R., III: Manhattan String Quartet

Duisenberre, Edward J.: Takács Quartet

Dukow, Bruce D.: Concertmaster, Hollywood Bowl Orchestra

Eanet, Nicholas: Mendelssohn String Quartet

Eicher, Bruno H.: Associate Concertmaster, Atlanta Symphony
     Orchestra
Evans, Ralph: Fine Arts Quartet
Farris, Kelly: Concertmaster, Spokane Symphony; Professor,
     University of Eastern Washington
Finclair, Barry: Concert Artist
Fischer, Simon: Author; Musicologist
Fitzpatrick, William: Professor, Conservatoire Maurice Ravel, Paris
Foster, Martin: Professor, University of Quebec; former member,
     New York String Quartet
Froschauer, Daniel: Vienna Philharmonic
Fulkerson, Gregory: Concert Artist; Professor, Oberlin Conservatory
Georgieva, Mila: Concert Artist
Gluzman, Vadim: Concert Artist
Gomyo, Karen: Concert Artist
Greenspan, Bertram: Concertmaster, Reading Symphony; Professor,
     Rowan College
Gringolts, Ilya: First prize, Paganini Competition
Grossman, Eric: Concert Artist
Gudmundsdottir, Gudny: Concertmaster, Iceland Symphony
     Orchestra
Guillen, Manuel: Concertmaster, Queen Sofia Chamber Orchestra;
     Professor, Royal Conservatory, Spain
Gutman, Michael: Concert Artist
Harada, Koichiro: Founding member, Tokyo String Quartet;
     Professor, Toho School, Japan; Conductor
Haupt, Charles: Concertmaster, Mostly Mozart Orchestra
Hayden William P.: Professor, University of South Florida
Heard, Cornelia L.: Professor, Vanderbilt University; Blair Quartet
Heichelman, Palle: Concertmaster, Royal Danish Opera
Hill, Janet Lyman: Concert Artist
Hirosawa, Jin: Concertmaster, Tokyo Philharmonic
Honda-Rosenberg, Latica Concert Artist; Silver Medal, Tchaikovsky
     Competition
Hou, Yi-Jia: First prize, Sarasate Competition
Huang, Wanchi: Professor, Tung Hai University, China
Hutchinson, Henry: Concertmaster, Puerto Rico Symphony;
     Professor, Puerto Rico Conservatory
Ikeda, Kikuei: Tokyo String Quartet; Professor, Yale University

Ishii-Eto, Kimbo: Conductor

Jakovcic, Zoran: Essex Quartet

Joiner, Lee D.: Professor, Wheaton College

Juillet, Chantal: Concertmistress, Montreal Symphony

Kamiya, Michiko: Concert Artist; Gold Medal, Hannover
    Competition

Kang, Hyo: Professor, Juilliard School; Founder and Director, Seoul
    Chamber Ensemble; Sejong Soloists

Kantor, Paul: Professor, University of Michigan

Kaplan, Mark: Concert Artist; Professor, University of Southern
    California

Kardalian, Sarkis: Assistant Concertmaster, Seattle Symphony
    Orchestra

Kashiwagi, Kyoko: Amernet String Quartet

Kato, Tomoko: Concert Artist; Silver Medal, Tchaikovsky
    Competition

Kawakubo, Tamaki: Concert Artist

Kawasaki, Masao: Professor, Juilliard School; Concert Artist

Kawasaki, Yosuke: Concert Artist

Kella, John: Professor, New York University

Kennedy, Nigel: Concert Artist

Keylin, Misha: Concert Artist

Kim, Benny: Concert Artist

Kim, Bok-Soo: Concertmaster, Korean Broadcasting Symphony
    Orchestra, Seoul

Kim, Chin: Concert Artist; Professor, Mannes College of Music

Kim, David: Concertmaster, Philadelphia Orchestra

Kim, Martha Potter: Violin Teacher

Kobayashi, Laura: Professor, University of Nebraska

Koch, Nanna R.: Concertmaster, Württembergisches
    Kammerorchester

Koornhof, Piet: Concert Artist

Kopec, Patinka: Professor, Manhattan School of Music

Krakauer, Barbara: Concert Artist

Kuppel, Reto, M.S.: Assistant Concertmaster, Bavarian Radio
    Orchestra

Kwon, Yoon: Concert Artist

Latvala, Johannes: First Concertmaster, Finnish National Opera

Lee, Christopher C.: Former Concertmaster, New Jersey Symphony

Lee, Rachel: Concert Artist
Lee, Sung-Ju: Professor, University of Arts, Seoul, Korea
Lee, Yura: Concert Artist
Leshin, Richard: Professor, University of Southern California
Levin, Ida: Concert Artist; former member, Mendelssohn String
    Quartet
Lewis, Brian D.: Concert Artist
Li, Chuan Yun: Concert Artist
Lin, Cho-Liang: Concert Artist; Professor, Juilliard School
Lippi, Isabella M.: Concert Artist
Lowe, David T.: Professor, Bethany College
Lu, Si Qing: Concert Artist; First prize, Paganini Competition
Lupien, Denise: Concertmaster, Orchestre Metropolitan du
    Montreal
Maehashi, Teiko: Concert Artist
Mann, Nicholas: Mendelssohn String Quartet
Manoukian, Catherine: Concert Artist
Martin, Janice: Concert Artist
Mathe Ulrike-Anima: Concert Artist
Matsuyama, Saeka: Concert Artist
Mayforth, Robin: Lark Quartet
McAslan, Lorraine: Concert Artist
McDuffie, Robert: Concert Artist
Menard, Pierre: Vermeer Quartet
Mendoza, Alejandro: Professor, Manhattan School of Music
Meyer, Julian D.: Professor, Temple University
Meyers, Anne Akiko: Concert Artist
Midori: Concert Artist
Milenkovich, Stefan: Concert Artist
Milewski, Piotr J.: Professor, University of Cincinnati
Miller, Anton M.: Artist in Residence, Lehman College
Mintz, Shlomo: Concert Artist; Conductor
Mishnaevski, Alexander: Principal Violist, Detroit Symphony
    Orchestra
Mori, Takayuki: Professor, California State University
Moye, Felicia: Miami String Quartet
Mugavero, Amy: Concert Artist
Murvitz, Moshe: Assistant Concertmaster, Israel Philhamonic
    Orchestra

Mussumeli, Bettina C.: Concertmaster, I Soloisti Veneti
Nikkanen, Kurt: Concert Artist
Oakland, Ron: Concertmaster, American Ballet Theater
Ofer, Erez: First Concertmaster, Philadelphia Orchestra
Ohtsu, Junko: Concert Artist
Okumura, Tomohiro: First prize, Naumburg Competition
Oundjian, Peter H.: Conductor, Caramoor Festival; Tokyo String
    Quartet
Pan, Philip D.: Concertmaster, Jacksonville Symphony
Park, David H.: Assistant Concertmaster, Utah Symphony Orchestra
Park, Julie: Concert Artist
Park, Min Jung: Professor, California State University
Park, Tricia: Concert Artist
Payne, Ellen A.: Principal Second Violin, New York City Opera
Peabody, Paul: Concert Artist
Perlman, Itzhak: Concert Artist
Perlman, Toby: Music Administrator; Founder, Perlman Music
    Program
Perry, David: Fine Arts Quartet; Professor, University of Wisconsin
Peskanov, Mark: Concert Artist
Picketty, Marianne: Concert Artist
Plum, Sarah: Concertmaster, Saarländisches Staatstheater Orchestra
Pollit, David: Conductor, Greenville Symphony Orchestra
Prunaru, Liviu, Concert Artist
Quint, Philip: Concert Artist
Rathnam, Odin J.: Concertmaster, Harrisburg Symphony Orchestra
Risely, Martin D.: Concertmaster, Edmonton Symphony Orchestra
Robilliard, Virginie: Concert Artist
Rosenthal, Paul: Music Director, Sitka Summer Music Festival;
    former faculty, University of Alaska
Rozek, Robert: Professor, University of Miami
Rubinstein, Jerrold: Professor, Royal Conservatory of Music, Brussels
Salerno-Sonnenberg, Nadja: Concert Artist; First prize, Naumburg
    Competition
Sanchez-Zubert, Eduardo: Conductor, Orquesta Sinfónica de
    Xalapa, Mexico
Sarch, Kenneth: Professor, Mansfield University
Sassmannshaus, Kurt: Conductor; Chairman, String Department,
    University of Cincinnati

Sato, Shunsuke: Concert Artist
Sato-Oei, Eriko: Co-Concertmaster, Orpheus Chamber Orchestra
Savaldi-Kohlbert, Bat-Sheva: Concertmaster, Jerusalem Symphony
Schwartz, Sergiu: Concert Artist; Professor, Harid Conservatory,
    Florida
Shaham, Gil: Concert Artist
Shank, Leslie J.: Assistant Concertmaster, St. Paul Chamber
    Orchestra
Shevelov, Ramy: Concert Artist
Shih, Michael: Magellan Quartet
Shiran, Ora: Concert Artist
Silberman, Matthew: Professor, Bucknell University
Silversteen, Rosemary: Professor, Del Mar College
Smirnoff, Joel: Juilliard String Quartet; Professor, Juilliard School
Sohn, Livia: Concert Artist; First prize, Menuhin Competition
Sokol, Mark: Professor, San Francisco Conservatory; former member,
    Concord Quartet
Sporcl, Pavel: Concert Artist
Statsky, Paul: Professor, Cleveland Institute of Music; Interlochen
    Academy of the Arts
Steiner, Oliver: Professor, Georgia State University
Stern, Kay: Concertmaster, San Francisco Opera Orchestra; former
    member, Lark Quartet
Stern, Michael: Conductor
Stern, Mitchell: Professor, Manhattan School of Music; former
    member, American String Quartet
Stillwell, Corinne: Harrington String Quartet
Strauss, Axel: First prize, Naumburg Competition
Suchecka-Richter, Magdalena: Professor, New England Conservatory
    of Music
Sumi, Eriko: Concert Artist
Sung, Janet: Concert Artist
Suwanai, Akiko: First prize, Tchaikovsky Competition
Suzumi, Kishiko: Concert Artist
Swensen, Ian: Professor, San Francisco Conservatory
Swensen, Joseph: Principal Conductor, Scottish Chamber Orchestra
Szeps-Znaider, Nikolaj: First prize, Queen Elisabeth Competition
Takezawa, Kyoko: Concert Artist; First prize, Indianapolis
    Competition

Tanaka, Naoko: Professor, Juilliard School, Pre-College Division; Concertmaster, Orpheus Chamber Orchestra

Tanase, Ion: Concert Artist

Taylor, David: Assistant Concertmaster, Chicago Symphony Orchestra

Taylor, Lyndon J.: Principal Second violin, Los Angeles Philharmonic

Taylor, Seth: Associate Concertmaster, Landstheater Eisenach, Germany

Taylor, Shirien K.: Principal Second Violin, Metropolitan Opera Orchestra

Teal, Christian: Blair Quartet; Professor, Vanderbilt University

Tecco, Romuald: Concertmaster, St. Paul Chamber Orchestra

Toda, Yayoi: First prize, Queen Elisabeth Competition

Trynchuk, Carla L.: Assistant Professor, Andrews University

Tsung, Nancy H.: Professor, National Institute of the Arts, Taiwan

Turban, Ingolf: Concertmaster, Munich Philharmonic

Urushihara, Asako: Concert Artist

Vaghy, Dezso: Vaghy Quartet, Canada

Vaghy, Tibor: Vaghy Quartet, Canada

van Zweden, Jaap: Conductor; former Concertmaster, Amsterdam Concertgebouw Orchestra

Vaz, Dominic: Associate Concertmaster, New York State Theater

Velin, Jean-Claude: Concertmaster, Toulouse Symphony

Wang, Linda: Concert Artist

Wang, Xiao-Dong: First prize, Menuhin Competition

Waterman, Ruth: Concert Artist; Lecturer

Weilerstein, Donald: Professor, Cleveland Institute of Music; former member, Cleveland Quartet

Wilson, Nancy J.: Professor, Mannes College of Music

Winograd, Peter: American String Quartet; Professor, Manhattan School of Music

Wyrick, Erick: Concertmaster, New Jersey Symphony

Yim, Won Bin: Professor, University of Cincinnati and Juilliard School

Ying, Timothy: Ying Quartet

Yonetani, Ayako: Professor, University of Central Florida

Yoo, Scott: Conductor; Concert Artist

Zelkowicz, Isaias: Associate Principal Viola, Pittsburgh Symphony

Selected Bibliography

Auer, Leopold. 1980. *Violin Playing As I Teach It*. Reprint. New York: Dover Publications. Original edition, New York: Frederick A. Stokes, 1921.

Epstein, Helen. 1987. *Music Talks: Conversations with Musicians*. New York: McGraw-Hill Book Company.

Feldman, David Henry. 1991. *Nature's Gambit: Child Prodigies and the Development of Human Potential*. New York: Teachers College Press, Columbia University. Original edition, New York: Basic Books, Inc., 1986.

Galamian, Ivan. 1962. *Principles of Violin Playing and Teaching*. 2d ed. Englewood Cliffs, New Jersey: Prentice Hall.

Green, Elizabeth A. H. 1993. *Miraculous Teacher: Ivan Galamian and the Meadowmount Experience*. Reston, Virginia: American String Teachers Association.

Kenneson, Claude. 1999. *Musical Prodigies: Perilous Journeys, Remarkable Lives*. Portland, Oregon: Amadeus Press.

Kolneder, Walter. 1998. *The Amadeus Book of the Violin: Construction, History, and Music*. Translated by Reinhard G. Pauly. Portland, Oregon: Amadeus Press.

Langer, Ellen J. 1997. *The Power of Mindful Learning*. Reading, Massachusetts: Addison-Wesley Publishing Company, Inc., Merloyd Lawrence.

Menuhin, Yehudi. 1997. *Unfinished Journey: Twenty Years Later*. New York: Fromm International Publishing Corporation. Original edition, *Unfinished Journey*. New York: Alfred A. Knopf, 1977.

Roeder, Michael. 1994. *A History of the Concerto*. Portland, Oregon: Amadeus Press.

Roth, Henry. 1997. *Violin Virtuosos: From Paganini to the 21st Century*. Los Angeles: California Classics Books.

Salerno-Sonnenberg, Nadja. 1989. *Nadja on My Way*. New York: Crown Publishers.

Schonberg, Harold C. 1988. *The Virtuosi*. Reprint. New York: Random House, Vintage Books. Original edition, *The Glorious Ones*. New York: Random House, Times Books, 1985.

Schwarz, Boris. 1983. *Great Masters of the Violin*. New York: Simon & Schuster.

Slenczynska, Ruth, and Louis Biancolli. 1957. *Forbidden Childhood*. New York: Doubleday and Company; London: Peter Davies, 1958.

Steinhardt, Arnold. 1998. *Indivisible by Four: A String Quartet in Pursuit of Harmony*. New York: Farrar Straus Giroux.

Stowell, Robin. 1993. *The Cambridge Companion to the Violin*. New York: Cambridge University Press.

Wechsberg, Joseph. 1972. *The Glory of the Violin*. New York: The Viking Press.

Index

Page numbers in italic indicate photographs. Photographs of Miss DeLay appear on pages 2, 25, 27, 31, 35, 40, 41, 55, 75, 117, 151, 202, 205, 223, and 224.